LIT BIZ 101

HOW TO GET HAPPILY, SUCCESSFULLY PUBLISHED

Also by Raymond Mungo

FAMOUS LONG AGO
TOTAL LOSS FARM
BETWEEN TWO MOONS
TROPICAL DETECTIVE STORY
RETURN TO SENDER
COSMIC PROFIT
CONFESSIONS FROM LEFT FIELD
HOME COMFORT (with the People of Total Loss Farm)
MOVING ON, HOLDING STILL (with Peter Simon)
RIGHT TO PASS (with Paul Williams)
MUNGOBUS

LIT BIZ 101

HOW TO GET HAPPILY, SUCCESSFULLY PUBLISHED

Raymond Mungo

A DELL TRADE PAPERBACK

A DELL TRADE PAPERBACK
Published by
Dell Publishing
a division of
The Bantam Doubleday Dell Publishing Group, Inc.
666 Fifth Avenue
New York, New York 10103

ISBN: 0-440-50023-0

Printed in the United States of America
Published simultaneously in Canada

August 1988

10 9 8 7 6 5 4 3 2 1

MV

This book is dedicated to Barbara Fukiko Yamaguchi
(1924–1985)
Artist and patron of literature and the arts

Acknowledgments

I'm deeply indebted to the many authors, editors, publishers, booksellers, and book distributors who shared their Lit Biz experiences with me. Every published author, it seems, has a wonderful tale of how that first book or story got accepted and was brought to life on the printed page.

For invaluable and inspired assistance, I particularly thank Susan Moldow and Judy Davidoff, who edited this book, agent Luis Sanjurjo of International Creative Management, who represented it, and the faculties of Lit Biz 101 in both Carmel, California, and Seattle, Washington: Alan Furst, David Brewster, Dan Levant, Robert Kaplan, George Bennett, Gordon White, Peter C. Miller, William Minor, Michael E. Clark, Penelope Sky, Jonathan Drake, Robert H. Yamaguchi, William Webb, and Frank Gibson.

LIT BIZ 101
The Business of Literature

CONTENTS

Introduction:

Welcome to the Class   *XV*

Welcome to *Lit Biz 101*, sit down and have a cup of coffee. It's not a creative writing course, but a comprehensive seminar in what happens to your work between typewriter and bookstore counter. From your desk to the reading public; the myth of the successful author; the urge to publish; a community of minds; one writer's life, the roller-coaster ride; surviving self-employment in the literary arena; how to use this book.

CHAPTER 1:

Nonfiction Books, or Facing the Facts   *1*

Advantages of writing nonfiction; journalism and reportage; ghostwriting; what is creative nonfiction?; first-person narrative; autobiography and biography; travel and entertainment; humor; restaurant review guides; photography and art; how-to books; collaborations; anthologies; cookbooks; the nonfiction book market; the editor as target; the query letter; how to write a good query (with samples); the importance of contacts and how to cultivate them; the rejection letter; the book proposal and cover letter; follow-up; delivery date; illustrations and photos; travel expenses; non-fiction in review.

CHAPTER 2:

Fiction, or Making It All Up   24

Fiction is stranger than truth; the cult of personality; reaching the fiction editor; contacts, contacts; read what's out there; short stories; sample query letter; beyond the query letter; the finished ms.; trends in best-selling fiction; the first novel; paperback originals; the second novel and beyond; genre fiction; pornography; procrastination, discipline, and writer's block; avoiding distractions; muscling into print, dignity intact.

CHAPTER 3:

Poetry, Children's Lit, and Screenwriting   38

Other forms of writing; poetry and making a living; which poets do; income sidelines; grants for poetry; where to submit your poetry; sample query letter; poetry distribution; writing for children; age level and children's lit; querying the children's editor; query or finished manuscript?; illustrations; trends in children's lit; screenwriting and ulcers; peddling your script; the Hollywood schmooze.

CHAPTER 4:

"When Writers Get Together, All They Talk About Is Money" 52

Getting paid for your writing; the literary contract and what to watch out for; defining the terms of the contract; subsidiary rights; getting a good, fair contract; a sample literary contract, with comments; conclusion.

CHAPTER 5:

The Writer and the Law   94

Legal considerations; libel and defamation; obscenity; protecting your ideas (copyright protection); legal warranties and indemnities; disputes between author and publisher; disputes between author and author; disputes between publisher and publisher; if you get hauled into court.

CHAPTER 6:
Money and Perks 103

Royalties and how to collect them; magazine and newspaper collections; accounting and bookkeeping; limitation on income; work-related deductions; literary perks and fringe benefits; the publisher's lunch; expenses-paid travel; selling your own remainders; intangible benefits; pension and insurance protection; feast or famine; retirement, lack of.

CHAPTER 7:
Agents and Whether You Need One 112

What a agent does; finding an agent; agents for sale; nontraditional agents; the rep as agent; the bookseller as referring agent; multiple submissions.

CHAPTER 8:
Manuscript into Type 117

Lit Biz Production Lab; the ideal manuscript; "do I need a word processor?"; choosing a computer and software program; pros and cons of working on a computer; choosing a printer; electronic bulletin boards; typewriters old and new; the production schedule, step by step; notes on the production schedule; the copy editor's role; typesetting; timetable deadlines; the index.

CHAPTER 9:
The Publishing Process 127

The launch schedule; the catalog announcement; positioning; brochure and advertisement copy; publicity planning; promotion planning; day of publication.

CHAPTER 10:

Major Publishers: Going for the Gold   *131*

Advantages of having a major publisher; your friendly editor; when you lose your editor; big-house production blues; "sell" a book by its cover; control over manuscript; hard cover or paperback?; trade *vs.* mass-market paperbacks; backlist, midlist, or listless; major *vs.* small-press publishers, an author's guide.

CHAPTER 11:

Small Presses and Self-Publishing   *141*

Advantages of small-press publishing; approaching the independent publisher; how big is "small"?; where to find small publishers; the friendly editor and publisher; jumping from small to major; secondary distribution; Bookpeople; self-publishing *vs.* vanity presses; making it yourself; notes on self-publishing; a word about university presses; promoting your small-press and self-published book; the personal appearance.

CHAPTER 12:

Newspapers and Magazines, for Ink-Stained Wretches 152

Paying the rent; researching the market; different kinds of magazine and newspaper rights; fiction in magazines; nonfiction articles as book proposals; the magazine query letter; sample query letter; daily newspapers; weeklies; types of magazines; doing business with a magazine; mistakes not to make with editors; magazine excerpts; magazine payment.

CHAPTER 13:

Publishing Your Own Magazine   *160*

An outlet for your own work and for contact with other writers; editorial content; advertisers; keeping to a schedule; subscriptions; magazine distribution, major and secondary; staples or glue, glossy or newsprint?; publishing book excerpts; small magazine network.

CHAPTER 14:

On the Shelf Between Austen and Zolotow 166

Bookstore economics from the author's point of view; what you should do; direct sales by reps; meeting your publisher's representative; wholesale distributors; chain bookstores; are small bookstores extinct?; sales tactics to booksellers (A) if you're published by a publisher and (B) if your book is self-published; "I can't find it in the bookstores!"; on the shelf between A and Z.

CHAPTER 15:

Self-Promotion, the Writer's Best Friend 173

Publisher's *vs.* author's promotion; a self-promotion success story; a self-promotion sob story; the rigors of the road; the ABA booksellers convention; small-press fairs; regional bookseller conventions; working the convention floor; blurbs; criticism and reviews; the "big book" campaign: different kinds of media; the publisher-sponsored publicity tour; TV and radio talk shows; radio-phone publicity; print publicity ideas; lecture and college circuits; promotional giveaway ideas; bookstore promotion; great self-promotion, a parting tale.

CHAPTER 16:

Owning a Bookstore 188

The author as bookseller; markets and locations; knowing the market; discounts; the (dismal) economics of bookselling; how booksellers find their merchandise; returns and credits; sidelines, or how the croissant saved Faulkner; remainders; building a loyal clientele.

CHAPTER 17:
Lit Biz 201, 301, and 401 195

A Lit Biz joke; writers' associations; writers' workshops; writers' colonies; correspondence schools; grants; teaching writing instead of writing; pomp and circumstance.

SPECIAL SECTION:
How to Submit 200

A thumbnail sketch on how to submit your nonfiction, fiction, poetry, children's literature, screenwriting, and newspaper and magazine writing.

SPECIAL SECTION:
Simple Things Nobody Ever Told You 205

A miscellany of odd facts about the business of literature.

ADDENDA:
Lit Biz Reference Sources 208

A. Other books and periodicals
B. Organizations, associations, and services for the writer

GLOSSARY OF LIT BIZ TERMS 217

INDEX 223

Introduction
Welcome to the Class

Lit Biz 101, or The Business of Literature, is based on a course I've given a number of times with a faculty of professional writers, editors, and publishers. It's a series of seminars designed to teach aspiring writers the fundamentals of how writers make a living. Many people, we found, have written or are writing a book, but need the basic information on how to get their work published, get paid for it, and protect their rights as authors. *Lit Biz 101* is an introduction, you might say, to the mechanics of the publishing business. It's not a creative writing course; we don't pretend to teach you how to *write*, only how to *sell* what you've written and how to pursue a successful publishing experience with your chosen publisher.

We define publishing terms as we go along and in the *Lit Biz* Glossary at the end of the book. If a "trade phrase" used in the text is unfamiliar to you when you first encounter it, you can look it up there in a glance.

From Your Desk to the Reading Public

The concept of *Lit Biz 101* is simple: We follow your written work—and explain the process by which it successfully reaches an audience—from the moment it leaves your typewriter to the moment it's sold over the bookstore counter, examining the business in between: contracts, royalties, book production, taxes, reviews, promotion, movie rights, book clubs, and more. Our faculty has included published authors, both novelists and non-fiction writers; book and magazine editors; a lawyer and accountant who specialize in writers' needs; a publisher's rep, i.e., book salesperson, and a retail bookseller. In recent years we added a computer expert to teach about word processors and whether we really need them. Guest lecturers have included agents, screenwriters, and celebrity novelists.

This book recreates the Lit Biz 101 class in written form so that you can take advantage of the advice of professionals in selling your work. So let's not waste any time. Pour yourself a stiff cup of black coffee, or whatever *you* use to put yourself in a writing mood, and crank that first piece of foolscap into the typewriter or boot up that software. I'll wait till you have something on paper: a book, an article, or proposal.

There! That was fast. Now you're wondering how to get your worthy prose out before the reading public. And here's where the fun begins.

The Myth of the Successful Author

Over the years we've seen many types of would-be authors in the various Lit Biz 101 classes, proof perhaps of the old cliché that everybody has at least one book inside the inner soul. Women formed the majority of our student bodies and indeed, statistically, women are more apt to write than are men, just as women are more dedicated readers. Ask any bookseller. Some estimate that they sell 80 percent of their books to female customers. Our students ranged in age from eighteen to seventy-four, and in professional writing experience from none at all to a considerable publication history. Many of these students have since published their stories or books using our techniques of talent, charm, smart negotiation, aggressive but dignified self-promotion, and, yes, a dollop of old-fashioned good luck.

How many times have you said, or heard others say, "My life has been so interesting, I could write a book"? As a published author, I hear that line all the time. When that stranger beside me in the airplane or lounge extracts the information that I write books for a living, the reaction is almost universally one of admiration, even awe. Writing is perceived as a glamorous career, full of freedom, travel, fame, and riches. Of course that's a misperception in many respects: Most writers are underpaid and obscure rather than rich or famous, and there's no pain quite so excruciating as facing that lonely blank page.

But there's more than a grain of truth to the splendid mythology. A successful writing career offers self-employment, the freedom to get up in the morning when you choose and work at your own pace, the opportunity to meet and interview interesting people or travel to exotic places. The biggest drawback to a writing career, even a fairly successful one, is that the income is sporadic and fluctuates wildly between feast and famine. It's a rare author who hasn't been forced to do some other line of work at times just to keep dinner on the table.

The Urge to Publish

In any case, the urge to publish comes from some deep-seated emotional center in the writer's heart and mind. For the genuine writer it's not enough to toil in solitude, putting those precious words down for posterity or one's grandchildren. The thrill of seeing your name in print, your thoughts published, is still the greatest boost in the world to the dedicated scribe. No proliferation of movies, TV, video cassettes, and computers is ever going to eliminate the intimate pleasure of reading—and writing. Literature offers a dialogue between two minds, the author's and the reader's, that is more personal and effective than any other medium.

And personal stories are still the number one kind of book people want to write, whether in nonfiction or fiction. The advice given to young Katerina by her mama in Kathryn Forbes's best-seller of long ago, *Mama's Bank Account*, is still true: "Write about what you know." You don't have to be a movie star or national politician to have a fascinating story to tell. The late William Saroyan achieved world recognition for his tales of Armenian people living small-town lives in California, and Erma Bombeck regales millions of readers with the travails of middle-aged motherhood.

Fiction and nonfiction appear to be equally represented in the vast pool of unpublished work. But other, more specialized types of writing may interest you, and we'll cover them all, including:

- children's books, a highly specific market, which we'll talk about in Chapter 3;
- poetry, for which there is a real but limited market;
- genre fiction, such as romances, Gothics, murder mysteries, and science fiction;
- topical nonfiction, the journalistic approach to contemporary issues;
- and of course how-to and self-help books, which are so broadly popular nowadays.

Writers are naturally also interested in newspapers, magazines, scriptwriting, and ghostwriting as extra avenues of income that keep them going while they work on the Great American Book.

A Community of Minds

Although writing is a solitary activity, there's a concrete benefit to all writers in personal contact with other writers as well as editors and publishers. One of the main benefits of the Lit Biz 101 course to our students is simply that it provides them access to editors and published authors who may be willing to read their manuscripts and answer their questions. A personal relationship with an editor or any other professional in the book business, from an agent's secretary to the manager of a bookstore, is highly desirable for the aspiring writer. It's virtually a waste of your postage to mail a manuscript "over the transom" to a publisher who has never heard of you. This book will discuss all kinds of tactics for approaching editors, some traditional and others boldly original.

Imagine yourself, while you are reading this book, sitting around a big table stacked high with publishers' catalogs, freely shooting the bull with Rosemary Rogers, Kurt Vonnegut, or whoever is your favorite author, or floating your book or story idea into the ears of a sympathetic professional who can guide you into print. We've taken pains to include every aspect of the literary business here, so that all of your concerns and questions are thoroughly addressed. Check the Index for easy access to specific points that are troubling you, and use our Addenda, Lit Biz Reference Sources, to locate more information and/or get in touch with publishers.

Through *Lit Biz 101* you will be introduced into a community of minds. You can find out what you need to know to nudge your work into the light of day. We urge you to overcome any shyness you may feel about promoting your own work. No matter what anybody tells you about the difficulty of getting published and the almost insuperable hardships of trying to make your living as a writer, remember that every published author was once a struggling unknown. Every successful writer had to endure the frustrations of getting started in this racket, and had to *believe* in the work and plug away at it diligently and without despair even when the world paid little notice. The odds may be highly stacked against your getting a million-dollar advance and a movie "package," but nothing ventured is certainly nothing gained. I like the way W. Somerset Maugham put it:

"I began to meditate on the writer's life. It is full of tribulation. First he must endure poverty and the world's indifference; then, having achieved a measure of success, he must submit with a good grace to its hazards. He depends on a fickle public. . . . But he has one compensation. Whenever he has anything on his mind, whether it be a harassing reflection, grief at the death of a friend, unrequited love, wounded pride, anger at the treachery of someone to whom he has shown kindness, in short any emotion or any perplexing thought, he has only to put it down in black and white, using it as the theme of a story or the decoration of any essay, to forget all about it. He is the only free man."

Or *woman.*

One Writer's Life, the Roller-coaster Ride

Writers tend to be afflicted with large egos. I could sit and tell you stories about my Lit Biz adventures, triumphs, and disasters as long as you'd be willing to listen. But I'll keep my personal history brief. It serves not so much to toot my own horn as to establish my credentials as an instructor in literary business and illustrate some of the concerns you will face as you graduate this course and lurch into your publishing career.

Like most of you, I realized a burning desire to write very early in life, and was an avid reader from childhood. Indeed, although some authors claim not to read much, most of them are voracious readers, and reading itself is almost an essential adjunct to writing. Particularly when we are young, we learn from reading the masters, but I admit I first started to read to escape from the drabness of a mill town in Massachusetts. I was the bookworm, the "brain" of the class, the puny, bespectacled young scholar. (You know the type.) At the age of five or six, after some observant relative had given me a toy typewriter and printing kit for Christmas, I bcgan producing a family newspaper and peddled it around the neighborhood. (Or "pedaled" it, to be precise, on my bike.)

Even then I was impressed with the power of the pen and used it ruthlessly to broadcast complaints about my sister and brothers. I can remember a monumental fight with my older sister after I'd defiled her name in juvenile print. Teachers in grade school encouraged my predilection toward writing, and my first articles were published in high school and college newspapers. At seventeen I landed my first paying writing job as cub reporter for the *Lawrence* (Mass.) *Eagle Tribune* on the morning edition (night shift) at $60 a week. It was thrilling to write obituaries and hang around with the old-timers in the city room every midnight.

After college, where I edited the *Boston University News,* I co-founded an international underground and college press syndicate called Liberation News Service. Based in Washington, D.C., LNS had 500 subscribing newspapers and a million readers within a year, but we were just cranking sheets of offset printing out of an old press in our basement. The operation was entirely homemade, and my articles brought me precious little income, but I was twenty-one, starting out, willing to publish anywhere, and just grateful to be reaching an audience.

So it is with most writers, excluding those rare overnight sensations who create headlines like "Publisher Bids $1 Million for First Novel by Unknown Writer." (Beyond the simplistic headline, however, you usually discover the "unknown writer" has published several books under a pseudonym, or at least has written some articles or stories.) You write for any audience you can reach, no matter how local, noncommercial, or unglamorous. You write in the hope of catching the eye of that one person somewhere who can elevate your status and increase your readership. You write for the exposure and the sheer love of *writing*.

Case in point: Those homemade articles for LNS got around and attracted the attention of a book editor, Arnold Tovell, at Beacon Press in Boston. Beacon in 1967 was a small, religious (Unitarian-owned), politically progressive house. Tovell asked me for an anthology of the best of Liberation News Service and I produced one, but it was off the mark. No sale. He then suggested I try writing the story of the LNS myself, which I did under the title *Famous Long Ago*. I was paid an advance against royalties of $1,500 on a payout schedule, which meant I actually received $750 in advance and another $750, ten excruciating months later, when the book was finally written. Arnold Tovell, bless his soul, came in person to my remote Vermont farm, slept on the couch, and suffered the rigors of the outhouse in order to nurse me through the agonizing final chapters.

The book did well from the start. *The New York Times Book Review* praised it, and Pocket Books bought the mass-market paperback rights for $25,000—real money in 1970. It seemed to be the tip of the iceberg. My second book, *Total Loss Farm*, was promptly sold to a major publisher for hardcover (Dutton) and mass-market (Bantam) publication for exhilarating figures, and Robert Redford bought the film option for *Famous Long Ago*. I was twenty-four and flabbergasted. Fellow writers warned me that my fall was imminent. The critics don't let you get too high before they shoot you down, I was told.

Unfortunately, the soothsayers' bleak prophecy proved correct. My first novel, *Tropical Detective Story*, was a resounding flop in the marketplace. But all told, there have been eight books in the past fifteen years, all published by major houses, several in the Book-of-the-Month Club's Quality Paperback division, and some translated and published abroad. There have been years of good income and years of scraping by. I've written articles for major national magazines and poems for tiny literary quarterlies. My career has also included some ghostwriting, screenplays that were bought but not yet made into movies, many reviews, and some advertising and promotional writing.

Surviving Self-employment in the Literary Arena

My first book was published while I was in my early twenties, and made enough money that I foolishly believed I could retire for life, in the sense of never again having to hold a nine-to-five job. Of course I was dead wrong. The money was quickly spent, the audience for the kind of hip/stoned books I wrote dried up, and by the age of twenty-seven I couldn't support myself and my family on my writing income alone. So with two friends as partners, I opened a bookstore, Montana Books, in Seattle, and eventually owned three bookstores and a small-press publishing company. For seven years these literary endeavors supported me while I continued to write. I took up a casual practice of literary agenting and succeeded in selling other people's manuscripts to the publishers even when my own stuff wasn't moving. We became book distributors and consolidated a group of Seattle-area small presses into one warehouse. By the age of thirty-two I was captain of a literary empire, with a thriving small press, a giant warehouse, three bookstores, fourteen employees, and a life so full of stress and business that there was no time left for writing.

Post-divorce, I kicked it all in and moved to California, carrying only what would fit in my car. Since then I've written three new books in Carmel and enough newspaper reviews, magazine articles, newsletters, brochures, ad copy, and software documentation to again make a reasonable living from my writing alone. I have just turned forty.

So don't quit your job just yet. Not even if the publishers advance you twenty-five grand. But know that, yes, it's possible to make your principal living as a writer. It's even possible to get rich and famous as a writer, though for every one who does there must be a million who don't. The odds are lousy, but if you've got the bug, nothing's going to stop you from trying. If you've got the talent, perseverance, good luck, and inner stability to tough it out, you can see your work published and a royalty check in the mailbox. Ya gotta believe.

How to Use This Book

This book is designed to be read from start to finish like any other book. Its organization flows from the inception of the work—your writing, in various categories—to the contract, the production work, promotion, and marketing, etc., all the way to the bookstore sale. But, from experience with the Lit Biz 101 class, we recognize that some of you will be more interested in one subject than another, or have urgent concerns with particular questions. Therefore, we've provided the tools for you to quickly look up a specific item.

Use the Contents, Glossary of Lit Biz Terms, Index, and Lit Biz Reference Sources to locate or cross-reference your concerns. Remember that there is some overlapping of material—the procedure for submitting a letter of inquiry to a magazine editor, for example, is similar but different in significant ways to that for submitting a letter to a book editor. There are many exceptions to the rules for submitting material to a publisher, but the book will always state the general rule first and useful exceptions will follow. The "How to Submit" chapter offers a simple guide to preparing your writing for submission to publishers. Case histories and other anecdotal material appear in boxes throughout the text.

1 | Nonfiction Books, or Facing the Facts

Advantages of Writing Nonfiction

If you are thinking of writing nonfiction, you have at least this advantage: nonfiction books are easier than fiction to sell to a hardcover publisher, they sell better to the public, and are likelier to remain in print and generate royalties.

Having said that, we have to add several qualifications. *Some* fiction sells better than any nonfiction (except, perhaps, for the incredibly popular autobiography *Iacocca* or Bill Cosby's *Fatherhood*—novels by established titans like James Michener or Robert Ludlum are automatically, it seems, on the top ten of any best-seller list). Fiction offers greater motion picture and television possibilities; everybody loves a great novel, and even one best-seller could make you rich for life. But so-called first novels are anathema to a publisher's financial coffers; most, indeed almost all, are unprofitable.

Nonfiction books can be marketed to a publisher from an outline and some representative chapters, whereas most editors will want to see a completed novel before considering it for publication. In this chapter we're going to talk about researching the nonfiction book market, finding out what editors are looking for and what the public is interested in reading, and getting your nonfiction work out into the marketplace.

But let's start at the simplest level, by defining what a "nonfiction" book is. Strictly speaking, nonfiction is that which is true or based on fact. You may express your opinions freely, but you may not invent or make up things. From there we can easily break nonfiction down into separate categories: journalism, that is the straightforward reportage of factual events; ghostwriting, in which you write somebody else's story; "creative nonfiction," a vaguely defined concept always used by foundations and writers' grant agencies, which includes essays, opinion, and poetic prose; first-person narratives, or what-happened-to-me; autobiography and biography; travel and entertainment; humor; how-to books; collaborations and anthologies; and cookbooks. Let's look at these categories individually:

Journalism and Reportage

Journalistic nonfiction books involve someone or something in the news, and of course the more widespread the publicity, the greater the value of the potential book contract. But your topic needn't have been a national or world news item if it is, in itself, a good study of some contemporary issue that affects many people (for example: a cancer victim's story, a child kidnapping story from the parents' point of view, any story of courage and tenacity overcoming some tragic misfortune). As with all news, timing is essential—you want your book to come out on the shelves while the issue is still timely and not overworked to death—and, unfortunately, bad news still sells better than good.

Bad news can even be good news for the writer and publisher. The eruption of Mount St. Helens in Washington State in 1981, for example, was a natural catastrophe that made a small press, Madrona Publishers of Seattle, into a "booming" concern, no pun intended. Dan Levant, president of Madrona, rounded up the best reporting and photographs on the volcanic eruption and rushed *Volcano* into print. It became a national best-seller. There followed a rash of imitators, but Madrona reaped the rewards for being there first.

Violent crime such as murder, serial killing, and assassination, lumped together in the "true crime" category by publishers, is guaranteed to fascinate the public and therefore sell. Truman

Capote may have made his greatest impression on American readers with *In Cold Blood*, the story of two perverted killers. More recently we've seen best-selling books about Gary Gilmore, Son of Sam, and Charles Manson's "family." Wherever tragedy befalls us, some journalist is right behind, and if the tragedy happens to befall you personally, you've got the inside story.

Investigative reporting in books has been popular since the Woodward and Bernstein Watergate series, which sent a whole generation of students to journalism schools in search of the glamorous life of a reporter uncovering government wrongdoing. (Ha! The average reporter is an underpaid stiff whose assignments are rarely more glamorous than city council meetings.)

At any rate, your journalistic nonfiction book will be judged on the merits of how well you prove your argument, so make your research thorough and try to interview all concerned parties. This process of getting to the truth of a matter is tricky, because the deeper you delve into it, the more complex the situation becomes. Different people will offer contradictory accounts of an event, simply because they perceived it differently or because they have something to hide. If you let your own opinion get in the way of "objective" reporting, you're not only ignoring one of the first rules of journalism, but you're leaving yourself vulnerable to critics who might dismiss your work as biased or who might sue you for libel. Be careful, get the facts, or at least all the variant versions of them.

Ghostwriting

A large percentage of best-selling celebrity works and autobiographies are ghostwritten. The writer works with the celebrity and actually does all the writing but takes a subordinate credit, or gets no public mention of his/her contribution. However, he or she always receives some payment and often a share of the royalties. So when you see a book that loudly proclaims it's "BY FAMOUS BASEBALL STAR" (or MOVIE STAR, POLITICIAN, TV PERSONALITY, etc.) there's usually a line in much smaller type that reads, "*With* Joe Ghostwriter." (Although a true definition of a "ghost" is one who gets no credit and is known only to the celebrity.)

What this means is that if you can convince someone famous to let you write his/her book, you probably have a good chance of selling it to a publisher on the strength of the celebrity's name, even if yours is not well known. Some ghostwriters, however, are thorough professionals who specialize in the craft and work with a succession of different collaborators, from diet doctors to former presidents to cinema idols.

Ghostwriting and collaboration are not the same thing. A pure collaboration involves two or more people working with equal status and credit. Occasionally a celebrity author will collaborate with a professional writer, but more often the famous person will hire a ghost.

---

*Most people realize that celebrity books are written by ghosts, but few understand how many other kinds of books and articles are assisted by, or written by, unnamed ghostwriters. Every professional writer will sooner or later entertain an offer to write something for someone who has thoughts or experiences he wants to see in print but lacks sufficient writing ability. Textbook editor Penelope Sky and I had a small business in Carmel, California, called Autobiographies, Ink. For a modest fee we would write, edit, and produce any person's autobiography in an elegant bound edition suitable for copying and/or giving to friends or grandchildren. We found that senior citizens were usually willing to pay for this highly personal service in order to have a family history to pass on to their heirs. Berkeley novelist Thomas Farber (*Curves of Pursuit*) ghostwrote memoirs for a former top-security government official in Washington, D.C., to keep himself in the black while working on his own fiction. As politicians hire speechwriters, corporate presidents often hire ghostwriters to handle everything from memos to correspondence. And we'll never know what percentage of nonfiction books are written by ghosts.*

Ghostwriting offers very little ego gratification but can be an invaluable source of support income to the working writer. It requires the writer to subsume his or her identity completely, taking on the voice and concerns of the employer, or "principal" author.

There is no industry standard for ghostwriters' pay. It depends completely on negotiations between the publisher, the celebrity, the ghostwriter, and the agents and lawyers who represent the celebrity and the ghostwriter. Generally, though, the celebrity will receive the lion's share of the royalties and the ghostwriter the remaining portion. Some ghostwriters even accept a flat payment with no share of the royalties, but that's likely to be a bad mistake. What if the book sells a million copies and you've settled for a $10,000 fee?

Collaborations

Collaborations involve two (or more) authors, or an author and an illustrator, working together on a book. They tend to work best when the artists know each other's work and temperament and have a mutual vision of the work. Each partner should be contributing a unique *aspect* of the book, but some writers' collaborations have been so pure that the reader can't distinguish one stylist from the other. An important point: Collaborators should establish at the outset, in the language of the literary contract, exactly what percentage of the rights and royalties each will receive. In a case of pure collaboration, the split may be 50-50, or an equal amount to each author. But that's not always the case. The share of rights and money is a negotiable item, and one that should be determined and agreed upon before the work begins in order to avoid misunderstandings (or even lawsuits) later.

(What Is) Creative Nonfiction?

The category of "creative nonfiction," a term that is often used by writers' organizations like American PEN or agencies that issue grants to writers, like the National Endowment for the Arts, is rather maddeningly hard to define. It's easier to say what it is *not*: It is not journalism, not the straightforward narrative chronology of events. Yet some kind of nonfiction assignments can fall into the "creative" category if the author has tackled the subject with a good deal of personal style. (A good example is Annie Dillard's *Pilgrim at Tinker Creek.* It's not only a book about nature, but about the author's interaction with nature, a symphony of personal observation.)

Creative nonfiction typically includes essays, opinion, and poetic prose. But what is "creative" and what is not is still a matter for subjective judgment in many cases. And while creative nonfiction is good for getting grants, it tends to be less commercially viable than other forms of nonfiction. Most publishers don't want to bring out a collection of essays because there is little popular demand for the form.

First-Person Narratives, or What-Happened-to-Me

If something extraordinary has happened to you (and, come to think of it, doesn't something extraordinary happen to just about everybody at least once in life?) *and* you have the ability to write about it, you've possibly got a first-person narrative nonfiction book. The most successful books in this area have an inspirational tone: they reveal how the author overcame anorexia, cancer, alcoholism, or some other tragic setback.

Personal Narrative

Lynne Sharon Schwartz, a well-known novelist, lost her New York apartment in a fire and wrote her first nonfiction book about how she and her neighbors fought the landlord, Columbia University, which refused to help its burned-out tenants relocate although it controlled 4,500 other apartments. The tenants eventually won their case. The book is We Are Talking About Homes.

The trick here is to convince the publisher that your first-person experience is interesting enough to gain a wide readership. If the book is to substantially cover all or a major portion of your life, it qualifies as autobiography; if it focuses on one dramatic event in your life, such as Schwartz's fire, it's personal narrative.

Autobiography and Biography

These two compadres are still among the most popular nonfiction books. Your autobiography—the story of your own life, written by you—will appeal to a publisher in direct proportion to the extent that you have: (a) been famous; (b) hung around with and know the intimate secrets of famous people; (c) experienced unusual or historically dramatic events, or (d) lived an ordinary life but managed to find universal truths in it.

People who become fabulously rich by their own efforts seem to have great autobiographical potential, as everybody loves a success story. Those who live to be extremely old are interesting because they are a link to a time gone by. And folks who have overcome enormous adversity, such as confinement to a Nazi concentration camp or diagnosis of a fatal disease, have interesting autobiographies. But personal fame or some connection to the famous and newsworthy crowd is still the best qualification for writing your own life story and getting it published.

Biography is another matter of course. Nothing can stop a writer from compiling the story of another person's life, even if unauthorized by the subject or his heirs. People love to read scandalous unauthorized biographies of movie stars and other media idols, like Kitty Kelley's book on Frank Sinatra, *His Way*. If the star objects, the attendant publicity could make the book sell even better, or so conventional thinking goes. Publishers are in danger of legal liability with an unauthorized book based on the life of a living person, and they will insist that you verify your sources. Biographies of deceased persons are a safer business, but not entirely free of litigious possibilities if the subject has living relatives.

Long-dead subjects pose no such problems, as everyone else in their biographies is long-dead also. If you could assemble the true but little-known story of an elegant marquise in seventeenth-century France who lived a riotously decadent life and seduced two kings, you'd have quite a yarn and an action-packed biography. You might even have a best-seller.

Travel

The professional travel writer is a rare species but a lucky one, we tend to think. But even an amateur traveler can write a book about exotic experiences on the road or even at home. Consider beginning your career as a travel writer for the Sunday newspaper travel section—most of them do use free-lance contributions—and how about writing up your own city for one of the many travel guides published by American Express, AAA, Frohmer's, and so forth? Many of those publishers use "stringers," local writers who submit work to a central editor. Check our "How to Submit" chapter for special guidelines on how to query editors.

And if you've lived through a marvelous adventure, you may have found great material for a whole travel book. Most of us, for one reason or another, can't run around the world on a luxury liner (or even a tramp steamer) but we love to read about it. Give me any travel book by Jan Morris, Thor Heyerdahl, or Henry Miller and I feel as if I'm taking the journey with them. Novelist Paul Theroux took us on a memorable armchair tour of Asia in his travel book *The Great Railway Bazaar*, for instance.

But, seriously, can you easily find a publisher for your travel book merely because you had a fascinating time in Europe? Of course not. The special grace and writing skill possessed by a Jan Morris is a unique gift. Even if her *experiences* abroad are not all that earth-shaking or unusual, she has the ability to paint an oil on canvas with words; she makes you *feel* the places she's been, she notices small details, overhears snatches of conversation. She lets the reader in on the adventure of seeing new places, something every successful travel book must do.

Humor

The humor concept book and other "nonbook" books, such as cartoon collections, are a special but large market. People who would never buy and read a serious book will do both for a funny book, especially at Christmastime. The publisher's litmus test here is simply whether your book makes editors laugh. If it does, it may make readers laugh, although there's no guarantee. The occasional blockbuster humor book, like *The Preppie Handbook*, is convincing evidence of the huge readership possible when you strike America's funnybone.

But as any stand-up comedian can tell you, a writer who can turn out funny jokes is one of the great wonders of the world. Those who are very good at it can potentially make a great living "doctoring" comedy scripts or authoring funny books. But the competition is fierce and no laughing matter. What is hilarious to one person may be offensive to another or, worse yet, just plain flat and unfunny.

Restaurant Review Guides

If you think of yourself as an expert on fine dining, and particularly if you can get your restaurant reviews published in a local newspaper or magazine, you may consider authoring one of the restaurant review books that are now so popular, especially in major cities and resorts. But technically you don't need any kind of official culinary degree to set yourself up as a food critic; most of the restaurant guides we see on the West Coast are self-published or produced by small presses. Out-of-towners will definitely buy any good-looking book that offers an insider's critique of dining and/or entertainment.

Photography and Art

It's a bit heretical to classify photography and art books as "entertainment" when they can be high art forms. We mean no disrespect. A photographer or artist who has achieved enough recognition to have his/her works published in book form is invariably both talented and widely recognized. Photographer Ansel Adams and artist Georgia O'Keeffe, both recently deceased, are good examples of visual artists whose books were best-sellers in their field.

The market for art and photo books is a special, rather rarefied one. Because of high production costs, these volumes tend to be more expensive than other books. They're often sold at Christmastime and given as gifts. Also, some people who think they don't have time to read books do buy picture books for the pleasure of the images, because they admire the artist's work, or because the book makes a fine decoration for the coffee table.

If your nonfiction book contains a lot of visuals, you can expect a higher risk factor and resistance from a publisher. From a bookseller's point of view, photo and art books are an elegant curse and blessing at the same time: they're costly, customers can absorb them in ten minutes standing up in the bookstore, they sell slowly and get shopworn. But when Christmas rolls around and people are willing to pay $50 to $100 for a fine book, the bookseller enjoys a brief period of relative affluence.

How-to Books

How-to, or self-help books, are so popular now that *The New York Times* maintains a separate best-seller list for these titles. Any book that breaks ground in a how-to category that captures the interest of the general public has an excellent chance of success, even if it originates with a small press or self-publishing venture.

How-to books fall into numerous categories, including but not limited to:

- diet
- health
- psychological self-help
- marriage and love
- sex
- exercise
- home/auto repair
- decorating and entertaining
- business and career success

If you can "do it," and teach somebody else how, you could have a gold mine.

Gen MacManiman of Fall City, Washington, was in her fifties, and had no publishing history, when she wrote Dry It, You'll Like It, *which sold well over 400,000 copies in paperback. She and her husband, Bob, had designed a wooden food dehydrator on their farm, which they manufactured one at a time for a small clientele consisting of friends. Those same friends often asked Gen for copies of her recipes. Years of experimenting in the kitchen had taught her how to dry every imaginable fruit and vegetable and even some kinds of meat.* Dry It *developed as a cookbook for owners of food dehydrators and included blueprints for building one's own dehydrator.*

The initial press run was 1,000 copies. Once the book took off, Gen was reprinting it in quantities of 25,000 at a time. She published the book out of her own living room, maintaining her office and book storage space at home and employing a printing press in nearby Seattle. She used this printing press although she knew that she could get the book printed much cheaper out of state. She even turned down an offer from Bantam Books for the rights, saying, "Why should I collect a ten percent royalty when I've already got a forty percent publisher's share by doing it myself?"

Anthologies

Anthologies are a writer's backup. These collections of disparate writings by many authors on a common theme (even if it's as vague as "new American essays") provide small income for the author but a continuing life for the work and an opportunity for the beginning writer. That is, it may be easier for you to sell a publisher on an anthology of previously published work, edited by yourself, than on a new work by an unknown writer. (As I mentioned earlier, my very first book started out as a commission for an anthology of the "best of Liberation News Service.") Most anthologies are for use in classrooms, so themes that are "teachable" are most likely to be published.

Anthologies reprint work that has already appeared in a book or periodical so the author generates a *little* extra income from the piece, frosting on the cake, although the original book publisher (if the anthologized piece is an excerpt) usually handles the negotiations and takes a small percentage of the payment. If you are trying to put an anthology together, you'll have to clear permissions and bring in the work at a price low enough to make the book profitable to the publisher.

Once you *are* a published author, it's an honor to have some part of your book, or one of your articles or essays, included in an anthology. And it's especially fun and gratifying when the professor who edits the book includes classroom questions and composition assignments based on your work.

Cookbooks

Last, but far from least in this nonfiction roundup, are the cookbooks. There seem to be an infinite number of them, but that doesn't stop publishers from producing more every year. When trying to sell a new cookbook to a publisher, you should be prepared to demonstrate that yours is an original approach, a kind of cookery not already represented in book form. In short, you need an angle. When electric crock pots were new, then-tiny HP Books of Tucson, Arizona, hit the national best-seller lists with *Crockery Cookery*. Vegetarian and ethnic cookbooks abound, and these days microwave recipes are particularly popular. Publishers are eternally looking for what's new in cuisine.

Fictional Nonfiction?

Nowadays we even see novels whose characters include actual historical figures (E. L. Doctorow's Ragtime *or Richard Miller's* Snail*), which blurs the clear distinction between what is fiction and what is not. These are "factional" books, a curious hybrid of fiction and nonfiction.*

The Nonfiction Book Project

Once you've got an idea for a nonfiction book, you've got to research thoroughly two important markets: Which publisher is right for this book and who are the readers going to be? If you were writing, say, on the CIA's role in Central America, you wouldn't offer the book to Sunset Magazine Press, which does books on gourmet dining and home decorating. You'd need to find a publisher who is already doing serious political books, *and whose point of view is compatible with your book.* If you take a pro-CIA, conservative stand, perhaps National Review Press would be interested, but if you're writing a muckraking, anti-CIA exposé, you'd find a warmer reception at Beacon Press.

Find out what publishers are interested in and what editors are looking for. It's as easy as keeping up with what's being published, which you can do best by reading *Publishers Weekly,* the trade magazine for the publishing industry, every week, even if it takes most of the week. *Literary Market Place* (hereafter *LMP*) and *Writer's Market* are both excellent resources for telling you simply the specialties of each publisher, the kind of books that publisher is interested in, and the names of some of the editors, so that you don't waste your time and money sending your "Cajun Kitchen" cookbook to a publisher who does only sexy soap-opera novels in paperback. Many other sources and resources are listed in the Addenda, Lit Biz Reference Sources.

All publishers are not alike. Hardcover publishers, for example, adhere to a different standard for choosing books than paperback houses do, just as hardcover royalty rates are usually higher than paperback ones. And publishers who do both hard cover and paperbacks may offer you the so-called hard/soft contract with different terms for each kind of edition. Every publisher has its own in-house style book and rules governing the submission of manuscripts. Before you decide to solicit a given publisher, find out as precisely as possible what it requires of its authors and what kind of publishing the firm is involved in—hard cover, trade paperback, mass-market paperback, or some combination of all three. (Mass market are the rack-sized paperbacks available at airports and at the supermarket, as well as in bookstores; trade paperbacks are generally larger and more costly and aimed at a smaller and more specific audience. Check the Glossary and Chapter 14, on book distribution, for more on the differences between publishers and distributors.)

Understand who your potential readers are. A publisher is going to be a lot more interested in your manuscript if he thinks he can identify the market precisely. This is an area in which nonfiction has great advantages over fiction. A novel is rather generally aimed at readers of novels, but a book on skiing has a built-in skier market.

Obviously, the publisher is going to be more interested if your targeted potential readership is a large one, but even matters of fairly esoteric interest can produce a profitable book if marketed very specifically to the limited readership. This book you have in your hand, for example, is written for the person who wants to sell his or her writing; millions of people are in that group, so naturally Dell hopes it will sell. (But Dell doesn't hope so nearly as fervently as *I* do! It has hundreds of titles to promote, while I have just this one. We'll get deeper into this in Chapter 15, "Self-Promotion, the Writer's Best Friend.")

Okay, once you've found a list of publishers who might be interested in your book because it fits their "line," and you've established who precisely is going to be interested in reading it, you're ready for the assault.

HOW TO SUBMIT: For a summary of the following guidelines, see our Special Section, "How to Submit."

The Editor as Target

Your first task is to get the attention of an editor, to get that person to at least *read* your work. Naturally, these creatures called editors are constantly under siege from thousands of people just like you and me; your typical New York major-house editor sits in an office stacked from floor to ceiling with manuscripts waiting to be read, and your best chance to get a sympathetic reading will result from having a personal relationship with the editor. I'd go so far as to say a personal obligation owed from editor to author is even better. If there's some clever way you can get an editor in your debt, you sly devil you, do it.

Starting at a basic level, let's assume you live in Garrison Keillor's Lake Wobegon, Minnesota, far from any publisher's office, and you don't know a soul in the publishing business. How are you going to crack Simon and Schuster? How are you going to introduce yourself and your book idea?

It's pointless to address your manuscript to Simon and Schuster, simply. Remember that your research in *LMP, Writer's Market, Publishers Weekly* and other sources has already given you the names of some editors. Alternately, you may see, for example, that Publisher A has brought out a book that is in your field, so you can call that publisher and ask the telephone receptionist for the name of the editor of that book. Such information is routinely given over the phone, and then you can address that person with your initial query. Since you've uncovered an editor's name through a mixture of careful reading, chicanery, and outright gall, use it in your query letter. Always include a stamped, self-addressed envelope for their response.

The Query Letter

In some cases it's advisable to telephone the editor directly. But even if you're a great talker and the editor is willing to take your call, he or she will still ask you to write a cover letter and query and/or send a proposal. Generally, editors are too busy to take calls from unknown authors, so the *query letter* is your best initial thrust. Editors do read their mail, of course, and a brief letter that succinctly describes the book you're writing, the reasons why this publisher should be interested, and the market you're writing for may very well generate an interested response. I strongly recommend to our Lit Biz 101 students that they hold an initial query letter down to *one page*. Puh-leeze. Even if your topic is so complicated and intricate that it would take ten pages to fully describe it, you can write that fuller description once you've got an editor on the hook and interested. Editors have time to read a one-page letter, and a quick-punch description of what you're up to may pique someone's interest even if it's a totally "cold" contact—that is, someone who doesn't know you from Adam or Eve.

(At one point in my career I turned down what my mother called a "golden opportunity" of a full-time editorship at a major house, McGraw-Hill, simply because I realized there would be query letters and manuscripts landing on my desk all day long *that I'd be obliged to read,* and I feared there'd be no time left over in which to *write.* If nothing else, editors are paid to read potential books. And if your idea is a good one, and well presented, there's no reason why you shouldn't be able to interest an editor.)

How to Write a Good Query Letter

Follow this simple formula, then add right-brain personal charms of your own:

1. Describe the book you're writing.
2. State why this publisher should be interested.
3. Identify who the potential readers are.
4. List your prior credits and publications, if any.

A sample query letter follows. Relate your book to the editor's specific interests and the publisher's specific needs, and point up the market this book will appeal to.

Sample Query Letter

J. P. Author
150 Main Street
Yourtown, CA 99999

December 1, 1987

Mr. Gilbert Editor
Major Publishers, Inc.
Madison Avenue
New York, NY 11111
Dear Mr. Editor:

I am currently at work on a book about the computer software industry and the many changes it is undergoing in the current economy. Since your firm publishes the excellent Personal Computing Series of books, I feel sure that you would be interested in reading my manuscript with a view toward acquiring and publishing it.

My targeted readership is the vast pool of individuals who are now using a personal computer at work or in the home. The book discusses many of the new software products available to readers and rates them according to quality and price. I will cover over 500 such products in the book, which will contain approximately 250 pages (double spaced) of text plus index and glossary. I expect to be able to deliver the final manuscript within a year, on December 1, 1988.

My writing has appeared here in Yourtown in the <u>Yourtown Gazette</u>, which runs my personal computer column, "First Byte." I enclose a copy of the most recent column. I am employed as a copywriter for the Fabulous Software Development Group, Inc.

Please let me know if my book seems right for you. I have enclosed a S.A.S.E. for your response. I would be glad to forward to you the full proposal and several sample chapters. Thank you for your attention, and I look forward to hearing from you.

Sincerely yours,

J. P. Author

The Importance of Contacts and How to Cultivate Them

Of course it is immensely preferable if you have had some earlier contact with the editor or have an acquaintance in common who can provide an introduction, and that is the arena in which the big-city folks have it over the rest of us. If you want to be a published writer, New York City is still the best place to be, and Los Angeles still has the most work for screenwriters. A kind of teeming community of publishing is going on in these places, and if you're there, you're far more accessible than in Lost Corners, Nevada. It didn't hurt my cause as a young writer that I was operating out of Boston, Washington, and New York City. Since 1973, however, I've lived on the West Coast, where small presses are numerous but the life-style can be conducive to falling out of touch with New York. I need periodic trips back East to keep abreast.

Your job, then, is to meet editors any way you can, it's that simple. If distance and inexperience inhibit the possibility of a three-martini publisher's lunch on Madison Avenue, use the public mails, the phone lines, even a dramatic telegram (NOVEL FINISHED. SENDING FEDERAL EXPRESS. NOTIFY PROMOTION DEPARTMENT).

If your sister-in-law's cousin once published a book with Harper & Row, get a reference to his editor. Many published authors are so vulnerable to flattery that if you write to praise their books, they may be willing to read your stuff.

> *Go to readings, writers' conferences, library events, regional book fairs, and booksellers' conventions, anywhere where you have a chance of encountering editors and/or published authors. You won't come to their attention unless you're willing to speak up!*

The story of author Gretel Ehrlich is a good example of absolute pluck overcoming relative obscurity. She had published essays in *The Atlantic* and *Vanity Fair,* so she was hardly an unknown writer, but she'd never had a book published when she submitted *The Solace of Open Spaces* to an editor at Henry Holt & Co. (formerly Holt, Rinehart and Winston; things are constantly changing in the publishing world). It's a book of essays on the Wyoming wilderness, where Gretel, a vigorous and brave soul and fine writer, lives among sheepherders and ranchers. Not having heard from the editor for a time, she flew to New York City from Wyoming and called the guy to announce that she was in town for a few days and needed an immediate assessment of her work. The overworked editor hadn't touched her manuscript in months, of course, but he read it that night on the commuter train out of New York and offered her a book contract the following morning! She didn't have an agent, so the publisher arranged one. The book appeared in November 1985.

I don't recommend this bold approach unless you live with ranchers in Wyoming and have had your pieces in *The Atlantic* and *Vanity Fair.* You could wind up in Times Square with nobody to call, waiting on Western Union for money from home. (I've been there.)

The Rejection Letter

Your query letter is likely to produce one of two reactions from the editor: either a rejection letter or an invitation to submit a full book proposal and sample chapters (or, in some cases, the book manuscript itself). Nearly every author has received rejection letters, and you can't let them discourage you to the point of quitting writing or you'll never make it. What's important is the *kind* of rejection you get:

—A preprinted, impersonal, unsigned rejection letter is the ultimate rejection, of course. It means nobody at the publishing company took the trouble to give you a personal reaction to your work.

—A personal letter giving a critique of your work is much better; at least you can learn one editor's response to your work, and the criticism may be helpful.

—A personal letter rejecting the work but expressing interest in seeing it revised, or in seeing more of your work, is better still: The editor has left a door open and essentially invited you to continue to submit more. You're "still alive" with that house.

The Book Proposal and Cover Letter

If you've elicited positive interest from an editor, you'll probably be asked to submit a proposal and some sample chapters from your nonfiction book in progress. It may seem odd, but initially most editors would rather read a proposal and some sample material than a whole book; again, it's a question of time conservation. Editors also enjoy the process of working *with* the author on a nonfiction book, and it often helps if the editor is involved with the project from its inception. Your book outline, sample chapters, and a cover letter that details the mechanics of the book and whatever publishing credits you may have must be impressive enough to convince the editor that you have the ability to deliver a publishable book, so consider this proposal carefully and send what you consider your most polished work.

Elements of the book proposal:

1. Chapter by chapter outline of the book. The outline portion of a good book proposal is not much different from outlines you may have written in school. You want to list the chapters in order and indicate briefly what material each will contain. If your chapters have subdivisions or other internal organization, include them here, but succinctly.

2. Sample chapters from the book. A few representative chapters, not more than fifty pages, is about right.

3. Cover letter stating various mechanics of the book. The cover letter addresses all the marketing and contractual issues: date of delivery, illustrations, length, travel expenses, promotional possibilities, etc., anything that helps the publisher see the value in your book. If there are to be illustrations, you should specify who will provide them and who will pay for them. (More about this shortly.) Indicate a schedule with a delivery date and some rough estimate of length. You may want to add some paragraphs about the physical production of the book, its intended market, your promotional abilities (are you willing to hit the talk-show circuit? is your uncle the chief buyer for B. Dalton's national chain? can you generate local reviews and appearances in bookstores? etc.) and anything else that gives the editor a fuller picture.

Some book proposals are just three to five pages while others are framed in a glassine binder, illustrated with photographs, and printed on heavy rag content, 80-pound bond stock. You can get as fancy as you like, but don't let your book proposal grow into half a book; it's still got to be readable in a short time and present a thoroughly planned, well-thought-out overview of your proposed book.

Follow-up

If you're asked for a proposal, follow up using the guidelines above. But what if you don't get any reply at all to your query letter? Your follow-up should be a second letter reminding the editor that you are waiting for a response and generally reiterating the content of your initial query and of your book. *But,* don't send that follow-up letter until you've given the editor a decent amount of time. Typically, a major publishing house will take one to three months to reply.

The too-good proposal: a cautionary tale . . .

There have even been cases in which a book proposal was so terrific that major publishers fought over the right to buy a first-time author's book without seeing a word of actual text. As a literary agent, I represented an author who proposed a book on how to fix old cars—all makes and models of American-made vehicles. It was called Save This Car *and the proposal was dazzlingly complete and handsomely produced. The book "package" included a top-flight graphic designer so that the author was selling not only the text but a complete book set up for the printer, with illustrations, engine diagrams, a full index. Three major New York publishers wanted the book, and it was sold for an advance of $17,500 to the author and another $10,000 to the illustrator/designer. (Half paid on signing, the other half on delivery of an acceptable manuscript.) But not one word of the book ever got written!*

The would-be author of Save This Car *took his money and made a down payment on a small house and farm in Nova Scotia, from which he stalled and procrastinated. When no manuscript at all had appeared after a year's time, I drove up there and found him, deep into the snowy wilderness, unable to move from his cold-comfort farm because he couldn't get his car started! After two years his editor in New York was fired from the job and nobody else at that publishing house seemed to remember* Save This Car. *To my knowledge, the author neither returned the advance money nor wrote the book.*

However, even if he ever decided to write it, he wouldn't set any records for lateness of delivery. A former editor of mine at Dutton once reported receiving a manuscript in 1973 that had been signed to a contract in 1922!

But don't count on this working for you! The terms of any standard literary contract leave the publisher the right to collect back any advance money paid out for undelivered material. Publishers can and do take non-delivering authors to court.

Delivery Date

You don't want to be a *late* deliverer, so be sure the timetable you describe in the query letter and book-proposal cover letter is realistic. The delivery date (the date by which you propose a final manuscript will be in the publisher's hands) should give you a reasonable amount of time to do the work, based on your personal writing speed. The deadline *can* be crucial in a nonfiction book, particularly if your topic is of current news interest or if another book on the same topic is forthcoming from a competing publisher. Missing your delivery date may constitute grounds for rejection of the manuscript and return of advance moneys. If you're going to be late finishing a manuscript, let your editor know as well in advance as you can.

Illustrations and Photos

Many nonfiction books require illustrations, photos, graphs, charts, or other visual documentation. There is no standard policy in this regard, so the question of who provides and who pays for any illustrations is open to negotiation. The proposal should make your requirements regarding these terms clear. Payments for illustrations can range from a flat fee all the way to a partial royalty; in some cases the publisher will issue an advance to the author on condition that he/she must provide the artwork with the manuscript, but other times the publisher will pay the illustrator separately. A standard example of the latter is the children's book field, in which the illustrator's contribution is sometimes equal to or more important than the author's.

Travel Expenses

If the writing of your nonfiction book will require travel expenses connected to your research, again you should make that clear in the cover letter with your proposal. Be advised, though, that publishers very rarely are willing to give an author an expense account. (Magazines more often do.) Most publishers will expect you to pick up your own travel expenses out of the advance on royalties. The advance should therefore be adequate to cover those expenses unless you plan to subsidize your own publisher, in the sense of paying for your own travel in the faith that future sales of the book will make it worthwhile. Many authors do so, and it can be worth the gamble.

Nonfiction in Review

We've had a long look at nonfiction books, how they are sold to a publisher and what kinds, or categories, they fall into. But the discussion is hardly complete, of course. In chapters to follow we'll look at the literary contract, the agreement between author and publisher to publish a book, the distribution process by which books are sold, the role of the literary agent, and the business of selling nonfiction articles to magazines and newspapers, among other topics. If there were a single most important bit of advice to leave you with here, it would be simply this: Make sure you really know what a given publisher is likely to be interested in before making your approach or proposal. Take the time, do the research, to find out the differences between publishing houses and their specialties. The more accurately you can pinpoint the editor who is going to be interested in your manuscript, the more likely you are to sell your nonfiction book to a publisher.

2 | Fiction, or Making It All Up

They say that truth is stranger than fiction, but nothing could be stranger than the fiction market. It's potentially quite lucrative, of course, but the general trend is that first novels (the author's first published full-length fiction work) don't sell well enough to earn a profit for the publisher. So by what miracle do they continue to get published at all? Aside from the long-shot (but real!) chance of a best-seller, major houses will bring out a new author's novel from pure admiration for the work, a feeling of responsibility to the tradition of fine literature in print, or the expectation of a modest reward and an interest in "investing" in that author's future success.

In any case, you get the picture: It's more difficult to sell a novel than a nonfiction book, and the marketing of a first novel is risky. Nonetheless, every novelist's career starts with the first one, and almost every major publisher brings out first novels, so take heart! While it's a difficult hurdle to overcome, it's hardly impossible.

"Fiction" defined here is absolute invention, a story that is the product of your imagination and entirely made up. Although you may be using real people you know as models for your characters, they should be sufficiently disguised to qualify as fictitious. Almost every novel carries an author's disclaimer (usually on the copyright page, the left-hand page on the other side of the title page) asserting that "This is a work of fiction.... Any resemblance to actual persons, living or dead, is entirely coincidental." Here we have a very fine line, which sometimes leads to the courts. (See our discussion of libel in Chapter 5, "The Writer and the Law.") The best fiction has a lot of truth in it—that is, the made-up story reflects true experience or advances a true understanding of life—and all fictional characters, even outlandish creatures in a science-fiction novel, are based in the author's composite experience of real people he or she has encountered. *But* if your main character bears a striking resemblance to Uncle Harry and is portrayed as an alcoholic and compulsive gambler, you'd better move Harry to another state and make him physically opposite to his "real" self. Naturally, don't call him Harry. Better yet, make him a woman.

Novelists are an eccentric breed. No other kind of writer has the broad freedom to invent a personal universe and people it with imaginary characters. An essential part of writing a good novel is having a highly personal style, and successful novelists develop personal followings. Vast numbers of people rush out and buy every new title from James Michener, Kurt Vonnegut, James Clavell, etc. When you buy an Agatha Christie novel, you know what you're getting. The trick, of course, is to build up that kind of name recognition, which takes some years and a lot of patience. Vonnegut, for example, published his first six novels while still working for General Electric as a public relations writer.

The Cult of Personality

The cult of personality is the novelist's popular support. Unlike nonfiction books, which can sell because of the subject matter and not the author's name, novels sell because readers are devoted to their favorite novelists. The exception to this is genre fiction, such as romances, Gothics, mysteries, and science fiction; a certain reader will buy a particular *type* of novel and read hundreds of them. But even with genre fiction, favorite authors get preference.

Publishers are not above exploiting a famous novelist's name in order to push other books. Pocket Books has a series called "Harold Robbins Presents" of novels written in the Harold Robbins *style* by lesser-known authors. The name "Harold Robbins" appears on the cover in much bigger type than the real author's byline. And how many times have we seen novels described as being "in the tradition of (Famous Author)" or a "cross between (Famous Author) and (Famous Author)"?

All is fair in your drive to make your name and novel a household term and bedside necessity. Here's how:

Reaching the Fiction Editor

The initial outreach to fiction editors is the same as for nonfiction editors: careful research of the fiction market through our old friends *LMP, PW, Writer's Market,* and of course the various magazines and quarterlies that publish fiction, followed by the query letter or call. The query letter describes your novel (or collection of short stories) as colorfully but succinctly as possible. However, the process of getting published from that point is distinctly different from nonfiction.

For starters, the book proposal (outline, sample chapters, and cover letter) is just an initial step with fiction. Whereas a nonfiction book can be sold from an outline, most editors would need to see a whole, finished novel in manuscript before deciding for sure whether to publish it. It takes a lot more time to read a novel than a proposal, so the hardest part of your task is finding an editor who's willing to give you a serious reading.

(We are referring to the marketing of fiction by a previously unpublished writer. Naturally, a writer who's already *had* novels published may be able to win a contract on the strength of a proposal alone. Some best-selling authors like Danielle Steel and Sidney Sheldon may be able to get a contract on the strength of a *title* alone, but we're not in that elite class—yet!)

Contacts, Contacts

Refer back to the previous chapter's discussion of the importance of contacts. What is true for nonfiction is equally so for fiction. If you admire the novels of a given writer, and feel that your own fiction belongs in the same genre or is similar in style, you could find out who the novelist's editor is and approach him or her with your query letter. Notice that when people describe a novel they often compare it to other, more famous novels, or the writer to other novelists: "It reads like an Arthur Conan Doyle mystery, with a twist of Steven King"; "Her style is reminiscent of the late Jacqueline Susann. . . ." It might definitely help you to be in touch with any published novelists you can meet through writers' workshops, book fairs and conventions, or creative writing classes at your local college or university. Many accomplished fiction writers do seminars, workshops, and classes to supplement their writing income. And don't overlook the many "little" magazines that publish fiction; through them you might get in written or personal contact with other fiction writers and fiction editors.

Read What's Out There

There are as many ways of writing a steaming potboiler of a novel as there are successful novelists. Jackie Collins doesn't read like Arthur Hailey. Beginning novelists have to look at their own experiences and consider what they like to read, as both will influence their own work of fiction. It's worth repeating the ancient advice that you should write about what you know. And naturally you'll know more about different genres of fiction if you read them. After you read a large number of romance novels, for example, you have a definite sense of the formula that is followed in producing novels in this genre.

Short Stories

The traditional avenue to the novel is the short story. Although the market for short stories has shrunk in major magazines and books, it is still alive and healthy in smaller reviews and literary quarterlies, and is actually thriving in special categories such as science fiction and fantasy and mysteries. It may help your ambitions as a novelist to have had some of your stories published, even in esoteric journals for little or no pay. Agents scan literary journals and papers, as do editors, looking for new talent.

Novelist Bill Minor, one of the Lit Biz 101 faculty, spoke to our students about "how to stick with stories that get passed up twenty-three times but eventually get published." He displayed complex tables showing where he had submitted each of his stories over a period of five years. He'd obviously taken the time to read a lot of publications and knew which ones might be able to use his kind of story. About half of his stories were accepted, some after being returned many times, and the remainder are still being offered; when a story comes back in the mail, Minor tries to ship it out again (with a good cover letter) to a new magazine the same day. That takes some of the sting out of being rejected, he said.

The point to be taken from his approach is that perseverance does pay off. The marketing of fiction takes a long time and requires massive internal confidence. Jack Kerouac, in an early stage of his career, termed his many unpublished novels "books published in Heaven."

Both *Writer's Market* (an annual book) and *Writer's Digest* give you some information about magazines that publish short stories. Using those two sources plus *LMP* and other resources listed in our Addenda chapter, you may determine who the fiction editor is, what length stories he or she prefers, and how much they pay. Whereas thirty years ago every major publication used short stories, and Americans waited eagerly for their weekly serials in *The Saturday Evening Post*, today few national publications are interested in short stories. We still have *The New Yorker*, *Esquire*, *Vanity Fair*, *The Atlantic*, and *Harper's*, of course, but much of the short-story market has gone to smaller presses, nonprofit literary reviews, and academic reviews like *The Massachusetts Review* or *The Sewanee Review* and category magazines like science fiction and mysteries.

Books of short stories have suffered a terrible decline in popularity also. Fewer are now published and it's extremely rare when one of them lands on the best-seller lists. There will always be short-story writers (Leonard Michaels, Isaac Bashevis Singer, John Updike, Ray Bradbury, Spencer Holst, Joyce Carol

Oates, for instance) but I doubt that any of them can make a living from their brief fiction alone. You have to complement your short-story output with the occasional novel, teach creative writing at a college, or receive grant and foundation subsidies to make ends meet.

Sample Query Letter

The query letter for fiction is quite similar to that for nonfiction in that you need to identify the nature of your book, its intended market, and your qualifications or credits. But you have more leeway in which to be personable and can take a more creative approach generally. Novelists are even permitted to be a bit eccentric.

Sample Query Letter

Storm LaRue
1000 Fashion Lane
Beverly Hills, Calif. 99999

June 12, 1987

Ms. Jean Germaine
Ravishing Books
00000 Wild West Blvd.
Hollywood, CA 99999

Dear Ms. Germaine:

As a great admirer of the romantic novels of Beverly Brandywine, especially <u>Crashing Toward Tomorrow</u> and <u>Destiny at Dusk</u>, I congratulate you on publishing her work. I don't mind admitting that my own novel, <u>Westward from Sundown</u>, was partially inspired by Brandywine's finest moments, although of course my style is original to me.

<u>Westward from Sundown</u> begins in Tahiti in 1934 where my heroine, Jane Roe Stanwell, is born out of wedlock to a proper aristocratic Englishwoman and an itinerant adventurer. She grows up in the simple, idyllic life of the South Pacific, but is cast into austere British society in western Australia at the age of nineteen after her mum dies and a distant branch of the family sends for her. Her

adjustment to "civilized" life includes a tempestuous affair with Stanley Blake, industrialist tycoon, world-traveling philanderer (oh, yes, he's married—several times), and overwhelming lover.

But Jane is meant for greater horizons than this man's attentions. Through Blake she eventually sails to England and discovers a fortune in inheritances from her mother's family. Endowed with social status and unlimited funds, this one-time island primitive who scavenged for starfish with little dark-skinned Polynesian girls is elevated to a position from which she can destroy Blake and her mother's enemies. . . .

Well, I can't give away the plot in a query letter, but I hope you'll be interested in having a look at <u>Westward from Sundown</u>. My stories have appeared in <u>True Hearthrob</u> and <u>Beverly Hills After Dark</u>. Let me know if you'd like to see the novel or a few chapters from it. I'll be eagerly waiting for your reply (a S.A.S.E. is enclosed herewith), as I expect to finish the manuscript this month.

Faithfully yours,

Storm LaRue

Beyond the Query Letter: The Finished Manuscript

If your query letter has succeeded in interesting the editor, who may ask to see a sample chapter or two, you'll probably still have to submit an entire novel to get a first contract. *For that reason, we don't recommend that the beginning fiction writer pursue a contract until the novel is finished, or nearly so.* You want to be able to present the finished manuscript as promptly as possible once you've extracted an editor's promise to read it!

Trends in Best-selling Fiction

Given all the inherent disadvantages in trying to sell your fiction, the rewards are still potentially great. Best of all is if your novel fits into the current trends of great popularity and is tailor-made to be turned into a movie or TV miniseries. It's regrettably true that not as many publishers are looking for highbrow, "serious" fiction as eagerly as for steamy potboilers with strong, romantic characterizations, plenty of adventure and sex, and a lot of *dialogue*. The latter may well be the key to selling your novel to the movies, since dialogue makes it much easier for the scriptwriter to transform the book into visual dramatic form.

Look at the fiction best-sellers in the Sunday newspaper or *Publishers Weekly*. These blockbusters do not happen accidentally but as a result of the publisher's enthusiasm for the novel and advance planning for promotion and advertising. Movie or video tie-ins can increase a novel's sale enormously. Some novels are sold to the movies before publication, while others are actually "novelizations" based on a film in production. It would be nice to say that these best-sellers are great literature, but they usually are not. The snooty reviewing establishment might call it junk, but readers devour the soft-core romance/adventure books of Jacqueline Susann, Harold Robbins, Rosemary Rogers, et al. Once in a blue moon a novel of high literary merit (such as Margaret Atwood's *Handmaid's Tale*) becomes popular despite its quality. But if you want a sure-fire best-seller, your best chance is with a book that's loaded with sex and thrills, based on an identifiable theme (Hawaii, Monaco, the oil industry, whatever, the more romantic the better), and calculated to entertain. If your novel is more prosaic, quieter, of better quality, you're to be congratulated but warned of a tougher market and a greater need to promote yourself. (More on promoting novels in Chapter 15, "Self-Promotion, the Writer's Best Friend," but the main thing is to use your personal style to attract readers.)

The First Novel

With your first novel you take whatever publishing arrangement you can get. (Not to deny the one-in-a-million chance of a spectacular "launch" by a dedicated publisher convinced of your present greatness and future marketability.) The amount of money you get paid is likely to be small, as little as $2,000 in advance even from a major house, and—here's the rub—the promotion budget may be even smaller. Publishers know that it seldom pays to advertise first novels, unless they are manufacturing a grand introduction to a Major New Talent. You, the novelist, are left with a disproportionate share of responsibility for promotion, getting the book in stores, getting reviews, perhaps even soliciting a paperback reprint publisher.

You do want your novel to come out first in a cloth binding (hard covers) simply because paperback books are not as often reviewed in the press. The importance of reviews is covered in Chapter 15. (The public has quite the opposite predisposition, choosing paperbacks over hard covers by a ten-to-one margin or better. See our chapter on "Owning A Bookstore." As we say in the trade, "nobody" buys hardcover fiction, but hard covers really help attract reviews.) With a first novel, too, you should be more willing to entertain the possibility of a small press house than with a nonfiction book. Smaller presses are doing a lot of fiction, and some (like The Fiction Collective in New York, which specializes in publishing first novels) have proved that it can be marginally profitable. For more information check Chapter 11, "Small Presses and Self-Publishing."

Paperback Originals

If your novel is a paperback original (that is, published for the first time as a paperback with no preceding hardcover edition), don't despair about the difficulty of attracting reviews! Bigger newspapers now feature "roundup" review pages in which new paperbacks are reviewed in brief—about one paragraph per title. *Publishers Weekly* now has a separate section for reviews of paperback originals. And smaller newspapers and magazines may be just as willing to review the book as if it had been in hard cover. After all, the public mostly buys in paperback, and the smaller journal won't have the same exacting standards as practiced at *Time* or *The New York Times*. The trend is turning toward paperbacks and away from the rigid code of reviewing hard covers only.

But, more than reviews, word of mouth acclaim is still the best advertising for first novels. If people like your story well enough to urge the book on their friends, you've got the beginnings at least of a *following*. It happened to Tom Robbins with his first novel, *Another Roadside Attraction*. He was working as a newspaperman in Seattle when it was quietly published by Doubleday to little notice. The paperback rights were sold to

Ballantine for a minuscule advance, but the book gradually developed a cult following of ardent readers and just kept selling and selling until it made its author famous.

The Second Novel and Beyond

But it was Tom's second novel, *Even Cowgirls Get The Blues*, that made him rich. "When I sold the first book, I had no experience and gratefully took a ridiculously small royalty. I wound up making something like two and a half cents on every copy sold in mass-market paperback," Robbins said. But by the second book, he had some experience and reputation and a strong agent.

Ideally, all second novels should be sold for six-figure advances, but not all novelists have the appeal and good fortune that Tom Robbins enjoyed. How much you can get for your second novel is in direct proportion to the market success of your first one, and the extent to which you're seen as a promising talent and therefore a good investment for the future. Even an encouraging showing could be enough to boost you into a higher category of advance and promotion moneys. What precisely is an "encouraging showing"? Believe it or not, 5,000 copies sold in hard cover would be a fine total for a first novel, and the publisher would not actually *lose* money on sales in that vicinity. In fact, 5,000 copies is probably close to a typical print run for a first novel from a major publisher, barring that rare one that gets a big push because it's been sold to the movies or otherwise is being packaged as a mass-market bombshell.

Learn from the Mistakes You Made with Your First Novel

Did you settle for an inadequate royalty (under 10 percent in hard cover, under 6 percent in paperback) because you were so anxious to see your work published that you'd sign anything, and did? Did you let pride get in the way of simply forcing all your friends and relatives to buy a copy? Did you fail to thoroughly exploit every possibility of a bookstore autographing party, radio or TV talk-show appearance in your vicinity out of some embarrassment? Did you neglect to offer your novel for excerpting and reprinting to every magazine that uses fiction? Don't make these mistakes again. Learn from the agony you experienced the first time around.

Genre Fiction

"Genre fiction" incorporates all those novels that are developed around a specific theme, including:

- Westerns—novels set in a Wild West environment, cowboys and coyotes.
- Men's adventure novels—hard-driving action, war and guts
- Mysteries—who done it, and how
- Romances (contemporary or historical)—love stories set in the present day or in some period of the past, like Victorian England
- Historical novels—stories set in a period of history, with plots revolving around royalty, power, saga
- Science fiction and fantasy—plots from the outer worlds of the imagination
- Gothics—tales of horror and old castles
- Young adult fiction (for adolescents)—teen novels

Most genre novels are written according to a formula. They are churned out by the dozens by "production writers" who often use pseudonyms to disguise the fact that they write so many. How fast you can write may determine your suitability for this form. If you've spent nine years polishing the first hundred pages of a novel, you'll never make a living writing genre fiction, but some people have a drawer full of completed manuscripts.

Genre fiction is almost always published in mass-market paperback format only, and pays lower royalties and advances than "prestige" hardcover fiction. In addition, genre novels seem sentenced to a very short shelf life, as these books are recycled and replaced with fresh titles by the distributors every month.

The formula for a genre novel will vary somewhat from publisher to publisher, but you can pick it up just by reading a few selections from the publisher's list. And don't assume that it takes little talent to write these formula tales: Many an author capable of better work has produced genre fiction for the income, and many have tried and failed.

Genre fiction can still provide writers with a good living (and readers with vast enjoyment) because these novels are so hugely popular. Prolific authors can turn out a number of them, often several a year, under various names. Occasionally a genre writer will even be raised to the heights of literary respectability. Philip K. Dick's science-fiction novels, all published as cheap paperbacks, are regarded more seriously since the author's death. The same is true of Jim Thompson's output, which consisted mainly of crime thrillers of the 1950s (with titles like *A Hell of a Woman* and *The Getaway*) that have been recently republished by Black Lizard Books as quality paperbacks.

What's the best-selling genre? Romance novels are eternally hot. Westerns have an avid readership (look at the success of a Louis L'Amour), and mysteries and science fiction/fantasy have enduring appeal to their fans. A careful perusal of your local bookshop should tell you which publishers are interested in your particular genre fiction manuscript, while our reference sources (such as *Writer's Market* and *Writer's Digest*) will give you editors' names, length requirements, and a general pay scale.

Each of the genre categories has a rather strong writers' association (the Mystery Writers of America, Western Writers of America, etc.) and these groups publish newsletters that contain the names of editors and other tips on getting your genre work published. For addresses of these associations see the Addenda, "Lit Biz Reference Sources."

Pornography

Hard-core pornography has to be considered a genre, but these novels pay least of all and are *always* written under a pseudonym. Many otherwise fine authors have resorted to porn for a quick buck and to fend off the wolves from the door. Anais Nin wrote sexually explicit stories for a rich patron, now collected in her beautiful *Erotica* series, but her work is not considered porn anymore and is published by a reputable house.

Procrastination, Discipline, and Writer's Block

Novelists and short-story writers *seem* to struggle with writer's block more than nonfiction writers do. Perhaps it's because they're involved in the ultimate creative process of invention. The muse doesn't necessarily speak up on demand, and many an hour of good writing time is spent pacing the floor, doing trivial housework that could wait a day (What? I haven't vacuumed the rug today! Better do it now and write later. . . .), or otherwise procrastinating. Authors defend these habits as a kind of "warm-up" for the writing work.

When you sit down to the typewriter or word processor for the first time in a day, it may help to perform a few rituals in order to get in the mood. Dashing off a few letters tends to serve; if you don't have any correspondence to answer, fire off a letter to the editor of your local newspaper expressing your opinion on some vital point like the doggie pooper-scooper ordinance or the threat of nuclear war. (If you live in a small town, your letters to the editor will probably be published, but it's a real coup if you can get your letter in *The New York Times* or another great big-city journal.) Make coffee or tea or some other beverage to have by your side. Add a short chapter to your daily journal or pay some bills. Vary this routine according to your own tastes.

Writing takes a great deal of self-discipline; good writing also requires inspiration. The way to beat writer's block is by subduing ego-consciousness, pushing the little critic in your head (the one who complains that your writing is insipid and reads like a fifth-grader's composition) far out of reach. Some writers use stimulants and depressants (like caffeine and alcohol) to help achieve this mental state. Be warned, though: It might seem romantic to drink and write, but it leads to accidents! Meditation and other mental therapies work for some people, and some prepare by running or jogging a mile before sitting down to work.

Avoid Energy-Sink Distractions

What's an "energy-sink" anyway? It's anything that distracts you from writing and *drains your energy* for creative work: hence a sink. The most fiendish of these is the telephone, which breaks your writing chain of thought. Most authors work out some freedom from answering the damn thing, either by hooking it up to a tape-recording answering machine or having an answering service or family member take messages. Television, newspapers, and magazines can be real energy-sinks, even if they do provide valuable input. Schedule time for reading *after* you've written for the day, with the exception of that morning newspaper you may need to get started. A VCR is a handy tool for recording television broadcasts you can watch later.

Muscling into Print, Dignity Intact

Muscling your fiction into print while retaining your dignity is like performing a high-wire act. You've got to master the balance. You have to pursue editors relentlessly until you get someone to read your work, but in so doing remain friendly, ingratiating, and charming in your letters and contacts. Editors understand the enormous challenge of writing a novel and getting it published—the odds are rather stacked against you from the first—and will appreciate the fact that your tenacity may also make you a greatly inspired salesperson for the book once it's out.

Good luck to you and your great American novel!

3 Poetry, Children's Lit, and Screenwriting

Aside from the broad division of literature into fiction and non-fiction, there are other and distinct kinds of writing for pay, which we'll consider here. The first is poetry, the grandest of literary forms and most specialized of markets. Children's literature includes both fiction and nonfiction written for the young reader. Screenwriting, or writing for the movies or TV, is potentially the most lucrative assignment of all for those few who make the big time.

Poetry and Making a Living

"Hail to thee, blythe spirit, bird thou never wert." But thou must be a bird of another feather in order to make it in the poetry world. Contrary to reports otherwise, poetry is not dead in the least, but *in the U.S.A.* it's been reduced to perhaps the toughest buck in Lit Biz. In the Soviet Union, in parts of Europe, in Japan and India, poets are revered as living national treasures, poetry books sell well to the general public, and the ancient art of verse thrives. In this country we have millions of amateur poets, thousands who are published by small presses and vanity houses, and a tiny handful who actually make a living at it. Poetry magazines, usually nonprofit entities, are frequently published by or affiliated with a university and they help keep the art alive. Also, a number of foundations offer grants to poets.

The human spirit, even in America, can't live without poetry, nor will it ever have to. But you have to begin with the understanding that poetry alone is unlikely to provide any writer with a comfortable income.

> *Which poets make a living from it?*
> *You can probably name for yourself the few poets who are capable of supporting themselves by their writing. Robert Penn Warren was named the national poet laureate in 1986, our first ever (Britain has had a poet laureate position for more than 250 years). Since Robert Frost died, only a handful of poets have actually become famous in this country. One such was Allen Ginsberg. Dating from the first publication of* Howl *by City Lights Books, he has eked out a living at poetry while augmenting his income with readings and personal appearances on college campuses at fees that range up to several thousand dollars an evening. Robert Bly does well conducting seminars and readings. Donald Hall is an excellent poet who recently published an essay stating that he does, indeed, make a living from poetry that would be adequate to survival, but of course he also writes journalism, essays, and novels (*Fathers Playing Catch With Sons) *and has taught college English courses.*

Income Sidelines for Poets

So if you're writing poetry, plan to do something else to actually pay the rent. One of the more poet-friendly occupations is the one Verandah Porche found in Vermont. Porche had her first book of poems (*The Body's Symmetry*) published by Harper & Row but makes her living as artist-in-residence for the Vermont Council on the Arts, teaching poetry to kids in the public schools. Poetry in the Schools is a national program but it is administered separately by each state and the guidelines for eligibility vary from place to place.

Many other poets have taken advantage of the program, so check your local requirements.

"What I do is I squirrel my way into the school system," Verandah said. "I spend every August on the telephone soliciting school principals all over the state. It's up to me to generate my own gigs; you really have to perfect your manner, know how to relate to kids, and have a product to offer. Still, I always feel like a cut-rate carpet dealer.

"Poets who want the *luxury* of getting paid have a break with this program," she added.

Grants for Poetry

Since most of the poetry magazines are nonprofit and can pay little or nothing, they and the poets themselves rely on subsidies in the form of grants, fellowships, and awards. The American PEN Center (47 Fifth Avenue, New York, N.Y. 10003) cares about poetry and publishes an excellent book called *Grants and Awards Available to American Writers* (14th edition, 1986–87) that contains listings of poetry grants and prizes. The book costs $6.00 for individuals, $9.50 for libraries or institutions, postpaid. Anybody can order the book, but you have to be nominated to become a member of PEN, and you must be a published writer to qualify for *most* (not all) of the grants listed.

Another excellent source of help is Poets & Writers, Inc. at 201 West 54 Street, New York, N.Y. 10019. Poets & Writers keeps addresses for each state arts council and over 640 sponsors of readings and workshops nationwide. You may telephone between 11 A.M. and 3 P.M. (EST) weekdays or write to them.

For more information on grants see Chapter 17, "Lit Biz 201, 301, and 401."

Where to Submit Your Poetry

A few major national magazines still feature poetry, but the competition is intense and most of them are swamped with more verse than the eye can read. Submitting your poems to highbrow journals isn't likely to be effective until you have established a reputation in the smaller poetry press. A large percentage of American poetry is self-published, and some of that is even profitable. Big Sur, California, poet Ric Matsen has supported a family and fine home through poetry alone. He publishes the books himself and sets up a vigorous schedule of college readings and public appearances at which he sells his own books, autographed. (For more on such self-promotion, see our chapter on "Self-Promotion, the Writer's Best Friend.")

You need to read and keep up with the poetry journals, of which there are hundreds—many connected to a university or other academic institution. The aforementioned Poets and Writers, Inc. publishes a "Newsletter," also at 201 West 54 Street, New York, N.Y. 10019, which serves as a good clearinghouse for poetry news; it also has a book called *The Writing Business*, with a strong emphasis on poetry.

As with any other kind of literary submission, you should send your poetry where you think it will be most appreciated. That means read the poetry journals you find in your library or sophisticated bookshop and know what kind of poetry they like to publish before you write your cover letter and submit a poem. A cover letter sent with poetry is not the same as a query letter sent to interest an editor in a full-length book. Since there is no effective way to *describe* poetry in a letter, the poet usually includes at least one poem with his or her first inquiry. The letter should generally describe you and your poetry background (where you've been published, simple autobiography, perhaps some personal background or even whimsical observations). And once you have had a few poems in print, there's no harm in trying for the prestigious few national magazines (like *The New Yorker* and *The Atlantic*) that keep to the practice of including poetry in every issue and pay a reasonable sum to the author.

In general, the small poetry journal will pay you a token fee ($10 to $100) if it is subsidized by a college or foundation grant that provides payment for authors. Often enough, though, no payment at all is available, and one writes for the love of poetry itself, the exposure, and hope of further success.

Professional poets (and, yes, there are many) in the United States are often heard to bemoan that the poetry journals are all controlled by cliques, members of which publicize each other's work and turn a blind eye toward newcomers. I doubt it's that bad, but there is certainly such a thing as a reputation within poetry circles, without which your work may attract little attention. The trick is simply to find the editor who will give your poetry a sincere reading and not simply toss it onto the pile of "slush" (unsolicited submissions).

Sample Query Letter, Poetry

Jaime Rhymer
1111 Keats Street
Stratford, Avon, U.K.

Mr. Howard Pentameter
Poetic Patterns Magazine
1111 Sonnet Lane
University of the East
New York, NY 10000

Dear Mr. Pentameter:

I received Issue Number Nine of <u>Poetic Patterns</u> and eagerly devoured the new work. Particularly good were your own sonnets on the seasons in the East, and the new haiku from Maui.

I've been hard at work on my new series called "Ovulations" and on the epic poem "Baccalaureate," which uses the imagery and terminology of undergraduate academia as a metaphor for a heroic journey.

I'm pleased to enclose a selection from "Baccalaureate," which I hope you will agree belongs in the body of work and in the spirit of <u>Poetic Patterns</u>. Keep up the good work.

By the way, my work has appeared in the <u>Stratford Observer</u> and the <u>Poetry Quarterly</u> of the University of Leeds, and my first volume of poems is being prepared by Poet on Avon Press here.

Cordially yours,

Jaime Rhymer

If you do break into an established poetry clique, you're likely to enter into a long relationship with your editor; there might be correspondence and even criticism flowing from editor to poet before a piece is actually bought and published. The follow-up for poetry can be more personal, more intense, than that for prose.

And if you *don't* break into the clique of your choice right away, start your own clique! Poetry, more than any other form of writing, is frequently self-published or published by a small press representing a few poets who band together. Put out a few sixteen-page chapbooks (small pamphlets), distribute them in local bookstores, and before you know it, other poets will be applying to join your clique. Believe it.

Poetry Distribution

Bookpeople in Berkeley, California, national distributors of small press books, stock many poetry titles and a careful reading of its catalog will give you further knowledge of which publishers are involved with poetry. (Write to 2940 Seventh Street, Berkeley, CA 94710.) Be advised that many poetry publishers are tiny one- or two-person operations. University presses (notably Yale) still publish distinguished poets, but the general rules in poetry seem to be: (A) there is no disgrace in publishing your own work or going with a small press for no money, since money is not expected or important, and (B) successful (in the sense of income-generating) poets *must* have show-biz qualities, the ability to give public readings and lectures.

Writing for Kids

The children's book field is an enormous part of publishing, and the rules of the business are quite different from the rest of the industry. Whereas even a popular novel might be on the shelves for only a year, a successful children's book can last indefinitely, through many editions and decades. Also, because children's books are shorter, successful children's authors frequently enjoy lifelong careers wherein they can write dozens or hundreds of titles. So although the advance payments on children's books tend to be lower than for fiction or nonfiction, the prospect of steady royalties is very appealing.

But it takes very special qualities to create a good children's book. There is a widespread and very wrong idea that it's easy to speak to kids because the language is simple. Most adults write for children from an *adult's* point of view, and that doesn't make it with children's book editors or, presumably, with children.

The rare author who can put him or herself into a child's mind, a child's perspective, is the best writer for a child reader.

In our society girls read more than boys do, so the beginning children's writer might do better addressing girls' concerns. But of course the really *great* children's literature cuts across all gender (and age) distinctions, while the vast majority of it is organized by age level.

Age Level and Children's Lit

It's important to distinguish levels of age readership for kids. The back cover of most children's books states the age group the book is intended for. Books for very young children rely more on illustrations, for example, while books for teens (such as Dell's "Seniors" series) may be considered a variation of genre fiction written for young adults.

Age level is determined by quite specific guidelines involving the level of vocabulary sophistication of the average child:

—Ages 1–4—Preschool level, mostly illustrations with simple words and ABCs in text;

—Ages 4–8—Early readers, elementary text with large and frequent illustrations;

—Ages 8–12—Middle school-level vocabulary, with fewer and smaller illustrations, and introduction of chapters;

—Ages 12–up—The teen-level readership presumes a vocabulary at adult level, and illustrations are not necessarily included, but the book addresses concerns and interests of young adults.

Note the importance of illustrations at different age levels. Young adult paperback books are usually published under an imprint—the Dell Laurel-Leaf line, Scholastic Press's Point books, Avon's Flare, and Bantam's Starfire line, to name a few. These young adult novels tend to run about half the length of a typical adult novel, and are often preoccupied with high school romance. S. E. Hinton, whose high school novels like *The Outsiders* and *Rumble Fish* have been made into films, is a popular author with a somewhat darker vision of reality.

At the middle school level it's easy to understand the charm of perennial favorite authors like Judy Blume and Beverly Cleary. They seem to understand perfectly how the eight- to twelve-year-old mind thinks. Who can resist the charms of Ramona Quimby and Henry Huggins, Cleary's series standards?

There's a very welcome trend today toward sophisticated and serious *nonfiction* books for children as well. We've seen some excellent sex-education books for preschoolers (some of these are objectionable to the religious right wing), a vast number of young people's history and contemporary issues textbooks, and books that educate teens about the dangers of drug and alcohol abuse. And, as always, there are series books about teen-idol musicians, actors, and sports heroes.

Querying the Children's Editor

As part of your query letter to a children's book editor, you should:
- State the age level of the reader you are addressing
- Indicate whether or not the book is to have illustrations (and who is to provide them)

Sample Query Letter, Children's

> Winifred D. Pueh
> 000 Main Street
> Anytown, U.S.A.

October 1, 1987

Sarah Sterling
Editor
Brownie Editions
Young Academic Publications
000 Michigan Blvd.
Chicago, IL 66666

Dear Ms. Sterling:

I enjoy the Brownie series of romance/adventure novels for girls eight to twelve years old, especially the mysteries starring the Dawson twins. My own book, <u>Strangers When They Met</u>, is directed to the same age level and vocabulary development.

Penny Lawrence, the heroine, is twelve and just finishing sixth grade when her parents decide she needs remedial education in summer school. Although dismayed at the very idea of French lessons in July, Penny soon changes her mind after meeting Rob LeBlanc, her dreamy instructor. (She calls him "Robear" in her mind.) Thirteen-year-old Jeremy Scott-Lyons is more than interested in Penny as well.

Things turn dangerous when the class makes its end-of-summer excursion to Quebec City in Canada for "life experience" in speaking French. Robear, it seems, is homesick for la belle France and must bid adieu to his students, but Jeremy has transferred to Penny's school from Central High for the fall. When Penny and Jeremy get stranded midair in the funicular, their knowledge of French really does save the day!

The manuscript is sixty-five pages long and requires illustrations suitable to this age level. May I send it to you for your perusal with an eye toward its possible publication by Young Academic Publications?

I do intend the Penny Lawrence stories to carry on as a series in the future. My earlier children's stories have been published in the "Small World" Sunday section of the Anytown Gazette.

Sincerely yours,

Winifred D. Pueh

Query or Finished Manuscript?

Determine the policy of the publisher you are soliciting in regard to first-time authors. While some publishers will still read and consider a full-length children's book manuscript from an unknown author, many others now discourage unsolicited manuscripts and prefer to work from a query letter. The Children's Book Council (CBC) offers this advice to the aspiring children's book author:

"Almost all children's book editors now assert writers should send a one-page letter of inquiry about their manuscripts before sending a book to a publisher. This suggestion about all books is especially appropriate in respect to nonfiction titles. Editors answer query letters."

CBC's pamphlet, "Writing Books for Children and Young Adults," goes on to say that your manuscript should be typed, double spaced, on white paper; that you should expect a waiting period of two to three months for an editor to read your material, and should always send adequate postage and a mailing label or envelope for return of your manuscript. The pamphlet can be obtained by sending a stamped, self-addressed envelope to the CBC at 67 Irving Place, New York, NY 10003. Not every children's book publisher follows the CBC guidelines, but they provide a good general standard.

Illustrations

When you submit your manuscript or query to the children's book editor, you face the special issue of *illustrations*, important to younger children's books. You have all of these options:

A. Submit the book without illustrations, leaving the publisher to choose an illustrator. Most publishers prefer to employ illustrators from "in house," on a free-lance basis.

B. Submit the book with illustrations, either your own or somebody else's, but leave the publisher the option of choosing another illustrator.

C. Submit the book with illustrations as a "package" that cannot be separated. Especially if you've illustrated your own story or worked with an illustrator in true collaboration on the book, this may be necessary for the integrity of the art.

Always specify whether the illustrations are intended to be in black and white or color. Color work, while essential to some children's books, increases the production costs of the book.

Illustrations may be represented by samples, a partial portfolio, or rough sketches rather than finished art. Be careful handling and shipping original art! Always insure it for fair value.

NOTE: Here we quote again the advice of the Children's Book Council:

"Authors of picture book texts should not submit illustrations with their manuscripts, unless they are, themselves, the illustrator. It is a pronounced disservice to a picture-book text if the submission is accompanied by pictures by someone other than the author."

This advice relates to our comment in option A above. Publishers generally prefer to employ their own illustrators. But if you are working with your own illustrator, you have to address the question of each person's share of the royalties. This can be a simple 50–50 split if each party contributed equal work and/or value, or any negotiated division. The book contract will state this arrangement in writing, but it's not a bad idea to have an agreement in writing between the two of you from the start—even if the illustrator is your trusted sister-in-law Flora.

Trends in Children's Lit

Children's books are not an easy universe but a magical one, and the potential is there for a steady relationship with a publisher and scores of books over the years. The children's book field is especially kind to series books, such as "Choose Your Own Adventure" or "Sweet Valley High." Many of us grew up reading children's series from The Hardy Boys to the Bobbsey Twins, which are currently being published again by Simon and Schuster in both reissues of the original stories and in new updated versions for older children. But publishers are forever looking for the latest *trend* or evolution in kids' books, and your best research will be done with children themselves. Close contact with kids—as a parent, teacher, or guardian—will tell you what they're interested in. Kids aren't usually shy about speaking their minds with trusted adults. Today's children's book field ranges from the traditional fairy-tale picture-book level all the way into serious juvenile novels about divorce, puberty, teen sex, drugs, and peer pressure. Consult the reference volume *Best Books for Children* and the shelves of your bookstore's children's section to see what's out there, what's selling, and which publisher might be interested in your story.

There are also any number of books in print on the subject of children's literature and/or how to write it. Consult the *Subject Guide to Books in Print* in your library or read *Children and Books*, 6th edition, by Zena Sutherland, Dianne L. Monson, and May Hill Arbuthnot (Foresman and Co., 1981), a 600-plus page volume the CBC calls "an invaluable introduction to the world of children's books."

Screenwriting and Ulcers

In our Addenda we've tried to provide you with a comprehensive list of important resources for more information on poetry, children's books, and screenwriting. Screenwriting in particular is a form of writing somewhat outside the core of literary business. It's writing that isn't meant to be read but performed. Scripts are not published but produced. For a deeper analysis of how to do it (and sell it) you might want to look into *The Complete Book of Scriptwriting* by J. Michael Straczynski (Writer's Digest Books) or Syd Field's *The Screenwriter's Workbook* (Dell Books).

Screenwriters write scripts for film or television. With the decentralization of the film industry, we now find screenwriters at work in all parts of the country, but the hub remains in Los Angeles, a city whose waiters include a high percentage of out-of-work screenwriters. As difficult as the book industry is to break into, selling a movie script makes it look easy. The publishing industry (usually) maintains some grip on sanity, but the film biz is utterly insane. When you finally sell a book to a publisher, it will almost surely see the light of day, but when you sell a script to a producer, the odds are still overwhelmingly *against* its actually going into production. That's because producers option rights to many more books and scripts than eventually obtain financing in this wacky world of the movies.

The screenwriter's intended market is a studio that produces either movies, television shows, or video cassettes. (Of course they are three different markets, requiring different types of films.) Studio executives who buy stories, scripts, and even "ideas" (which may be simple enough to explain in a paragraph) are fairly accessible through the query letter or telephone call, but in order to sell a script to a major studio, you have to be a member of The Writers Guild of America (WGA). *And*, in order to join the WGA, you must have already sold a script! Now that's Los Angeles logic. What happens, in reality, is that once you've persuaded a studio to buy your script, your agent (if you have one) gets you into the union at more or less the same time. If you don't have an agent but have succeeded in selling your work on your own, the studio may be able to find you an agent, just as publishers sometimes bring author and agent together.

Finding a theatrical agent is a trick in its own right, rather like finding an editor and publisher. Naturally the agents are looking for fresh talent and new ideas, and you approach them as you would any literary agent or publisher, with a letter of inquiry describing your work, which usually falls into one of these categories:

• Original treatment; this is a brief plot summary and overview of an original motion picture idea;
• Screenplay; a manuscript containing camera directions, descriptions, and dialogue of the motion picture, a "working script";
• Adaptation; a script that is based on an existing story or piece of writing;
• TV series concept; a document that describes the basic characters, concept, and plot developments of a series for television. Note when you are watching TV that a series' credits may read "Created by" one person but "Written by" another person. The creator gets a royalty for each show for having invented the concept.

Peddling Your Proposal: The Hollywood Schmooze

Have an idea for a great TV serial or movie? Write it up as in a book proposal, with a sample episode (TV) or scene (film) complete with camera direction and dialogue, and join the crush of would-be screenwriters peddling their projects to Hollywood by phone, mail, and in person. Remember, though, that unlike books, scripts tend to end up with multiple authors, and the system of determining credits for the main authors is complex beyond description here. If you are a sensitive soul who can't bear the knife of a blue pencil on your work, don't go into the screenwriting pool.

The casual, breezy Southern California style makes it somewhat easier to approach agents and producers, but it's still consummately difficult to see your scripting work produced on film for reasons of simple economics. A publisher can produce your book, depending on its size and/or complexity, for a manufacturing investment of as little as several thousand dollars, but any feature-length movie, no matter how low-budget, runs over six figures, and most cost many millions. When a publisher contracts to produce your book, almost invariably that publisher has the wherewithal to do so, but when a studio takes an interest in your script, it still must (in many cases) find investors and raise funds to pull off a production. An enormous, incalculable amount of energy is expended every day in the film industry over projects that never see the light of day. Some of them come close—incorporating several script revisions and even signing the actors and actresses—before falling apart for one reason or another, usually financial. The risk factor is relatively greater and the amount at risk substantially larger than in book publishing.

Turn to the "Special Section: How to Submit" for general guidelines on submitting screenplays and treatments.

Now let's go on to the "good part"—the intricacies of getting paid for your writing. As you've heard before, "when writers get together, all they talk about is money." It's a complicated subject when it comes to the literary contract, and one that yields as many opinions as there are speakers. What all writers agree on, however, is that one can never be overpaid. (Publishers naturally disagree.)

4 "When Writers Get Together, All They Talk About is Money"

The Holy of Holies: The Literary Contract

Your query letters, outlines, sample chapters, and proposals have succeeded, you've established a personal working relationship with an editor, and you're offered a literary contract. If you have an agent, it's supposedly his or her job to worry about the contract, but don't be fooled: It's *your* hide. With or without an agent, the terms of your contract hit you right where you live, in your bank account and household budget. Too many writers have been yoked to inadequate contracts out of sheer gratitude for any recognition at all. In Lit Biz 101 we acknowledge that publishers have a tough time making a profit, but writers are worse off by far. Most of them can't even eat without pursuing some other, if related, task.

The one major point we'd like you to remember about the literary contract is that most of its content is negotiable between author, agent, and publisher. Therefore, the better you understand the terms and general expectations of a contract, the better equipped you'll be to negotiate your own.

I do not mean to deny the great value of having a good agent. In fact, after reading this chapter, you may realize even more why it's worthwhile having one. Getting paid for your writing is the best part, if admittedly the trickiest, of being a professional. For the purposes of this chapter, you have already sold your book to a publisher and are engrossed in the awful business of collecting your due. Most books are "sold" by verbal agreement between editor and author, either in person or in letters. But the contract puts that agreement into legal effect. The most important document in your literary career may well be your contract, not your manuscript.

Defining the Terms of the Contract

Before we get into the contract itself, a representative sample of which is to follow, let's define the most important terms in it. These terms are also included and more thoroughly defined in our Glossary. You can read the definition of the term, then advance to the contract itself to see how it's used.

For starters, the *Contract* itself is simply an agreement, legal and binding, between the publisher and the author. Author agrees to write, and publisher to publish, a book, and they specify all the terms.

Advance or "advance against (or on) royalties" is the amount of money the publisher pays the author out front. (Also called a "guarantee.") It is usually paid in installments, conventionally half on signing the contract, the other half on completion of an acceptable manuscript. The advance is like a loan that must be repaid out of the author's future earnings on the book, earnings that are called royalties. (See clause 9A.)

Royalty is a percentage of the retail cover price of the book, which is paid to the author for every copy sold. If the author has a 10 percent royalty on a book that sells for $10 a copy, he or she receives $1.00 for every copy sold. (See Clause 9B.)

Rights are what an author sells a publisher. Rights equal proprietorship of the written material, plus the legal authority to sell it. In addition to primary rights, there are subsidiary rights, movie rights, foreign rights, and more . . . all of which we'll get into below. An author *grants* rights to a publisher in exchange for compensation in the form of royalties and/or advance. (See Clauses 2A–D, 11 A–B.)

Sales refer to the number of copies of the book sold, and are usually divided into categories of sales within the United States, export sales, including Canada, sales of foreign editions, and sales of reduced-price editions. "Gross sales" are the number of copies sold before the bookstores return unsold leftovers; "net sales" are gross sales minus these returned copies.

The *Statement*, or "royalty statement," is a document submitted from publisher to author on a regular schedule, showing how many copies of the book have been sold and how much royalty money (if any) is due to the author. (See Clause 12.)

Copyright is a legal registration of written work by the Library of Congress in Washington, D.C., which protects it from being illegally published or reprinted without permission of the author or person holding the copyright. Submitting your work for copyright protection is usually done by the publisher. (See Clause 8.)

The *Termination* clause explains the circumstances under which the publisher will surrender all interest in the book and end the contract . . . usually some time after the book goes out of print. (See Clause 14.)

Warranties are essentially the guarantees that an author makes about his writing to a publisher. The author guarantees that the material is original, not plagiarized, and that he or she has the right to sell it, and that it's not illegal. (See Clause 3.)

Delivery refers to the time when the author turns over a completed manuscript to the publisher. (See Clause 4.)

Option Clause is the clause in which an author agrees to give the publisher the first chance to negotiate to publish his or her next work. (See Clause 16.)

The *Agent* is the person who represents the author in negotiating the terms of the contract with the publisher, and who receives as a commission a percentage of the author's earnings. Payments will be made by the publisher to the agent. (See Clause 19.)

Reversion of rights occurs when a publisher returns the rights of a book to an author. (See Clause 15.)

A *Printing* is the number of copies of a book printed on the press at any one session. If the first *printing* sells out, the publisher will probably order a second printing, and if that sells out, a third, and so on. (Not to be confused with second or later *Editions*; a new edition means a book that has been revised from an earlier version.)

Stock refers to the number of books the publisher has on hand in its warehouse, as in "copies in stock."

Subsidiary Rights

Subsidiary rights are secondary, but frequently important rights, the most significant of which are briefly defined here. Again, see the Glossary for full definitions. Subsidiary rights refer to all potential uses of your writing other than the original publication as a book. The Authors Guild endorses the basic standard of a 50 percent division of paperback reprint rights and book-club rights, but authors should receive much higher percentages of performance, movie, and translation rights. A more detailed explanation of each of these follows. (See Clause 11, containing various kinds of subsidiary rights.)

Territorial rights. The publisher may buy rights limited to publishing the book in English for sale in the U.S.A. and certain other "territories and dependencies," usually the Philippines and Canada. The purpose here is to distinguish U.S. territories where English is the dominant language from British territories, including Australia. If the publisher buys "world rights," he is entitled to publish the book in other languages and countries. (See Clause 2A.)

Foreign rights. If there is to be a foreign-language translation and publication, the original publisher licenses the foreign publisher, who pays an advance on royalties and submits regular royalty statements like any other reprint house. (Except in cases where the agent handles the author's foreign transactions independently of the U.S. publisher.) (See Clause 11H.)

Performance (including movie) rights. Movie rights are the rights to make the book into a film. Performance rights also cover stage adaptations, TV movies, video cassettes, any medium that could adapt the work for performance. (See Clause 11I.)

Serial rights. "First serial rights" are the rights of first publication in a magazine or newspaper; if the material is to appear in your book, your agent or publisher can sell an excerpt to a periodical for appearance prior to book publication. "Second serial rights" are rights granted to a newspaper or magazine to reprint material that has already appeared in another periodical or in a published book. "One-time rights" give the periodical the right to use the material once, but no promise of exclusivity or first-time privilege. (See Clause 11A–B.)

Book clubs. Ever wonder why the book clubs can offer such bargains on new books? Well, the author takes a nosedive on the royalty rate for one thing! Still, writers never scorn the added income, prestige, and visibility the book club lends. The book club issues a contract to the publisher and pays some advance on royalties as a minimum guarantee. Mere admission to the Book-of-the-Month Club, Quality Paperback Book Club, the Literary Guild, or the Preferred Choice Book Plan does not make a book a best-seller or even a financial success. If your book is an "alternate selection," the club may sell only a few hundred or thousand copies. About half the book-club royalty goes to the original publisher. (See Clause 11E.)

Getting a Good, Fair Contract

What are the elements of a good literary contract?

1. *The most amount of money in advance that you can get.* Remember that the author is not required to refund the advance on royalties to the publisher if the book doesn't do well enough to repay it. (The author must refund the advance, however, if he or she fails to deliver a manuscript or breaks one of the warranties in the contract.) The advance is the minimum risk the publisher is willing to take on your work.

A significant percentage of books never earn their advance on royalties, so the advance is the only sum you as the author can count on. Even if you do earn further royalties, it's likely to be several years down the line, after the advance has been repaid.

Most authors believe the advance on royalties also directly affects the publisher's attitude toward spending money on promoting and advertising the book; the more money advanced, the more serious the investment. Publishers argue this point, but it is a logical assumption. Certainly when a book has been granted a huge advance (in six figures or more) the publisher will promote and advertise energetically; however, a book published on a smaller advance can sometimes be granted good promotion dollars because the publisher has confidence in its salability.

2. *The highest royalty rate you can get per copy sold.* Royalties are simply the amount of money you get for each copy of your book that the publisher sells, based on a percentage of the *retail price.* Exceptions exist for books that are sold for lower than the retail price, such as to book clubs for special editions. Your royalty per *hardcover* copy is likely to be between 8 and 15 percent, although royalties range as low as 5 percent and as high as 20 percent, and royalties for *paperbacks* are offered at a slightly lower version of this same scale. Each percentage point difference is, of course, money gained or lost to you, the author.

If forced to place a general standard on royalties, Lit Biz 101 would judge that a good medium standard for a *hardcover* book would be this:

—10 percent on the first 5,000 copies;
—12½ percent on the next 5,000 copies;
—15 percent on all sales over 10,000 copies.

A decent standard for a *trade paperback* edition would be in this neighborhood:

—6 percent on the first 10,000 copies;
—7½ percent on the second 10,000 copies;
—10 percent on all sales over 20,000 copies.

And a similarly acceptable standard for a *mass-market* paperback edition is:

—8 percent on the first 150,000 copies;
—10 percent thereafter.

As outlined above, the royalty rate for paperbacks is a bit lower than for hard covers. Both trade paperbacks (the more expensive, larger-sized paperbacks) and mass-market editions (the cheaper, smaller, rack-sized ones) command a royalty between 6 percent and 15 percent. A major distinction, however, is that trade PBs are sold only in bookstores, while mass market sells in supermarkets and other outlets.

3. *The best possible share of subsidiary rights.* In a case where the hardcover publisher sells paperback rights to a reprinter, the author and original publisher usually split the revenues (both advance and royalties) equally. These reprint rights are one type of *subsidiary rights* and the 50 percent split is standard in the

book business. But nowadays the pattern has been more and more toward a "hard-soft" contract in which the same publisher ties up both hardcover and paperback rights, resulting in the full paperback royalty rate flowing to the author and not split 50–50 with the hardcover publisher. We even occasionally see contracts in which the paperback publisher is the original publisher and sells hardcover rights to another publisher. We define rights as they come up in the contract below, and again in the Glossary for easy reference.

A Sample Literary Contract, with Comments

While there is a great deal of latitude and area for negotiation in the literary contract, there are also many "boilerplate" clauses that are fairly standard to all such agreements. You, as the author, or your agent representing you, want to negotiate as much as is reasonably possible. Special clauses that are added to the contract to reflect an author's particular interests are called "riders."

What follows is not any real publisher's literary contract but a composite contract based on the many real ones we've seen (and signed). Consequently, the order of times and wording may vary widely from the contract you receive for your book. This contract is meant to be an example of a fair, decent, middle-of-the-road agreement that is close to what you are likely to be offered. The Authors Guild in New York publishes an *ideal* literary contract from the author's point of view, but it's so slanted toward the writer that I doubt any publisher would sign it. You can write away for it (234 West 44 Street, New York, NY 10036) for your reference or edification.

Staying for the moment on the topic of negotiation, you should read the following contract with an eye toward all the clauses that are open to discussion, and remember that when you are starting out it doesn't pay to be *too* much of a stickler. The last thing you want is for the publisher to withdraw the offer because you or your agent are making unreasonable demands regarding the contract. At the same time, writers have been burned in the past and you don't want to settle for truly inadequate terms just because you're grateful to be published at all.

Like all legal documents, the literary contract tends toward repetitive, boring language and is set in small type. If you are familiar with literary contracts, skip over the fine print and read our Lit Biz 101 commentaries in italics, but if you are aiming for your first literary contract, it pays to read every word. In studying this fairly typical document you are also learning about various rights, obligations, and royalties.

The literary contract is your basic road map to payment for your book, as it outlines the publisher's responsibilities to you. Royalties are conventionally paid on a twice-yearly schedule, reflecting sales postdated to about nine months, less a "reasonable" reserve against returns. ("Returns" are those books sent back from the bookstore to the publisher after not selling for a period of some months.) The publisher decides what is "reasonable" as a reserve against returns, although the author may not always agree. Purchasers of other rights in the book, such as reprint, first and second serial rights, performance and translation rights, pay the publisher, who then pays the author his percentage in the twice-a-year royalty dispersal—and only *after* the full advance has been earned back.

By the time your book comes out, you're already in a hole— rather like being born with a handicap to overcome. Meanwhile, the publisher, who has assumed the whole financial risk of producing, manufacturing, and distributing your book, must try to recoup its investment. (All rights mentioned above, as well as all terms mentioned in the contract, are defined in the Glossary.)

Contract for Trade Book Publication

AGREEMENT made this _____ day of _____, 19__, between
_____Name____of____Publisher_, _____ Publisher's
Address_____(hereinafter called "Publisher") and _____ Name
of____Author_, _____Author's____Address_____(hereinafter
called "Author"),

Wherein PUBLISHER and AUTHOR hereby agree with respect to the work at this time entitled:

_____Name of Book (working title; hereinafter called "the Work")_____

Authors often change the title of a book during or upon completion of the writing process, hence the use of a working title in the contract. The working title is also the title under which the book was marketed to the publisher in its outline and proposal forms. If you are using a pseudonym, it should be noted here at the beginning—e.g., "Jane Doe, writing under the pen name Valerie Divine." For "author's address" use your safest, most permanent address. This contract may be paying you royalties years from now, after you've moved several times. If the author has an agent, the agent's name and address may also be included here.

As follows:

PURPOSE OF AGREEMENT

1. AUTHOR and PUBLISHER enter into this publication contract for the purpose of cooperation in the successful completion or revision, publication, and distribution of the Work, in the hope that both parties will thereby gain financial and literary enhancement. PUBLISHER, in order to cooperate fully with AUTHOR, agrees to provide AUTHOR free of charge with any reasonable amount of editorial or commercial advice regarding stylistic revisions to be performed by AUTHOR, organizational revisions to be performed by AUTHOR, or revisions by AUTHOR to facilitate the marketing and sale of the Work. AUTHOR recognizes PUBLISHER's interest in promoting and selling the Work, and will strive to satisfy any reasonable request by PUBLISHER for revisions or information needed for promotion purposes.

This is all fairly self-evident and politely put. Essentially, both author and publisher stand to gain from sales of the book, so they are pledging to work together

Continued

Continued

under "reasonable" conditions. The word "reasonable" turns up a lot in the standard literary contract, and it's one of those things that can't be precisely defined. As long as there really is a spirit of cooperation between author and publisher, there shouldn't be any problems.

AUTHOR'S GRANT AND DURATION

2. (A) AUTHOR grants and conveys to PUBLISHER the exclusive right to print, publish, and sell, and to permit others to print, publish, and sell the Work in volume form in the English language in the United States of America, the Philippine Republic, and Canada, and to sell the Work for export to all other countries of the world except for the British Commonwealth countries as named by the International Copyright Convention; for the entire period of any copyright or copyrights obtained upon the Work, in any country of the world, and for the entire period of renewal or renewals thereof, and in any event, for so long as moneys continue to be earned by AUTHOR or PUBLISHER on the Work.

2. (B) AUTHOR grants and conveys to PUBLISHER the exclusive right to license or sell the Work for publication by book clubs and for publication of a cheap or reprint edition by PUBLISHER or another publisher. Reprint by another publisher is subject to the approval of AUTHOR, such approval not to be unreasonably withheld or delayed.

2. (C) AUTHOR grants and conveys to PUBLISHER the exclusive rights to publish and to license the Work for publication in anthologies, selections, abridgments, digests, magazine excerpts, first and second serialization, and newspaper and magazine serialization or syndication.

2. (D) AUTHOR grants and conveys to PUBLISHER the exclusive right to print, publish, and sell, or to permit others to print, publish, and sell, the Work in all foreign languages throughout the world in book form and in magazines and newspapers.

*These are the author's "grants"—just as when you sell
a house, you grant the deed to the buyer, here the
author grants the publisher certain rights to his/her book.
These are the most important, primary rights, the rights
to print and publish the book. Other rights such as
movies will be discussed later in the contract. Note that
the English-speaking and -reading world has been divided by the International Copyright Convention so that
American and British publishers have their separate markets. In practical terms, this doesn't matter to you, as
author. If there is no British edition of your book, the
U.S. publisher is allowed to sell its edition over there.*

*As far as foreign rights go, usually your publisher or
agent handles foreign sales through a foreign agent, a
person based in the country where the translation edition is to be produced. The foreign royalties are generally
paid to the U.S. publisher, who then pays the author
whatever percentage of foreign moneys the contract calls
for. Note that this arrangement is not the same thing as
surrendering what are called "world rights." Generally
speaking, no author is advised to grant world rights to a
publisher.*

*Note in clause 2(A) that the author grants the right to
his or her book "as long as moneys continue to be
earned." This is not a perpetual grant. If the book goes
out of print, the author regains these rights—see clause
14(C), termination. Also see clause 11 for a comment on
additional rights such as serial and performance rights
with general guidelines on how much of these rights an
author can expect to retain. These clauses tend to miti-
gate the apparently sweeping and all-inclusive rights in
clause 2.*

AUTHOR'S WARRANTIES

3. (A) AUTHOR warrants and represents to PUB-
LISHER:

1) That AUTHOR is the sole owner, by right of
authorship or otherwise, of the rights herein granted;
that AUTHOR has fully notified PUBLISHER of the
authorship of the Work; that these rights are not
liable to any prior agreements, contracts, liens, or
encumbrances; that AUTHOR has disclosed to PUB-

LISHER any grants, subsidies, awards, or other amounts of money paid to AUTHOR to assist in the accomplishment or completion of this Work; and that AUTHOR has full right to enter into this publication agreement; and

2) That the Work contains no obscene, plagiarized, libelous, or illegal matter; nor any matter the publication of which will constitute an infringement or violation of any person's or corporation's common law rights, or rights of property or privacy or copyright; and

3) That AUTHOR has obtained or will obtain and give to PUBLISHER before the final date herein for the delivery of the manuscript to PUBLISHER, at AUTHOR's own expense, legally recordable written permissions to publish any copyrighted material to be included in the Work, signed by the copyright proprietors thereof; and

4) That AUTHOR has, prior to the execution of this agreement, informed PUBLISHER in writing of any and all claims of which AUTHOR is aware that AUTHOR does not have the full right to enter into this agreement or that the execution or performance of this agreement is a violation of any of AUTHOR's warranties herein.

These are the mighty "author's warranties" we defined a bit earlier. When you get a warranty on an appliance, it's like a guarantee the thing will work. These warranties guarantee the publisher that you, the author, have the right to sell this written work, that you didn't rip off somebody else's book, and that you're taking responsibility for the fact that there's nothing unlawful in the book. If you do quote some other work, such as including a poem by Robert Frost in your dedication, you need written permission. In the case of a deceased author like Frost, permission is given by his publisher (or his estate, if rights were reverted) in exchange for a

Continued

> *Continued*
>
> *fee. If the author is living, chances are you'd need that author's signature on a permissions letter or form your publisher can provide. (I say "chances are" because occasionally a living author will have assigned the copyright to the publisher, another person such as his agent, or another company.)*
>
> *Permissions can be free (let's say the author is a personal friend of yours), modestly priced, or exorbitant, depending on who you're dealing with. Popular recording artists, I'm told, tend to charge a mint for permission to reprint lyrics, but I paid only $25 for permission to reprint a Frost poem in an earlier book of mine.*
>
> *Legal issues such as libel and plagiaraism are covered later in Chapter 5, "The Writer and the Law."*

PUBLISHER'S ACCEPTANCE OF WARRANTIES

3. (B) PUBLISHER is under no obligation to make an independent investigation to determine whether the foregoing warranties made by AUTHOR are true and complete; however, any such independent investigation by PUBLISHER shall not constitute a defense to AUTHOR in any court action based on a breach of any of the foregoing representations and warranties.

AUTHOR'S INDEMNIFICATIONS

3. (C) AUTHOR will indemnify and hold PUBLISHER harmless of and from all suits, damages, settlements, fines, court costs, counsel fees, judgments, and recoveries arising out of any breach or alleged breach of the foregoing warranties and representations. In the event that any suit or legal action is threatened or imposed on PUBLISHER, PUBLISHER shall promptly notify AUTHOR and PUBLISHER shall have the right to defend against the same by counsel of its own choice at AUTHOR's expense and to compromise or settle the same at AUTHOR's expense if PUBLISHER deems it necessary to do so. PUBLISHER preserves the right to withhold, until the final disposition of any such suit or judgment, any and all sums due to AUTHOR and to apply the same in satisfaction of the indemnity herein provided.

This rather scary clause is standard, in some form or another, to every literary contract we've ever seen. It says that the author agrees to pay every cent of legal defense if someone should sue claiming the book is plagiarized, libelous, or whatever. In practice, however, such lawsuits are usually filed against both the publisher and the author, and frequently it's the publisher, not the author, who has the funds necessary to pay for defense and to pay for any judgment. But this clause officially leaves the responsibility with the author and, at the least, the publisher can withhold paying royalties until its court costs are repaid. The best advice we can give you is to make certain your book doesn't include anything that's likely to cause legal action against you— even if you have to hire a lawyer to review the manuscript before publication.

Most publishers check a manuscript for legal problems; the process is called "vetting." And many publishers now offer their authors indemnification insurance as well.

AUTHOR'S DELIVERY OF MANU- SCRIPT

4. (A) AUTHOR shall deliver to PUBLISHER on or before the *Date of Delivery* a complete and legible manuscript copy of the Work, satisfactory to PUBLISHER in form and content, double spaced, suitable for printing, consisting of not less than *Minimum Number of Words or Pages* nor more than *Maximum Number of Words or Pages* together with all photographs, maps, drawings, charts, or indices required by PUBLISHER.

4. (B) In the event that AUTHOR fails to deliver such a satisfactory copy of the Work to PUBLISHER on the date specified above, PUBLISHER shall nevertheless retain all rights to the Work herein granted when and if the Work is later completed unless PUBLISHER elects to terminate this agreement because of AUTHOR's delay in delivery, which PUBLISHER has the right to do at any time after the original delivery date by mailing AUTHOR a registered letter announcing such termination. Termina-

tion becomes effective *Number of Months* after AUTHOR's receipt of such registered letter unless AUTHOR has delivered a satisfactory manuscript in the above-mentioned time. If AUTHOR dies before the completion of the Work, PUBLISHER retains the right to publish the uncompleted manuscript of the Work without any revision or changes.

The key phrase in Clause A is "satisfactory to publisher in form and content." You'll note that the publisher has complete authority to determine whether the manuscript is satisfactory or not. The term is both vague and absolute. The publisher can find the book unsatisfactory for any number of (unnamed) reasons. However, the economic reality is that the publisher is also paying the bills and can't be expected to guarantee producing a book it hasn't seen yet.

Clause B says that you should be on time if you possibly can, but if you're going to be late, inform your publisher and get an extension in writing. Most publishers will understand and forgive if the delay is not unreasonably long and the book not urgent. Here also, the author agrees to a length of manuscript, minimum number of words or pages, and maximum number of words or pages. Don't deliver half or twice the amount of work as originally projected. The length of your manuscript is as important as the delivery date. If you come up severely short or extravagantly overwritten, you could create a serious publishing problem. Remember that illustrations, charts, all secondary materials add to the number of pages of your book and the cost of production. Keep the length closely within the confines of the terms of your agreement with the publisher.

The delivery date, length of manuscript, and number of months the author has to complete successful delivery are all points to be negotiated before this contract is drawn up. Give yourself the benefit of the doubt in this process. That is, if you think you can produce the book

Continued

Continued

*in six months, negotiate a delivery date of nine months
after the date of the contract—the extra few months
may come in handy if you have unanticipated problems.
If you expect the book to be 300 pages, offer a length
between 250 and 350 pages, giving yourself some leeway
from either direction. Three to six months is a reasonable extra time in which to complete delivery of a late
manuscript.*

*An easy thumbnail guide to length is this: The con-
ventional 8½-by-11-inch typing page, double spaced,
contains about 250 words and equals roughly one page
of book type. A manuscript of 200 pages equals 50,000
words; 250 pages is 75,000 words; 300 pages is 100,000
words, and so on.*

*As for "photographs, maps, charts, or indices" required
with the manuscript, be sure to negotiate in advance
just what is required. An index, for example, can be a
complicated piece of work requiring a great deal of time.
A children's book may require extensive illustrations.
Any visuals necessary to the completed manuscript should
be specifically mentioned in the contract.*

*Some contracts call for the author to submit two cop-
ies of the manuscript, others only one. In any case,
whatever you do, make a copy for yourself before sending anything through the U.S. mails!*

**AUTHOR'S
REVISIONS
AND
SPECIAL
EDITORIAL
SERVICES**

5. If in the opinion of PUBLISHER the Work as
submitted requires special legal or editorial services,
including but not restricted to typing, additional
research, additional checking with legal counsel, or
other special legal or editorial services, or if AU-
THOR fails to provide any photographs, maps, drawings, charts, or indices required by PUBLISHER,
PUBLISHER may perform or supply or retain others
to perform or supply the same and deduct the cost
thereof from AUTHOR's payments due or to become due thereafter.

6. PUBLISHER shall submit galley proofs of the
Work to AUTHOR prior to printing or publishing

the Work, and AUTHOR shall correct and return the proofs to PUBLISHER within thirty (30) days of receipt thereof. PUBLISHER shall not be obligated to accept any additions to or changes from the last version of the manuscript PUBLISHER has approved. Alterations in the proof made at AUTHOR's request, the cost of which exceeds 10 percent (10%) of the original cost of composition, shall be charged against any payments due or to become due to AUTHOR. AUTHOR shall pay in full for any corrections in the plates (other than printer's errors or changes made at the request of PUBLISHER) requested after the plates have been made in conformity with last page proof as corrected by AUTHOR.

Here are two areas in which the publisher is protecting itself by charging the author for extra work that may be required. In clause 5 the publisher gives you fair warning that if you submit a manuscript so messy that it has to be retyped, you're going to have to pay the typist; ditto if you've left out essential materials the publisher has to hire somebody to provide.

Clause 6 is telling the author not to rewrite the book after the manuscript stage! It's extremely expensive to make plates over in order to catch errors you may have missed in the galley proofs (see Glossary and Chapter 8, "Manuscript into Type"). Read those proofs carefully, and if possible have several other people read them as well. You are not penalized for printer's errors or typos, and although your publisher will also have someone proofread, it's the author's responsibility to spot errors in the proofs. No one is as sensitive to subtle errors as you.

PUBLISHER'S PERFORMANCE OR DELAYS

7. (A) PUBLISHER shall publish the Work in book form no later than *Number of Months or Years* after the date of delivery of a satisfactory manuscript from AUTHOR. PUBLISHER's failure to publish the Work within the period stated above shall not constitute a breach of this agreement if such

failure or delay was due to time required for special legal or editorial services as provided for in Clause 5 above, or due to war, strikes, acts of God, floods, fires, government restrictions, court orders, or other circumstances beyond PUBLISHER's control.

The number of months or years the publisher has to produce the book is a negotiable point, but the general neighborhood should be between one and two years. Certain books are so timely they are rushed into print in six months, but it usually takes about a year to produce a hardcover book. Every contract contains a standard exception in the case of labor unrest, "acts of God," and so forth. If a publisher's delay is caused by the typesetters' union going out on strike or lightning striking the printing shop, you, as author, are just out of luck . . . but read on.

7. (B) If PUBLISHER's delay in publication is in breach of this agreement, AUTHOR shall have the option to terminate this agreement by a written notice to that effect mailed to PUBLISHER by registered mail. Such termination shall become effective <u>Number of Month</u>s after PUBLISHER's receipt of such registered letter if PUBLISHER has not within such a period published the Work.

Again, a negotiable point. This clause gives the publisher a few extra months in which to bring out the book—three to six months is about right here. As author, you shouldn't object to a clause like this because all kinds of human problems can come up—let's say your editor falls ill or suffers a death in the family—and you'd want the same consideration if you were forced to delay the manuscript because of unforeseen problems.

7. (C) AUTHOR and PUBLISHER agree that
　　1. If AUTHOR fails to deliver a satisfactory manuscript in breach of this agreement, AUTHOR shall

at PUBLISHER's request promptly return to PUB-LISHER any payments made to AUTHOR pursuant to this agreement;

2. If PUBLISHER fails to publish the Work in breach of this agreement, AUTHOR shall not be required by PUBLISHER to return to PUBLISHER any payments or advances against future royalties received by AUTHOR.

3. Both parties furthermore agree that the only damages recoverable by AUTHOR shall be confined to the advance of <u>Number of Dollars</u> paid to AUTHOR by PUBLISHER, and that no other damages will be claimed by AUTHOR against PUBLISHER.

Simple enough, and fair—although some literary contracts obfuscate this point with a lot of legal terminology. Basically these clauses almost never present a problem except in cases of actual fraud or failure to produce on either party's part. If the publisher is honest and the author is capable of writing the book and willing to cooperate with requested revisions, both parties will likely bend over backward to cooperate in producing the book, even if publication is delayed. The advance money already paid is the whole amount the author can keep if the publisher fails to publish the book. Any payment due "on publication" would under those circumstances not be made.

COPYRIGHT

8. PUBLISHER shall register the copyright to the Work in the United States in the name of AUTHOR or any other name AUTHOR requests, and PUBLISHER retains the option to register the copyright to the Work in countries other than the United States. PUBLISHER shall take all steps required to ensure protection under the Universal Copyright Convention, and agrees to publish simultaneously in Canada. AUTHOR hereby authorizes PUBLISHER to take all steps required to obtain such copyright or copyrights, and PUBLISHER may obtain renewals of all copyrights obtained. AUTHOR irrevocably

appoints PUBLISHER his attorney-in-fact for this purpose and AUTHOR will, upon PUBLISHER's request, do all acts necessary to effect and protect such copyrights and renewals thereof. PUBLISHER shall print the appropriate copyright notice required by law to comply with the applicable copyright laws of the United States on each copy of the Work it publishes. AUTHOR and PUBLISHER shall have the right to jointly prosecute any infringement of copyright. The expenses or proceeds of a joint prosecution for infringement of the right to publish the Work in book form shall be equally divided between them.

The copyright is your document of ownership of the rights to the work, and copyrights on books whether in print or not can form the major part of a writer's estate. The actual certificate usually rests with the publisher but should be returned to the author if and when the book goes out of print and the rights revert to the author.

The current copyright term on a book continues for the life of the author and for fifty years thereafter. (That is, on books published since January 1, 1978; prior to that, term of copyright varied according to complex statutory rules. The usual term was twenty-eight years, renewable for an additional twenty-eight years.) The author's heirs are entitled to the royalties on the book up to the point where the copyright expires and the work passes into the public domain. Copyright laws have been revised several times in the past two decades: the Library of Congress in Washington, D.C., registers copyrights and can provide information about current regulations. One important change is that you can now take out a copyright on an unpublished manuscript, which wasn't possible until a few years ago.

The Universal Copyright Convention, mentioned earlier and discussed further in Chapter 5, is the agreement between U.S. and British publishers that carves the English-reading world into separate markets. Many U.S. publishers have a working relationship with a Canadian publisher for a simultaneous edition.

**ADVANCE
AND
ROYALTIES**

9. (A) As an advance against and on account of all moneys accruing to the AUTHOR under this agreement, PUBLISHER shall pay the AUTHOR the sum of <u>Number of Dollars</u> in the following manner:

<u>Number of Dollars</u> upon the signing of this agreement and <u>Number of Dollars</u> upon PUBLISHER's acceptance of a satisfactory manuscript of the Work. PUBLISHER shall notify AUTHOR of the acceptability or nonacceptability of the manuscript within thirty (30) days of PUBLISHER's receipt of the manuscript.

Obviously, the key figure here is the size of the advance. This particular contract, which includes hardcover rights, pays half of the advance when the author signs this contract and the other half when the manuscript is delivered and accepted by the publisher.

However, in contracts for original paperback books, the breakdown is frequently different. Many contracts pay one half on signing and the other half on publication, which is likely to be at least a year after the manuscript is finished, and as the advances get higher, the number of payments increases. Sometimes these installment payments extend well beyond publication of the book—which would seem to negate the meaning of the word "advance." In any case, the advance is the sum of money the author is guaranteed to receive, whether or not the book earns royalties sufficient to repay it.

Limiting the publisher to thirty days in which to deem a manuscript acceptable or nonacceptable is a negotiable provision in a contract. From an author's point of view, it's a valuable clause because otherwise the publisher could take a number of months to get around to your manuscript, while you wait in agony. As with the other deadlines in the contract, the author should be prepared to allow a reasonable extension of time in the event of delaying circumstances. For more on advances, refer back to Chapters 1 and 2, on nonfiction and fiction markets.

9. (B) PUBLISHER shall pay to AUTHOR royalties to be computed on the retail selling price of various editions of the Work as follows:

1. HARDCOVER EDITIONS

<u>Number</u> percent of the retail price on the first five thousand (5,000) copies sold;

<u>Number</u> percent of the retail price on the next five thousand (5,000) copies sold;

and

<u>Number</u> percent of the retail price on all copies sold in excess of ten thousand (10,000).

Remember our "fair" standard: 10 percent to 5,000; 12½ percent to 10,000; 15 percent thereafter.

2. TRADE PAPERBACK EDITIONS

<u>Number</u> percent of the retail price on the first ten thousand (10,000) copies sold;

<u>Number</u> percent of the retail price on the next ten thousand (10,000) copies sold;

<u>Number</u> percent of the retail price on all copies sold in excess of twenty thousand (20,000).

For trade paperbacks we place the rate at 6 percent to 10,000; 7½ percent to 20,000; and 10 percent thereafter.

3. MASS-MARKET PAPERBACK EDITIONS

<u>Number</u> percent of the retail price on all copies sold.

The mass-market royalty tends to be simpler. We suggest 8 percent to 150,000 copies and 10 percent thereafter.

4. SALES OUTSIDE THE UNITED STATES

Royalties on all copies sold in Canada and other export markets shall be 50 percent (50%) of the above royalties.

Different publishers have different ways of putting this, but royalties on export sales of the U.S. edition are always lower than domestic royalties. Some contracts will place this export royalty at the same figures, the same percent, as regular royalties, but base the payment not on the retail price of the book but on the net amount the publisher receives. Note that royalties on copies sold in Canada are always calculated at a lower rate than U.S. royalties.

**EXCEP-
TIONS TO
ROYALTIES**

10. The foregoing royalty schedule, however, shall be subject to the following exceptions:

**FREE AND
DAMAGED
COPIES**

10 (A) No royalties will be paid on copies given to AUTHOR or purchased by AUTHOR at discounts described herein, nor on copies given away for review or promotion (and not for resale), copies destroyed or materially damaged prior to sale, or copies sold at or below cost.

Obviously, the publisher can't afford to pay an author's royalty on books it is already losing money on.

**DIRECT
MAIL
ORDER**

10 (B) PUBLISHER shall pay AUTHOR a royalty of 50 percent (50%) of the royalty that would otherwise be applicable on all copies sold by PUBLISHER by means of direct mailings or newspaper coupon advertisement, and with such orders and sales not passing through bookstores.

Here, the publisher lowers the royalty because it has to pay for advertising and shipping/handling of single copies.

**SMALL
REPRINT-
INGS**

10 (C) PUBLISHER shall pay AUTHOR a royalty of 75 percent (75%) of the royalty that would otherwise be applicable on all copies sold from a reprint-

ing of two thousand (2,000) copies or less, made after two (2) years from the date of first publication if, in any one-year royalty period, sales of the Work do not exceed five hundred (500) copies.

> *Small reprintings are less profitable, but this reduced author royalty allows the publisher to keep the book in print and in circulation. Many contracts have some provision like this—often it's a 50 percent royalty cut. But this applies only after your book has been out for a couple of years and sales have trickled down to small numbers. This clause is much likelier to appear in a hardcover than a paperback original contract.*

LARGE DISCOUNT SALES

10 (D) PUBLISHER shall pay AUTHOR the stipulated royalty calculated on the basis of the price as received, and not on the retail price, in cases where the Work is sold at discounts of more than 50 percent (50%) but less than 70 percent (70%) on the regular retail price.

> *This is fairly self-explanatory. If the publisher sells the book for half price or less but at least 30 percent of full value, the author's royalty is based on what the publisher actually received. Read on.*

OVER-STOCK AND REMAIN-DERS

10 (E) PUBLISHER shall pay AUTHOR a royalty of 10 percent (10%) of PUBLISHER's charges on copies of the Work that PUBLISHER, after at least one (1) year from the date of first publication, deems it expedient to sell at overstock or remainder prices, that is at a discount of 70 percent (70%) or more from the retail price, except when these are sold at or below PUBLISHER's cost, in which case no royalty shall be paid.

PUBLISHER agrees to furnish AUTHOR, in writing by registered letter, with the first opportunity to purchase copies of the Work at overstock or remainder prices before offering such copies for sale to others. AUTHOR shall have a period of thirty (30) days from receipt of such written notice in which to offer to purchase all or some of such overstock or remaindered copies.

> *Remainders, or copies left over after the sales of the book have fallen to a level too low to be profitable, and overstock, or copies on hand in excess of what the publisher thinks it can sell, often do sell for less than manufacturing cost and hence bring the author no royalties. We do recommend that you negotiate to include a clause giving you the first opportunity to buy such copies, as the author is frequently in the best position to keep the book alive by selling the remaining copies one by one or reselling the rights to another publisher (if the book has gone out of print and rights have reverted to the author). If nothing else, you can use the books for personal promotion and gifts, as we will see in Chapter 15, "Self-Promotion, the Writer's Best Friend."*

BRAILLE EDITIONS

10 (F) PUBLISHER shall pay AUTHOR no royalty on copies of the Work translated into Braille and distributed or sold for the benefit of the blind.

ADDITIONAL AND SUBSIDIARY RIGHTS

11. AUTHOR hereby grants to PUBLISHER the following rights in the Work, in addition to the rights granted above:

FIRST SERIAL RIGHTS

11 (A) The exclusive right to publish or permit others to publish the Work in whole or in part in the English language in magazines and newspapers prior to the date of first publication by PUBLISHER or by other magazines or newspapers. PUBLISHER shall pay to AUTHOR *Number* percent of the net amount it receives from sale of these rights.

SECOND SERIAL RIGHTS

11 (B) The exclusive right to publish or permit others to publish the Work in whole or in part in the English language in magazines and newspapers after first publication by PUBLISHER or by other

magazines or newspapers. PUBLISHER shall pay to AUTHOR *Number* percent of the net amount it receives from sale of these rights.

> *The author should receive at least 75 percent of these first and second serial magazine and newspaper rights. Some publishers surrender the full 100 percent to the author when the author's agent handles the sale of such rights. You, the author, definitely want your income from magazine and newspaper excerpts to come to you in addition to book royalty rights, and those excerpts also publicize your book.*

ABRIDG-
MENTS

11 (C) The exclusive right to publish or permit others to publish abridgments or condensations of the entire Work in book form or in magazines or newspapers in one or more installments. However, PUBLISHER shall not without the approval of AUTHOR or AUTHOR's literary executor exercise this right in such a way that the Work's style is altered or the Work's paragraphs internally altered. PUBLISHER shall pay AUTHOR *Number* percent of the net amount it receives from the exercise of this right.

> *This clause relates to the possibility of your book's being condensed in a special edition such as the Reader's Digest series. The author's share of the proceeds should be 50 to 75 percent.*

PROMO-
TIONAL
EXCERPTS

11 (D) The exclusive right to publish or permit others to publish short excerpts or selections from the Work (including photographs or illustrations) for the purpose of aiding the publicity and sale of the Work. No royalties shall be paid on such permissions for publication without payment.

These free promotional excerpts are shorter than and not to be confused with first and second serial excerpts sold to magazines and newspapers. Occasionally the publisher may grant permission to reprint a small portion of the book to a reviewing publication or other promotional vehicle without pay or royalty.

BOOK CLUBS

11 (E) The exclusive right to publish or permit others to publish special editions of the Work for sale by book clubs, PUBLISHER shall pay AUTHOR *Number* percent of the net amount it receives from the exercise of this right, provided, however, that if PUBLISHER itself publishes a special edition or editions for sale by its own book club, it shall pay AUTHOR on the basis of the retail prices of copies actually sold to the public in accordance with the royalty schedule contained herein.

The author usually gets 50 percent of revenues from book-club sales or sometimes half of the normal royalty rate. As we've discussed earlier, no author should pass up a book club merely because the royalty per copy is lower. The advertising, exposure, prestige, and additional sales make the book clubs worthwhile. Although this contract addresses book clubs as a whole and single entity, some other contracts now distinguish between the hardcover book club and paperback book club, with a somewhat lower royalty to the author from the paperback club. Major clubs include the Book-of-the-Month Club, Quality Paperback Book Club, and the Literary Guild. There are also specialized book clubs for mysteries, fine art, history, war, etc.

REPRINT EDITIONS

11 (F) The exclusive right to permit others to publish paperback or other "cheap edition" reprint editions of the Work. PUBLISHER shall pay AUTHOR 50 percent (50%) of the net amount it receives from the exercise of this right.

As we noted earlier, the 50–50 split of these subsidiary rights to reprint editions is conventional in the publishing industry when the original hardcover publisher does not bring out its own paperback of the book. The percentage is a negotiable point, like every number value in the contract, but most hardcover publishers would insist on their half of these revenues because many a hardcover book that lost money still earned a profit in the long run thanks to reprint income.

Paperback reprints are either trade paperbacks, the larger books sold in bookstores, or mass-market paperbacks, the rack-sized books sold in supermarkets and other outlets besides bookstores. "Cheap edition" can also refer to an inexpensive hardcover reprint line (such as Outlet Publishers).

TEXTBOOK SALES

11 (G) The exclusive right to publish or permit others to publish the Work as a text for sale to educational institutions at a retail price of not less than one half the price of the regular trade edition. PUBLISHER shall pay AUTHOR with respect to all such textbook sales a royalty of 50 percent (50%) of the royalty that would otherwise be applicable.

Another negotiable point, but textbook royalties are invariably lower than trade royalties. For the most part, your regular trade book is never going to be published as a text, so this clause is irrelevant. Advantages of textbook authorship include: controlled academic distribution (one professor can assign many students to buy the book so sales efforts concentrate on reaching teachers); chance of long-term, steady sales and revised, updated editions; professional advancement in one's academic field.

Textbooks, by the way, operate on a different level from trade books meant for the broad reading public. Not only are the royalty rates and advances low, but the books take years of preparation and are sold to book-

Continued

Continued

sellers at a much lower discount—meaning less profit to the store. Most are sold directly to students through assignment in classes and school bookstores. Unless they are extremely successful, textbooks usually just supplement the teaching income of the professors who write them.

FOREIGN LANGUAGE EDITIONS

11 (H) The exclusive right to print, publish, and sell or permit others to print, publish, and sell the Work in all foreign languages throughout the world in book form and in magazines and newspapers. PUBLISHER shall pay to AUTHOR *Number* percent of the net amount received by it from the exercise of such right, except that if PUBLISHER itself publishes a foreign-language edition of the Work, PUBLISHER shall pay AUTHOR the same royalties as for the domestic market.

As we mentioned earlier, foreign rights sales are handled through foreign agents, who of course take a commission, and the publisher or your agent handles the expense of paperwork, negotiation, etc. Consequently, although the author gets the lion's share of these foreign revenues, say 75 percent or more, it is neither uncommon nor unjust for the publisher (or, in some cases, the author's agent) to get as much as 25 percent. From the author's point of view, it's an advantage to have your agent handle foreign rights and receive foreign payments, since they don't have to go through the publisher and be credited against any unearned advance money. (Foreign payments made to the agent go directly to the author after the agent deducts his or her commission.) Most agents turn payments over to the author quite promptly, whereas most publishers have a twice-annual payment schedule, as we shall see below.

**PER-
FORMANCE
AND
MISCEL-
LANEOUS
RIGHTS**

11 (I) The exclusive right in all countries and languages of the world to sell, lease, or otherwise dispose of the following rights, paying over to AUTHOR *Number* percent of the net amount PUBLISHER receives from such use, sale, lease, or other disposition: dramatic production, motion picture, radio, television, mechanical or electronic recordings of the text, and all other performance rights in the Work that could now be known but are not specifically mentioned anywhere herein and rights arising out of the Work that hereafter may be discovered, or come into being.

The agent controls these performance rights most of the time and the publisher seldom shares in them except to a token degree. It is not unusual for the author to receive 100 percent of performance rights, but in all cases he or she should get at least 75 percent. Once again, it's preferable to have your agent receive performance revenues for quicker payout to you as author.

**ACCOUNT-
ING**

12. Statements of sale or other income from the Work shall be compiled by PUBLISHER on or about April 30 for the period of the preceding July 1 to December 31, and on or about October 31 for the period of the preceding January 1 to June 30 of each year. Statements shall include a deduction for a reasonable reserve against returns. Such statements shall show the gross amount credited to AUTHOR, and PUBLISHER will remit with the statements royalty payments due for the period covered by them. The first statement of sales shall not be prepared until the Work shall have been on sale for at least six (6) months. Should AUTHOR receive an overpayment on copies sold but subsequently returned, PUBLISHER may deduct such overpayment from any earnings then or thereafter due to AUTHOR on this Work. PUBLISHER shall, upon written request from AUTHOR, cause either the public accountants employed by PUBLISHER or a certified

public accountant of AUTHOR's choosing to provide
to AUTHOR a certified copy of AUTHOR's royalty
statement or statements at AUTHOR's expense.

*Whoa! This is the most important paragraph in the
contract, after of course the Number of Dollars of the
advance. The publisher promises to send a statement of
copies sold including "a deduction for a reasonable reserve against returns." This is the notorious reserve against
returns clause, and it does put an important decision
entirely in the publisher's province, but almost no author can do anything about it, so there's hardly much
point in fretting over it.*

*The book business is one of few that operates with a
broad "returns privilege." A bookseller orders ten copies
of your book, sells four of them, and as long as a year
later has the right to return the remaining six copies to
the publisher for a full refund. The publisher may charge
a few percentage points and make the bookseller pay
return shipping costs, but the refund is still nearly total.
Imagine the havoc this policy has spawned! (See more in
Chapter 16, "Owning a Bookstore.")*

*Because the publisher has "sold" (i.e., shipped) 50,000
of your books doesn't mean that 40,000 of those won't
come back as returns. Depending on the returns policy
your publisher has, the period of sales limbo between
the bookstore's order and the cutoff date for returns
could be six months to a year and a half. Often the
royalties "owed" the author will be partially withheld
by the publisher pending the returns. There are also
occasional instances in which an author is paid his royalties only to find the returns have left him again in the
publisher's debt—and the publisher deducts the overpayment from the author's next royalty statement.*

*Note that the royalty statement of October 31 covers
sales from January 1 to June 30. That gives the publisher
all of July, August, September, and October to figure up
the numbers and mail your royalty statement and check.*

Continued

Continued

The April 30 statement covers sales from July 1 through December 31 and gives the publisher all of January, February, March, and April to do your statement. Despite this, beware that many publishers are not on time with their statements, just as many authors are late in delivering their manuscripts.

Often, if no royalty payment is due, no statement will be filed. But that's generally the case only with books that have been published for several years, when the income from the book has steadily diminished, and/or the advance against royalties owed is hopelessly greater than the income.

What you've got here is at its best a steady flow of statements and royalty checks. At its worst it is a flow of red-ink statements reflecting unearned advance money and/or books sold but waiting on the returns privilege. The system is complicated and, some would say, antiquated, but it doesn't seem likely to change much in the immediate future. An author can sometimes wait two years or more to collect a per-copy royalty on actual books sold—just as a publisher can wait that long to be certain "sold" books won't be returned!

As a small press publisher (Montana Books), I experimented with abolishing the returns privilege. We sold the books we published for cash (or check, of course) to booksellers who then owned them—no returns allowed. It simplified our bookkeeping enormously and we were pleased with the results even though it did cut into our sales about 25 percent. However, no major publishing company can take the same risks we took as a tiny, West Coast house.

AUTHOR'S COPIES

13. PUBLISHER shall present to AUTHOR ten (10) free copies of the Work upon its first publication by PUBLISHER and shall permit AUTHOR to purchase additional copies for AUTHOR's personal use and not for resale at a discount of 20 percent (20%) of the retail price on orders of one to four copies each,

and 40 percent (40%) of the retail price on orders of five or more copies each.

This clause is about standard, although in point of fact, most publishers will willingly give an author more than ten copies of the book—particularly if the author is promoting the book by giving copies to potential reviewers, interviewers, or other authors willing to donate some comment ("blurb") the publisher can use in advertising the book. It's wise to negotiate in advance for more than ten complimentary copies and, if you expect to be in the position of selling your own book (for example, at readings or appearances), work out a Premium Sales agreement with the publisher to create specific exceptions to the rule of discount author's copies "for personal use and not for resale."

For example, a Premium Sales agreement might state that the author is entitled to buy books at 50 percent discount for the purpose of selling them at his/her seminars and appearances on a college campus speaking tour.

**TERMINA-
TION OF
CONTRACT**

14. This agreement shall terminate and cease:

(A) If AUTHOR fails to deliver a satisfactory manuscript of the Work and PUBLISHER exercises its option to terminate this agreement for that reason; or

(B) If PUBLISHER fails to publish the Work at the time herein specified, and AUTHOR exercises his option to terminate this agreement for that reason; or

---

These two clauses are fairly obvious points. If the author failed to deliver, or the publisher to publish, there was never a book produced and the contract should be null and void. If the failure was the author's, he or she could be required to return the advance money to

Continued

Continued

the publisher; if the fault was with the publisher, the author keeps the advance.

Just what does "termination" mean in this context? It sounds so terribly fatal and final. It means the end of this agreement, the point at which the two parties break off their working relationship. But in fact, certain aspects of the contract, such as the publisher's collecting reprint or foreign royalties on the author's behalf, live on beyond termination. Those exceptions follow in Clause 15. You could say, at least in some cases, that it's never really the end.

(C) If PUBLISHER at a date at least two years from the date of first publication of the Work gives three months' notice by registered letter to AUTHOR of its intention to permit the Work to go permanently out of print, terminating PUBLISHER's rights to publish the Work; or

Some publishers don't give three months' notice, or any notice at all. Once a book is permanently out of print, however, the original contract almost always terminates.

(D) If PUBLISHER and AUTHOR at the same time mutually agree in writing to terminate this agreement on any terms; or

This occasionally does happen—for example, when an author agrees to write a book and finds after three years of agony at the typewriter that it's just not coming out right, or when publisher and author together abandon a book because another publisher has rushed out with a similar book they don't want to compete with. These are just a couple of the many possible reasons to terminate by mutual agreement.

(E) If PUBLISHER files a petition in bankruptcy or assigns its assets to creditors or takes refuge under state or federal insolvency laws, or if a bankruptcy petition is filed against PUBLISHER and granted by a court, or if PUBLISHER's business is liquidated; or

And if any of that happens, the author is just out of luck. If your book is already published when the publisher goes bankrupt, it can be almost worse. The books themselves may be seized as assets and sold off to remainder distributors in lots. In any case, you may find it difficult to interest a new publisher in the book once it's disclosed that thousands of published copies are sitting in the bankrupt firm's warehouse. And of course it's tough to collect any royalties that might be due you from a bankrupt publisher. If the publisher goes under before it brings out your book, you should be able to sell the rights to a new publisher without complication.

It's not worth worrying about this issue, however. Happily, bankruptcies in publishing are relatively rare, especially with major houses. I do have a friend whose first novel was published in paperback three months before the publisher went under. The books sat undistributed, unadvertised, and unread for years while the courts sifted through a protracted series of claims, credits, assets, and liabilities. My friend never saw another penny and had to accept payment in cartons of his own books. But, while I've met and known authors by the hundreds for twenty years, I've known only one who endured this particular problem.

(F) If PUBLISHER fails to keep the Work in print later than three years from the date of first publication, and if after written notice by registered letter from AUTHOR, PUBLISHER fails to place the Work in print and for sale with a period of six months from the date of such written notice. The Work shall be considered to be in print if it is on sale in a paperback or "cheap edition" either published by PUBLISHER or licensed to another publisher for reprinting.

The object here is to terminate the contract and thus return the rights to the author if the publisher doesn't keep the book in print. Although this contract earlier had the publisher promising to advise the author before the book goes out of print, many a book has gone quietly out of print, and if the author doesn't write to the publisher formally demanding that the book be returned to print or the rights returned, nothing at all happens and the publisher retains rights even years after the title has gone O.P.

That's not necessarily bad, however. Sometimes a publisher will decide to republish an old book for which it retains the rights. See the first paragraph of the next section for more on this point.

EFFECTS OF TERMINA-TION

15. When termination of the agreement occurs, by any of the means in section 14 above:

(A) All of the rights granted by AUTHOR to PUBLISHER herein, except the option on future Work described in Clause 16 below, revert to AUTHOR on PUBLISHER's receipt of a registered letter from AUTHOR requesting such rights reversion.

This is important. You or your agent has to write and request a document which states that the rights have reverted to you. Imagine that your book has been out of print for ten years but Publisher A never bothered to return the rights to you and you never bothered to write and formally request the reversion. In the meantime you've written a best-selling novel, and your new publisher, Publisher B, decides it would be profitable to do a reprint edition of your old book. But you find that Publisher A still controls the rights—and has six months after receipt of your written notice to bring out its own edition! (See Clause 14 F above.) This scenario is not all that unlikely. It can happen when an author has achieved newfound popularity or when a book is sold to the

Continued

Continued

movies or, unfortunately, when a famous author dies and the reading public goes back to his/her former works to assess the career.

What happens in a case like that? One of several courses is likely:

(a) Publisher A, in a spirit of cooperation, responds to your letter by simply mailing the certificate of rights reversion, and you go ahead and sell the book to Publisher B:

(b) Publisher A, exercising its control over the rights, negotiates with Publisher B and sells B a reprint right. Typically, the author gets 50 percent of the revenues and the original publisher the other half:

(c) Publisher A realizes the new value of your book and offers to bring out a new edition of its own, with a new advance on royalties paid to you. Often enough the original publisher is willing to give the author a new advance in the interests of keeping everybody happy and gaining the author's signature on a clause giving it extra time beyond six months in which to produce the book.

(d) Publisher A simply exercises its legal rights and rushes into print with a new edition of the book in six months or less. No new advance is paid, but royalties are due according to the percentages in the original contract.

Of these four possibilities, I tend to think that (d) is the least likely to happen. It's fairly difficult (and expensive) to rush a book onto the market in under six months. And there IS a kind of gentility and cooperation in the business of literature—although you couldn't blame a publisher for wanting to hang on to rights, or a portion thereof, of work by some red-hot author. The vast majority of such cases involve lesser "lights" and smaller amounts of money.

A final thought: Since you, as author, prefer option (a), that the original publisher will simply mail you the reversion paper, it might be wise to make your request

Continued

Continued

simple and brief, and NOT mention any interest from another publisher in the book! Once Publisher A knows of Publisher B's interest, option (b), a sale of reprint rights, becomes A's best bet.

(B) AUTHOR has the option to purchase from PUBLISHER all or part of the copies of the Work which PUBLISHER has on hand at the manufacturing cost thereof, and the plates of the Work, if PUBLISHER still has such plates, at the cost of composition and plating. If AUTHOR fails to exercise the right of such purchases within sixty days of the date of termination of this agreement, then PUBLISHER shall have the right to dispose of remaining copies of the Work and the plates of the Work free from obligation.

What are "plates"? In the old days they were heavy metal slabs, trays loaded with the actual lead type characters of the book. Since the advent of photo offset printing, the plates are on thin, pliable metal sheets, or even plastic. They are the mechanical means by which the book is printed. The advantage to owning them is that one can reprint the book from them without resetting it in type, an expensive process, and we've known more than one author who republished an earlier book that had gone out of print with its original house. Sometimes an author will buy the plates for sentimental reasons—an archival souvenir.

(C) Beyond the termination of this agreement, PUBLISHER shall remain liable to AUTHOR for all unpaid royalties or other moneys due to AUTHOR and PUBLISHER shall continue to receive payments from all third parties under contracts pertaining to the Work, paying to AUTHOR his share of such payments as provided in this agreement.

If your book should live on in some other edition after the original publisher's edition is out of print, you might be receiving checks from Publisher A for years after this contract has terminated. Assuming your initial advance on royalties has been repaid, the original publisher becomes your "holding company" for royalties from other editions, paying you every six months on a standard royalty statement.

OPTION TO PUBLISH NEXT WORK

16. AUTHOR agrees to submit to PUBLISHER an outline together with a representative sample chapter or chapters of his next book-length Work and give PUBLISHER the first option to publish it. PUBLISHER shall have a period of thirty (30) days after submission of the outline in which to notify AUTHOR by registered letter whether it wishes to publish such next Work and, if PUBLISHER wishes to publish such next Work, offer its terms. If within twenty-one days thereafter, AUTHOR and PUBLISHER fail to achieve a mutually satisfactory agreement, or if PUBLISHER fails to notify AUTHOR of its decision whether or not to publish such next Work, AUTHOR shall have the right to submit such outline to other publishers. However, AUTHOR shall not grant rights to such next Work to another publisher on terms equal to or less favorable than those offered by PUBLISHER.

Whew, the notorious Option Clause. This is the great bugaboo that worries writers from Day One, but an awful lot of energy is wasted in the worrying. This particular option clause favors the author in that he/she (or the agent) has negotiated a promise to submit only an outline, not a finished manuscript, of the next full-length work, and to give the publisher only a month in which to decide on it. Very often the printed option clause in the contract will state that the author has to

Continued

Continued

submit a complete manuscript of the next book for the publisher's first option, and it will not give the publisher any firm deadline. Obviously the terms of our sample contract are better and LIT BIZ 101 recommends that you negotiate similar ones.

Some option clauses will also specify a time frame before which the author can't submit another book. For example, the contract would state that the option book can't be submitted until at least thirty days after the current book has been published. Writers should try to extract from publishers an early decision on an option manuscript.

In practice, if an author is satisfied with his/her publisher, he or she will want to remain with that house, and vice versa. Sign the option clause, it won't kill you. Think of it as future security—at least you can be sure one publisher is committed to seriously considering your next work!

INTERPRE-TATION

17. This agreement shall be interpreted according to the laws and statutes of the State of *Name of State* regardless of the place of its execution and performance, and this agreement shall be binding on and benefit the heirs and assignees of AUTHOR and any successor in business of PUBLISHER.

Legal fine points, and nothing to worry about. State laws vary, and the publisher wants to assure that everything here complies with the local requirements of the state it's in. And of course your heirs (or any business that buys up your publisher) inherit this contract and/or its payments.

COMPET-ING WORK

18. AUTHOR agrees that during the term of this agreement he will not, without PUBLISHER's written permission, publish or permit to be published any work which is likely to compete with the Work provided for in this agreement or which is reasonably likely to injure its sale.

A simple protection for the publisher against the un-scrupulous author who would sell the same-basic-idea book to two different publishers. We don't object to this clause, it's reasonable, but we've never actually known an author to compete against him/herself in the literary marketplace. It wouldn't be smart. You do see authors writing, over and over, what appears to be much the same book: The New, Revised, All-Different Such-and-Such Diet Book. *(When Such-and-Such Diet became a national hit, suddenly the authors produced sequel after sequel, boldly proclaiming the name of the diet in every title. But that's hardly compet-ing against yourself.) This clause just ensures that you're not going to go out and publish a very similar book to the one this publisher is buying, thus tak-ing income away from the publisher if not from you personally.*

AUTHOR'S AGENT

19. AUTHOR hereby designates *Name of Agent, Agent's Address* as his exclusive agent with respect to the Work and hereby authorizes PUBLISHER to pay all royalties or other payments due or to be-come due to such agent. In return for services ren-dered by the agent in connection with this agreement, AUTHOR agrees to pay and authorizes said agent to receive and retain as its commission, *Number* percent of all moneys payable to AUTHOR through this agreement.

The typical agent's commission is 10 to 15 percent. More about agents in Chapter 7.

ADVERTISE-MENTS

20. No advertisements may be inserted or printed in PUBLISHER's editions of the Work without AU-THOR's prior written consent.

Good clause, this one, and negotiated well. In many contracts this clause will provide an exception for "house ads," in which the publisher advertises its other titles. A mass-market publisher once bound a stiff cardboard ad for Kent cigarettes into the middle of one of my books. When I complained bitterly I was told, "Relax, it's only for the New York and New Jersey markets!" Without a clause such as this one, there's nothing you as author can do about it, so be advised.

IN WITNESS WHEREOF, the parties hereto have duly executed this agreement the day and year set forth above.

Signed by Author	Signed by Publisher
Citizen of: _____	(Name and Title)
Social Security #:	

Conclusion

That, in essence, is the literary contract. Some will add original clauses, called "riders," which take up an author's unique, personal concern with issues not mentioned in the "boilerplate" above. For example, you could ask for a rider stating that the publisher agrees to a specific budget for advertising and promoting the book. That's a privilege reserved for highly commercial prospects, but many an agent has negotiated such a deal.

When you sign your first literary contract you are permitted the same level of celebration as a bar mitzvah, wedding, or wild birthday party. It's rather like seeing your kid graduate from college. If the writing of the book is like birth, the signing of the contract is coming of age. Your baby's out in the world now.

The contract is like a road map to your pot of gold, or at least pot of beans. Follow the map carefully and it will lead you to ensuring that you collect the earnings due to you, if not to riches. We'll concentrate on those earnings and consider some related money matters that spring from the contract in Chapter 6, "Money and Perks."

5 | The Writer and the Law

A very lucky writer will have no involvements with the law, no association with attorneys or bailiffs. But the terms of the literary contract clearly pay deference to certain laws of the land, including those surrounding libel, obscenity, defamation, copyright protection, legal obligations, author's warranties and indemnities. What follows is only a very general discussion of some complex areas of the law. If you need guidance on specific legal questions, you should consult your attorney or your publisher's attorney.

Libel and Defamation

"Libel" and "defamation" are more or less the same thing: a published false statement that is damaging to a person's reputation.

Libel suits are fairly uncommon in today's atmosphere of virtual license to print anything. Standing on line in the supermarket, you'll read headlines in "exposé" magazines like LIZ REVEALS TORRID AFFAIR WITH AMBASSADOR or DAD SLAUGHTERS FAMILY AFTER LOSING LOTTERY TICKET. . . . Who knows whether this kind of stuff is true or not? But these tabloids make for popular, entertaining reading, and libel suits against them are rare, expensive, and time-consuming. While the movie stars claim it's all lies, they seldom try to fight it in court. For one thing, a public figure as plaintiff has to prove that the false statement was deliberate or reckless, while a private figure must prove negligence; for another, the mere fact of filing suit is bound to create more publicity and spread the false statement further. It's often better to let the matter slide, trusting that most people know better than to believe *everything* they might read in a newspaper.

Nonetheless, libel is a serious matter. With all nonfiction, it's wise to stay within the limits of what you can reasonably prove, or at least confirm via tapes or notes from interviews with your sources. And what about "Deep Throat," the Watergate informer who remained anonymous? What if your sources can't reveal their identities? How do you know (and you'd better know) that what you've been told and reported is true, or at least from a "reliable source"? And if you're not absolutely sure of its truth, how can you protect yourself from a libel suit?

Remember that under the law *you and your publisher can be held responsible for information you publish while quoting a third party.* If you can't absolutely prove an accusation, you should have reasonable cause for presenting it within a piece of writing and be free of any charge of purposefully telling lies. Big publishers maintain a legal department of well-paid attorneys who comb over every word of some manuscripts (the process called "vetting," which we mentioned in Chapter 4) searching for possible liabilities; smaller publishers do not have a separate legal department but they do read with an eye out for potentially libelous passages. But small publishers are usually not rich enough to make it worthwhile for anyone to sue them. And chances are nobody is going to sue you, the author, unless your book makes a fortune and it's obvious that you are getting rich from it, and/or some person or other mentioned in the book (even fictitiously) takes offense. Good advice: As a safe rule of thumb, you should have at least two sources for every allegation you make in a nonfiction book, and you should never publish anything that you suspect is untrue, whatever its source.

And the way to go in a novel is to take more rather than less literary license in "fictionalizing" your friends and acquaintances (especially ex-spouses)—that is, alter any identifying features (not just physical but professional and geographical). Yes, you can be sued for libel if someone you know thinks a fictional character in your novel resembles him or herself and is portrayed in a negative light. BUT, and it's an important exception, you are on safer legal ground (although not immune to suit) if the fictional character is based on someone who is already a public personality rather than a private person known to you. Obviously, it's safer to fictionalize with details that are flattering, not unflattering.

For example, didn't Nora Ephron's best-selling novel *Heartburn* pretty clearly attack her ex-husband, Carl Bernstein? Didn't many of Jack Kerouac's novels feature thinly disguised characters based on Neal Cassady (road bum), Allen Ginsberg (homosexual), William S. Burroughs (drug addict), and other famous writers? Many people who are already celebrities in the public eye, like Carl Bernstein or Allen Ginsberg, have less protection under the libel laws than those who are ordinary private citizens. Not all celebrities, however, are in this category; they must have voluntarily joined in a public controversy. The reasoning behind this is that a public figure's life is open to widespread public discussion and depiction, and that such persons can presumably respond in print. But even public figures are protected against "known falsehoods," which all true fiction perforce contains. The truth is that we have a "gray," as opposed to black-and-white, clear-cut, situation with our libel and defamation laws. On the one hand, you can't make defamatory, false statements about a person; on the other hand, people do it all the time and get away with it. The odds are definitely in the author's and publisher's favor, but the safest bet is to take no chances. Don't say bad things about people in a nonfiction book unless you have very reliable information, and personally believe those things to be true, and don't portray fictional characters in an unflattering light who closely resemble real people you know. Remember, even celebrities can sue for known falsehoods.

Obscenity

Obscenity refers to published matter that is indecent or "repulsively lewd," to quote the Oxford Dictionary. Legally speaking, obscenity is material that appeals solely to the reader's prurient interest and has no countervailing social value. Fortunately (in my opinion), it is almost impossible to prove in the United States. What is obscene to one mind is mildly entertaining to another, and the laws have consistently favored freedom of expression since the big obscenity trials of the 1950s and 1960s. While Henry Miller's *Tropic of Cancer* and D. H. Lawrence's *Lady Chatterley's Lover* were banned here only forty years ago, we now have open sales of hard core sexually oriented literature, with very rare prosecutions.

Your publisher, however, might have a lot of trouble distributing your "obscene" material through certain channels and in some states. In recent years we've seen the Moral Majority people pursuing allegations of obscenity against some of the best-known and most-respected American writers, particularly when their books were taught in public schools. We've seen movements to ban and even burn offending books by Kurt Vonnegut, Joseph Heller, and J. D. Salinger, to name a few. While a novel may not be legally declared obscene, it can still be harassed and persecuted out of existence in some places. Civil liberties lawyers defend such works, while more conservative thinkers press to have them removed from libraries and school reading lists.

Under the Reagan Administration there's also been a so-called war on pornography, followed by the Meese Commission Report on Pornography. To date, at this writing, it's been more a campaign of intimidation than of legislation.

As an author, you have every legal right to describe a sex scene in explicit detail. Steamy, passionate love scenes that would once have been considered indecent are now an essential ingredient of any best-selling potboiler (see Chapter 2 on fiction) and are considered "soft core." Some (not all) "hard-core" stuff is legal, too, but limited to "adult bookstores." And when we're considering text alone (not photographs or illustrations) the line between soft and hard core can be very vague. Some sex will help your book sell, probably; too much sex may cause it to be hounded off the shelves.

Protecting Your Ideas (Copyright Protection)

Many people in the Lit Biz 101 classes have asked about how
they can protect their uncopyrighted work from being ripped off
by (imagined) unscrupulous New York and Los Angeles agents
and publishers. You've probably heard a variation on this story
yourself: "I wrote a novel about two bank robbers, a man and a
woman, in Las Vegas, and sent it to such and such a publisher.
They turned it down and sent it back to me with just a printed
rejection slip and six months later they came out with another
novel about two bank robbers in Las Vegas *using my plot and
just changing the names of the characters and some of the
writing! Can I sue?*"

Well, you could, but don't bother. It's extremely difficult to
prove that your uncopyrighted idea was ripped off. It's much
easier to take out a copyright on your writing since the new
copyright law went into effect in 1978. To copyright your material, just show the copyright symbol (©), the year, and your
name (the name of the person or entity who is holding the
copyright) on the first page of the manuscript. To *register* that
copyright, send for forms available from the U.S. Copyright
Office, Library of Congress, Washington, DC 20559. It's fairly
simple and inexpensive and the best part is that, since 1978,
your writing doesn't have to be published in order to be
copyrighted.

It's worth adding here that a great deal of the anxiety expended worrying about what some publisher or movie producer
is going to do with your idea, having stolen it, is wasted. "Ideas"
are extremely difficult to protect legally, and cannot be copyrighted. (Nor can titles, but if you use a well-known title of
somebody else's work, he or she could sue you for unfair competition.) By some synchronicity, different writers and publishers
in different parts of the world bring out books on identical topics
at the same time. Rather than worry too much about someone's
potential designs on your ideas, you as the nascent author should
make your material so original that nobody could steal it.

Although it might even be flattering to think so, don't dissi-
pate your creative energy by imagining that an army of unethical
plagiarists is out there just waiting to steal your precious ideas.

We don't deny that there's a certain amount of copycat activity going on, particularly in the Hollywood universe, where you can actually sell an "idea" for a picture written up in a short (one- or two-page) memo, and very successful books and movies often do spawn a host of imitators. But that level of commercial cloning is not the same thing as ripping off a book that hasn't yet been published. Copyright your stuff and send it out plainly marked with the cosmic ©!

Legal Warranties and Indemnities

As you saw in Chapter 4, the literary contract includes a clause for the author's "warranties and indemnities" in which the author promises that the manuscript is all legal and lets the publisher off the hook by agreeing to pay legal costs if there's a lawsuit. A "warranty" in this context means a guarantee in writing from author to publisher that:

—the author has the right to sell this material, hasn't already sold it to someone else;

—the book is original and not plagiarized and doesn't violate any copyrights;

—there's nothing obscene, libelous, or otherwise illegal in the book.

An "indemnity" is the act of legally exempting someone from responsibility; in this case the author agrees that the publisher is not responsible for paying to defend a lawsuit based on alleged violations of the warranties.

As we've noted before, in a typical lawsuit the plaintiff will sue both publisher and author, so both have some territory to protect. Following the old commonsense axiom that people sue only when the sued party is presumed to have enough money (or insurance) to pay a judgment, the plaintiff will likely be more interested in suing the publisher than the author. Few writers have as much to lose as their publishers do. Nonetheless, if your manuscript holds any *likelihood* of libeling somebody and your publisher doesn't already have a lawyer vetting it, it could pay for you to hire your own, just to have at least one professional opinion. A good lawyer should be able to protect your material from any risk of legal repercussions without being *too* nitpicking.

> *I once got into a wrangle with a pack of starched-collar Boston lawyers over the fact that my interview with an entrepreneurial young publisher on a Canadian island mentioned the fact that he had IBM computers in his house but no indoor plumbing.*
>
> *"This guy can sue us for saying he doesn't have an indoor toilet" was the rationale, as if it was some kind of crime. What the shysters of Beacon Hill didn't realize was that the young publisher was proud of not having an indoor toilet. He was an environmentalist who moved his business to a remote island, for Pete's sake. I did convince the lawyers to let me get away with it, but I could scarcely believe the pettiness of their worries.*

Avoid lawyers when possible, but when you find that you need one, try to locate an attorney who has some prior experience in representing authors and dealing with literary claims or contracts. If you have a regular or long-standing lawyer who handles your other business, but is unfamiliar with literary contracts and law, he or she may create more trouble than solutions. We've known of a few times when a publisher withdrew a contract offer to an author because the author's lawyer belligerently argued over the terms. However, a trusted attorney with some knowledge of literary matters could be your best adviser and de facto agent.

Disputes Between Author and Publisher

When you have a legitimate dispute with your publisher, in fact, you may be forced to hire counsel. Such disputes are rare but not unknown. The publisher may accuse the author of accepting money for a book he knew he couldn't provide (one is reminded of the Clifford Irving/McGraw-Hill case involving a bogus autobiography of Howard Hughes), or the writer may sue the publisher, alleging that his royalties have been improperly accounted or illegally withheld. Most such disputes allege that one side or the other is guilty of a *breach* of one or more of the terms of the contract, so as long as you're sure you've fulfilled the promises made in the contract, you should be safe.

A legal dispute between author and publisher can be as bitter and destructive as any divorce or bankruptcy action, and most people will go to great lengths to settle their differences out of court. As the old saying goes, the lawyers are the only ones guaranteed to come out of the courtroom winners. You have to pay them whether or not they win the case. And although authors are fond of describing their publishers as crooks (among other bad things), we don't know a single author who's ever successfully proved that the publisher bilked him out of his due earnings.

Disputes Between Author and Author

One of the most common kinds of legal dispute is between two authors and involves the charge of plagiarism. Every now and then there's a widely publicized plagiarism case, and in recent years we've seen startling admissions of guilt from well-known, established authors. Somebody will take an obscure novel that was published twenty years ago in England and essentially rewrite it, using much the same characters and plot and even scraps of identical dialogue but changing the title, the setting, and enough details to disguise the counterfeit.

Don't do it. Don't even think about it. The attendant bad publicity of a plagiarism trial could destroy your reputation as an author for good, not to mention your liability to the original writer for financial damages. I can't imagine why a reputable author would choose to plagiarize from another's work, but there's no doubt that it goes on. There are also cases of "unintentional plagiarism," in which an author reads something and then later—maybe years later—regurgitates it onto the page without realizing that it's coming from memory and not creation. However, you'd have a hard time convincing a jury that you unintentionally "remembered" an entire plot or book.

Disputes Between Publisher and Publisher

All kinds of legal problems can arise between publishers, but the most serious one is the unauthorized reproduction of copyrighted material—that is to say bootleg, or pirate, editions of your book. For decades, particularly in Asia, unscrupulous pirate publishers have been bringing out nearly identical hardcover editions of U.S. best-sellers without paying the author or original publisher a cent. They simply get one copy of the book, photograph its pages, and reproduce the whole work in a cheaply printed and bound edition for sale in Hong Kong, Taiwan, or Korea, at a fifth of the normal price. But American publishers have been more vigorous in suing these bandits in recent years, and the problem may be diminishing. It's not a problem, of course, unless your book is famous and successful enough to be worth pirating.

If You Get Hauled into Court

If you have the misfortune of being sued, the best position for you to be in is with your publisher right beside you, and all of its professional attorneys' wisdom at your disposal. Try every reasonable routes toward settling the issue by negotiation and compromise *outside* the courtroom. Goodwill and honesty usually go a long way. If you find that you unintentionally or inadvertently wronged another party, a mutually agreeable settlement will almost always be less harrowing, stressful, and damaging to your reputation than a public court case. On the other hand, if you know you're in the right, there may be times when you just have to defend yourself—with the full cooperation and backing of your publisher, you hope.

6 | Money and Perks

This chapter will take a more detailed view of basic money matters that affect the writer's life. As you may have already noted, the financial life of a writer isn't necessarily a lucrative one. The process of actually collecting your due and accounting for it to the tax people is more complex than when you're simply working at a nine-to-five job. But getting paid to write is one of life's sweet triumphs, and there's no compulsory retirement age.

Royalties and How to Collect Them

We don't mean to be facetious. An honest publisher will send your royalty statements and checks with regularity, and an honest agent will promptly forward them to you after deducting the commission. But none of us is shocked to hear an author claim that he or she was ripped off. Aldous Huxley once discovered that his trusted agent of years' standing had taken him for a bundle in six figures. The contract offers the author the remedy of hiring an independent certified public accountant to examine the publisher's books but in practice this is rarely done. Your best security is your publisher's good reputation and length of survival in the business and your best approach is to read and keep excellent track of all your royalty statements and your agent's accountings. To some extent you can verify your sales figures from independent sources (your editor, a friendly book-seller, or a publisher's sales rep, etc.).

Magazine and Newspaper Collections

Collecting for a magazine or newspaper placement you've sold is relatively simpler. If the periodical has bought first or second serial rights to an excerpt from your book, it will pay your publisher and the payment will be recorded on your royalty statement. If you sell a piece of writing directly to a periodical, find out whether that periodical's policy is to pay "on acceptance" or "on publication." "On acceptance," like "on signing this agreement" in the contract, means payment *within thirty days.* The publisher, like any business, will require about a month to do the bookkeeping and "cut" a check. After thirty days of waiting for a check you may write a polite inquiry to your editor; after sixty days you are entitled to raise your voice and/or grumble threateningly in your letters.

Payment "on publication" usually means within thirty days of when the article, story, or poem appears in print. Depending on the "lead time" of the particular magazine or newspaper (the time between the scheduling of a piece and its actual appearance in print), this system can delay your payment as long as six months. The periodical also protects its own interests by not paying for work that may, at the last minute, have to be cut or dropped because something more important came along.

Obviously it's better from your point of view to be paid on acceptance but we don't want to overstate the point. A sizable percentage of magazines and newspapers pay on publication and are completely reliable, and unless you can negotiate an exception to the rule for your work, you just have to accept the policy. Most major periodicals will provide you with a "kill fee," equal to about a third of your full payment, in the event that your piece has to be canceled.

Major periodicals sometimes offer the writer a contract for a piece. Naturally it is much shorter than the literary contract—usually only a page—and simply states what the article or story is about or is called, how long the piece is to be, what the deadline is, how much payment will be made, and how much the kill fee is. Such a contract works toward the author's benefit, of course, as you are guaranteed in writing of at least some payment.

Accounting and Bookkeeping

Accounting and bookkeeping are important legal duties. When it's time to fill out your tax return (see below), you'll need to have clear records of how much money you received in the tax year from each publisher. Your best record is the Personal Income Diary: Every time you receive payment for writing, record it in a special file called "Income, 19— (current year)." This file can be as informal and loose as a cardboard folder or as complicated as a software diskette file with crossfooting calculations. The basic idea is that you make a record of every check before depositing it in your bank account, indicating who paid, how much, when, and for what.

If your income from writing is substantial and you are fully self-employed, you probably need a professional accountant. Writers are entitled to many tax advantages, such as employment-related deductions, which may be too complex for mere scribes to understand, although we go into them below. A trusted accountant sometimes ensures peace of mind and a good night's sleep.

Limitation on Income

An author who expects considerable income from a book may also lower taxes by limiting the amount he or she receives from the publisher in any given year. A Limitation of Income clause is added to the literary contract, stating the maximum number of dollars the author will receive from the publisher in a year. Any moneys over that limit will be held in reserve for the author; the publisher is in fact acting like the author's savings bank by holding royalties that are due and paying them out at a certain sum annually.

However, if you're successful enough to have to worry about limiting your income, you're probably successful enough to take the full income and invest it in tax shelters that will pay a better return than the publisher can. Publishers don't offer to pay interest on royalties they are holding for you.

Work-related Deductions

It goes without saying that you should keep receipts and records of all your expenses. Part of your rent or mortgage payment is deductible if you maintain a working office in your home. Travel costs for a particular project are entirely deductible only if you are under contract or on assignment. Some forms of business entertainment are partially deductible—that's why publishers buy you lunch—and all your supplies, from paper clips to computers, are a write-off from your taxable income, as long as they are used for writing material that is eventually published. There is no federal minimum income to qualify you as a self-employed writer; I'm sure the IRS gets thousands of returns from self-employed writers who actually earned under $5,000 from it in a year yet had no other major source of income or alternate career.

Many of these pauperized writers have a patron, a fancy name for a person who is most often the spouse of the author. You know, the wife works so the husband can finish his novel, or the husband works while his wife completes her book. Sometimes the patron is an understanding parent or child, or a friend. I found my greatest patron in a sympathetic landlady who rents houses to artists and writers at lower-than-market prices.

Our best advice: Keep good records of your expenses and income, and hire a professional accountant if your annual income from writing exceeds $20,000.

Literary Perks and Fringe Benefits

Aside from the ten free copies of the book the contract promises, many other fringe benefits can derive from being a published author. There is some unwritten law that the author is entitled to a free copy of any other book published by the publisher. (Please don't be greedy, though. It's bad form to ask only for the $75 full-color art books.) A generous editor will give you carte blanche access to the shelves of new releases, but you shouldn't take more than a few per visit to your publisher's office. I generally won't take a book unless I want to read it myself, but once in a great while I've accepted a book because I knew someone else who would love to read it.

Books of other publishers are often free to you if you're willing to write a charming letter stressing your professional connection to the subject matter. Address your letter to the publicity director at the publishing house after locating his or her name in *LMP* or one of the other research sources. And do offer to submit a comment or, if you have a legitimate outlet, write a review. Reviewers and published authors often receive unsolicited free books.

Another great fringe benefit is lunch—not only the traditional publisher's working lunch that your editor treats you to, but all kinds of other lunches to which you may be invited. I've had lunch with any number of writers seeking advice on how to get published; the advice is free but I never pick up the tab. Also, authors frequently are guests of community luncheons sponsored by lodges, public interest groups, reading clubs, the PTA, you name it. If you're expected to give a speech, however, some honorarium or stipend should be added to the rubber chicken.

The Publisher's Lunch

The publisher's lunch with the author is one of the few surviving pieces of noblesse oblige left over from the good ole days when publishers coddled their authors more than they do now. It's a chance to enjoy socializing with your editor, but you should tailor your order to the probable limits of the expense account. It's rather like the free-book etiquette. If your publisher is a small one, the lunch may be in a modest establishment. If you're dealing with the editor in chief of a huge New York publishing firm that is running a first printing of 50,000 copies of your book, you could be permitted a steak and fine bottle of wine, or whatever your idea of luxury is.

The lunch between editor (or, sometimes, the publisher's publicity director) and author is a revered tradition, not to mention a tax deduction to the publisher. You may be invited to lunch, dinner, or drinks repeatedly, or even do your most serious work and negotiating over food and drink.

As a very young author I was privileged to have an editor who simply loved to have three vodka stingers and a lavish, two-hour lunch in gourmet restaurants. But nowhere have I found a more stupendous publisher's-lunch tradition than in Tokyo, where the same publisher has translated and published my last three books. One can be taken to a lunch that costs $200 to $300 a person, and it's only sushi and sake. (But what sushi, and what sake! And what a beating the dollar has taken when measured against the almighty yen!) You might wish your editor had taken you to McDonald's in the Ginza and spent ten bucks, giving you the hundreds he saved, but the Japanese are wonderfully hospitable toward foreign authors and insist on making a splash. Don't expect that level of dining from any U.S. publisher.

Expenses-paid Travel

Once you're published, travel may be at times free to you. The publisher may want to send you around the country promoting the book and speaking on talk shows, or universities and speaking bureaus may invite you to conferences, writers' workshops, and the like at their expense. The publisher's publicity tour occurs only at the time of publication of your book, and seldom lasts longer than three or four weeks, and it could hardly be called a vacation. It's grueling work, in fact, but often well worth it if you can really get the word out on your book. Writers' conferences and college speaking can be fairly renumerative and fun, depending on your personal preference—some writers hate to appear in public, while others thrive on the attention.

Selling Your Own Remainders

Clause 10 E in our literary contract provided that the publisher gives the author thirty days' notice in which to buy up any "remainder" copies of the book before they can be offered to another buyer. This is a good arrangement from the author's point of view because most publishers will sell off or destroy the remaining copies of your book without giving you a chance to buy them. It's important to have a clause like that because there are a lot of ways an enterprising author can peddle his or her own remainders or overstock books for reasonable gain. When the publisher decides to remainder your books it will send you a letter asking you to make a bid on the whole number of copies left in stock or to indicate whether you'd like to buy some, but not all, of them. The price of such leftover books, especially in great quantity, can be extremely low—10 percent of retail value is not uncommon.

A publisher may offer you a chance to bid on the remainders. But other publishers will simply ship you ten free copies and sell off or destroy the bulk of the inventory, giving you no opportunity to purchase it. So do insist on a good remainder clause to be sure.

Many authors sell their remaindered books at lectures and readings, sometimes to clubs after delivering a luncheon speech, to local bookstores, who can reorder directly from the author while the supply lasts, or by mail order via advertisements or flyers or catalog insertions. Take your cartons of leftover books to your local book distributor's warehouse and leave them on consignment. Use your imagination. If Thoreau could insulate his walls with unsold copies of *Walden*, it's no disgrace for you to be hoarding 2,000 copies of your book in the garage. I had a distinct advantage in owning three bookstores and a wholesale distributing and publishing business that shipped to several thousand other bookstores. I bought up remainders and overstocks on my own titles by the thousands, and sold them through my own literary enterprises.

At the very least a book is the most personal and appreciated gift you could present to someone—an autographed copy of your work, inscribed to the recipient with terms of love or admiration. The average American doesn't know a published author personally and there remains a mystique about the profession, as with actors or celebrities. (But, alas, we're not as glamorous as movie stars or rock musicians and don't rate that level of public adoration.) To one who is a serious reader, the gift of a book from the author is a great pleasure (and even someone who *doesn't* read might like to have it as a "collectible" item). The

writing does no good if it doesn't find readers, anyway. The pact
between author and reader—between *us*—is intimate and cher-
ished. Here's an unusual perk of being published that keeps that
bond alive!

Intangible Benefits

Aside from material fringe benefits, the author also gets a host
of spiritual and psychological benefits, which, one could say, are
better than money can buy. The thrill of seeing your name on a
published volume, of holding your book in your hands, weighing
it lovingly, is a pleasure greater than most material things.
Society as a whole tends to view you as an exalted person, and
you should view yourself as lucky—lucky to be published, lucky
to be self-employed, utterly and absolutely privileged to be able
to broadcast your thoughts and creative works to the general
public. Every person who reads your book is paying you a com-
pliment; some authors even get fan letters, offers of marriage, or
declarations of undying love from their readers. I once got a
letter from a reader who'd read my book on Japan and India
(*Return to Sender*) and promptly quit his job, collected his life
savings, and had gotten on a freighter bound for Yokohama.

Pensions and Insurance

The self-employed writer doesn't have the normal fringe benefits that salaried people enjoy: no pension, medical insurance,
dental health plan, or paid vacations go along with the standard
literary contract. If those kinds of material security are absolutely necessary to you, the writing business is not as highly
recommended as, say, a career with IBM.

Some of the writers' associations now offer group medical
insurance, but it's minimal coverage. Pensions for self-employed
writers simply don't exist. Naturally, what you *want* to do is set
up a personal security mechanism through an IRA, a good insurance plan, savings, home ownership, and/or investments—but,
sadly, many writers don't make enough money to acquire all
those things.

Feast or Famine

Material security is something that Lit Biz seldom provides in great measure. You have to be willing to subsist on the Feast or Famine standard of economics: prolonged periods of tight finances (if not absolute starvation) punctuated by occasional episodes of binge spending (following receipt of a royalty or advance check). The "binge" is oftentimes just a matter of catching up with overdue debt. It's extremely helpful to:

—have a friend or relative who will lend money to you in bad times, and recoup in flush times (a personal banker);

—pay essential bills, like rent or mortgage, some months in advance while the money's on hand;

—stock up on necessities, both office supplies and nonperishable household goods, anytime you can;

—project your future royalty payments realistically, allowing for the "reserve against returns";

—always be working on a new book, preferably under contract, before the preceding book is published.

Retirement, Lack of

If the lack of a pension or retirement fund is a disadvantage, it can also be turned around and considered another benefit. I like what John Coles, the former editor of *The Maine Times* and a fine author, had to say about it when he reached his sixties. "The great thing about being a writer is they can't force you to retire," he quipped. "As long as there's somebody out there who wants to read my stuff, I'm still in business."

7 | Agents and Whether You Need One

The role of the literary agent in the business of literature is that of a crucial middle negotiator between publisher and author. While some authors negotiate for themselves, and therefore pay no commission to an agent, the vast majority of serious professionals have some representation. If you know some authors, you may have noticed that they complain about their agents as much as about their publishers. A good agent does much more than just haggle over clauses in a contract; a powerful agent can make and shape a writer's career.

What an Agent Does

Obviously the agent's primary job is to negotiate the literary contract to the author's advantage. But agents also interest a publisher in your work, bring editors and writers together, and in some cases even wield a formidable editorial influence over their writers' output. Assuming the agent is an honest one, she or he can be the author's strongest ally in money matters, someone who helps you plan and direct your writing career.

An agent can sell the writer's services as a "ghost" or writer for hire on a book project he discusses with a publisher. Even for longtime professionals, this can be a serious career advantage. If Liz Taylor, let's say, needed a collaborator for her diet book, you'd appreciate somebody throwing your name into the ring.

The agent can sometimes get faster results than an author can manage on his own. The agent can skip the query-letter stage and direct a submission to a preselected editorial pool. He or she can sell your book idea via a phone conversation or lunch meeting. (Realistically, of course, this speedier method works only for authors who are already known from earlier work.)

Finally, an agent can turn a multiple submission (see below)—in which you submit your work to more than one publisher at a time—into an auction situation, in which one publisher bids against another for your manuscript.

We saw in the contract how many matters are wide open to negotiation—the author's share of movie rights, foreign rights, and other subsidiary rights, the terms of the option clause if there is one, the size of the advance on royalties and the royalty rates themselves. While you don't absolutely need an agent, most writers do benefit enormously from having one. First of all, the agent is likely to know much more about the intricacies of the publishing world as well as the contract than the author would; and secondly, the agent can take a hard line and argue for more money, a process that would be demeaning to the author's dignity if she or he tried to do it. Whereas you might accept a publisher's first offer in gratitude, your agent can wheedle and cajole to drive home a better deal.

Finding an Agent

Unfortunately, when you are starting out and relatively unknown, it is just as much a challenge to get a reputable agent to take you on as it is to get a publisher. As you would with an editor, you send an agent your query letter and samples of your writing and push toward getting a professional reading. *LMP* contains listings of agents, or you can get the book *Literary Agents of North America*, published by Author Aid Associates, at 340 East 52 Street, New York, NY 10022. You can also write to the Independent Literary Agents Association or the Society of Author's Representatives (addresses are in our Lit Biz Reference Sources.)

But, as with editors, agents are most often contacted via some referral or personal connection. The majority of an agent's new clients come by referrals from existing clients or from editors who put writers in touch. The networking extends, of course, to writers' conferences and booksellers' conventions, which the agents work systematically. Lit Biz 101 urges you to attend any and all kinds of writers' gatherings, where your chances of meeting an editor or agent are good to excellent.

Agents for Sale

Please note that there are now agencies that offer *manuscript evaluations for sale*—that is, who offer to read your book and give you a professional opinion for a nonrefundable payment in the neighborhood of $100. There is nothing illegal in the practice and Lit Biz 101 doesn't mean to impugn the integrity of those agents who charge a fee for such evaluations, but the business is relatively new and clashes with our basic philosophy, which is to make money with your writing—not pay for somebody to read it!

Nontraditional Agents

A publisher's sales rep, a well-known bookseller, or a published author of your acquaintance can serve as a kind of alternative agent. This is a function I've performed myself any number of times. Although I prefer to have my own agent haggle with the publisher over my pay, I'm not at all embarrassed to haggle over some other writer's pay.

A publisher's sales rep is in an ideal position to carry your manuscript to an editor for a reading because the rep is a human link between a major publishing house and your local bookstore, which she or he visits a couple of times a year. If you know a bookseller whom you regularly patronize, that person may be willing to introduce you to the publisher's sales rep.

The Rep as Agent

The publisher's rep can be a somewhat reluctant literary agent. Many of them have mailed a manuscript back to the home office that went on to get published, or even become a national best-seller. You can be sure that the rep who discovers a best-selling book is both proud and excited about it. Reps are a bit easier to approach than editors, and even if you live far from the East Coast publishing centers, there are likely to be some reps who visit or live in your locality. The key to meeting with a rep is your local bookseller, preferably someone you know personally and whose shop you regularly patronize. You can ask your bookseller for the name and phone number of the rep from whichever publisher you're interested in approaching and contact him or her directly. But the preferred method is to find out when the rep is scheduled to visit and arrange a personal introduction.

You have to take it easy on them, however. Reps are not editors, after all, and reading or transporting manuscripts is not part of their responsibility. Many will do so, though, if you have curried their favor and friendship, or if your book (as described by you) genuinely appeals to them. Better yet, if the rep should become wildly enthusiastic about the book, she or he might be able to buttonhole an editor and push for a reading.

And in fact an experienced bookseller can help push your manuscript into print, as she or he will know many reps and, perhaps, also editors in the business. The name of the game is *contacts*. Even if you don't know a soul in publishing, you probably know somebody who does. I hate to use the dreadfully overworked term "networking" twice in this chapter, but that is what you have to do when you're getting started: Form a network, have one acquaintance lead you to another until you find someone—an agent by any other name—who can represent you to an editor.

Multiple Submissions

Submitting your outline or book to more than one publisher at a time, by you or your agent, is fine as long as you are ethical and acknowledge up front, to all parties, that you're doing so. A book that is in great demand may even be sold at auction to the highest bidder. The agent, or in the case of reprint property the original publisher, entertains bids, via the telephone, from interested parties. The chances of two or more publishers wanting the same book are slim enough, and if you are in the position of having to weigh separate offers, consider yourself lucky.

The practice of multiple submissions is more acceptable now than it was years ago, but there is at least one decided disadvantage to it, which is that some editors will be less interested in your book if they think they might have to compete for it. Such competition tends to drive the price up, possibly scaring off a good publisher for the book, and there is always the real risk that an editor will spend hours reading the material and dealing with the author or agent only to lose the book to another house. That's wasted time. And that's why a few elite publishers still cling to the old-fashioned policy of not reading any manuscript that's been submitted to another publisher.

8 | Manuscript into Type

Lit Biz Production Lab

This chapter takes a look at the production process by which books are made. As with the sample literary contract in Chapter 4, we've created an authentic production schedule based on real production schedules used by publishers. We'll take you step by step through this process, explaining the technical words and terms as they come up. To begin with, you want your manuscript to be as nearly perfect as possible.

What follows are some sensible guidelines to preparing the kind of manuscript that a publisher can respect and work with easily. This topic alone could fill up a whole book, and there are numbers of manuals devoted to it. But here we'll look at the fundamentals of producing a professional-looking work, one which meets the standards necessary to the business of literature.

The Ideal Manuscript

Preparing the ideal finished manuscript is clearly your best insurance against major snafus in the production process of your book. The only acceptable manuscript is free of typos or misspellings and neatly typed (double spaced) with wide margins for corrections and plenty of white space for ease of reading. When we say "free of typos or misspellings," we mean *virtually* so; the maddening thing about manuscripts, even the best ones, is that a few typos are simply bound to slip through even repeated readings. But no publisher wants to tolerate a manuscript that is plagued with frequent mistakes of that kind. If you can't spell, find someone who can correct your spelling before you submit the work.

The first draft of your manuscript should be neat and clear both for the editor and copy editor. The copy editor will pore over every comma and semicolon, searching for typos, misspellings, poor grammar or syntax, and, of late, trying to weed out sexist or discriminatory language. A series of queries will be raised by the copy editor and they will be relayed to you by mail or phone, enabling a last chance for manuscript changes before the writing is set into type.

A designer must choose a typeface and style; there are literally hundreds of type styles to choose from in standard printing. Galley proofs will be submitted for the author's reading, and many typos and other errors have to be corrected. Finally you have "bound galleys," a once corrected (not final) coverless version of your forthcoming book that is used for promotional purposes. A series of deadlines prevail as the book moves through the production schedule toward day of publication; revising becomes more difficult as the manuscript takes more permanent form. Along the way you may have bleeding ulcers, but this process of birthing the manuscript is an exciting time, one you are likely to relish and keep fondly in your memory.

"Do I Need a Word Processor?"

Are word processors necessary? Do you need to have a computer to be a professional writer nowadays? Definitely not! But you'll find that many working writers have now turned to the software goddess who promises easy production, quick editing, and instant printout. Word processors make production writing about three times faster than the old typewriters could handle. They're especially useful (indeed, a miracle and a blessing) when it comes to complicated revisions. But no, you don't actually *need* one of these new contraptions even if you really are a production writer, working every day and meeting deadlines on a regular basis.

We live in the age of the computer, after all. Some major magazines and a few publishers now prefer their authors to submit manuscripts on diskette as well as on paper, but I haven't heard of any publisher declining to accept an old-fashioned typed ms. *Writer's Market* contains listings of magazines that urge you to submit your work on diskette only—"no printouts please"—but they are in a small minority.

While word processors offer many advantages, the world of computers and word-processing programs can be hopelessly confusing to the uninitiated. The real danger to the aspiring writer is that you'll lose six months or more of your precious writing time just adjusting to the machinery, figuring out the complex manual, and learning how to store your work without losing it.

Choosing a Computer and Software Program

Then there's the considerable issue of choosing which computer and word-processing program to buy. You walk into the computer store to find a bewildering assortment of equipment and software programs, each incompatible with the other. The hardware is the computer itself, the software is the disk you "play" on it (much like a phonograph record), and the industry standard seems to be set by IBM. (No offense to you Apple users out there.)

You don't have to buy an IBM computer, however, to use the "family" of software that works on IBM. There are a large number of "clones," cheaper machines that are patterned after the IBM and use the same software programs. I find the COMPAQ to be a good, solid computer at a low price, and it's portable. Friends of mine are happy with Kaypro, Commodore, and Epson machines. Probably the best approach is to try hands-on experience with a variety of brands. It is especially important when you are starting out to pick one that is simple and basic enough so that it won't confuse you or tie you to the instruction manual for months. You can always trade up to more sophisticated equipment later.

The software you choose matters almost more than the kind

of computer. IBM had to abandon its own first attempt at word-processing software, EasyWriter, because it was anything *but* easy to learn and use. Word-processing programs run from the "low end," cheaper ones like PFSWrite that are easy to learn but perform limited functions, to "high end," expensive packages like WordStar that can produce complicated layouts and lengthy documents but which are fiendishly difficult to operate. WordStar left me in tears. My own salvation came in Volkswriter, a medium-priced program that's truly simple to learn.

Pros and Cons of Working on a Computer

What does a word processor do, exactly? It allows you to type on a display screen and then print out your words on paper. You can move the little video words around much faster than words typed on paper, and when you make a mistake you can wipe out the error and replace it swiftly and neatly. Because you no longer have the hassles of white-out fluid (which takes a long time to dry) or correction tape (flaky and messy), the revising and correcting process is much faster. And you can move whole blocks of type around in the manuscript, taking some paragraphs out of one chapter and moving them to another, without the old-fashioned scissors-and-paste method.

There are also certain frightening disadvantages. All of these marvelous gadgets are expensive, although the price of computers comes down a bit every year. Until you are a thorough professional getting paid real money for your writing, it may not be cost-effective to get yourself a computer. If you should somehow lose power due to an electrical failure, you could lose all the work you'd put into the computer *since the last time you stored it.* We recommend storing your work every couple of pages or so, as you go along, and always creating a "backup" disk, or copy, of each day's work before closing down the computer at night. There are a thousand potential ways to crash a program or lose a file, so you're well advised to have copies of everything.

One little floppy disk holds enough files to constitute a medium-length book—several million characters. Be careful not to overfill your disk; some software will let you overflow the limit but you won't be able to retrieve the work later.

Choosing a Printer

Your choice of a printer is important, since the printer quality will reflect in the appearance of your manuscripts. Again, you can "trade up" later but you don't want to start out with the lowest-level dot-matrix printer, either. Some publishers might refuse to even read your work if it's poorly printed, faint, or otherwise difficult on the eye. Find something that produces a sharp, clear type equal to or better than a modern office typewriter face.

Electronic Bulletin Boards

When you hook your computer up to a telephone using a modem, you can contact other "hackers" out there in electronic fantasy-land and read and write messages on electronic bulletin boards. The growing popularity of this kind of written communication may portend something for the future. We've been told by industry analysts to prepare for the days when people will read "books" off a computer screen. When the earth's forests are stripped bare, when we're all safely in outer space, these prophets claim, books of paper, board, and ink will be unavailable, impossibly expensive, antiques. Forgive us, however, a small tear. We like the old-fashioned hardcover book with a silk bookmark bound in.

The bottom line is probably this: There is most likely a computer and word processor in your future if you write. Take it from one who successfully resisted the things, indeed hated them, for the longest time, only to surrender in the end. It may be years away, you may not need it yet. But the damn things are coming down in price, and once you start writing on a word processor, you do get addicted.

Typewriters Old and New

For now, however, the new generation of electronic typewriters, with easy self-correcting backspace key, may be all you need. Many of these machines double as computer printers and some have extensive memory features. You can type a letter once and print out a hundred copies.

Or you may not be able to tear yourself away from that battered old Royal standard you've had since 1940, anyway. Although I use it only for labels nowadays, I've got a thirty-year-old typewriter that I love like a brother. It's the original IBM Executive, circa 1955, a massive elephant that's too heavy to carry and takes an antiquated ribbon available only at the largest office-supply stores. But it got me this far and I can't turn it out into the cold.

Whether typed on a battered manual machine or printed via laser-jet technology, your completed manuscript now goes through the production schedule described below.

The Production Schedule, Step by Step

1. *You and your editor.* Before the manuscript enters the production process, you and your editor have reached agreement on its final content. If legal work was required, it's been done, and any permissions necessary to quote from copyrighted material have been gotten in writing.

2. *Manuscript to copywriter for jacket copy.* Copywriter reads manuscript (and in the case of a reprint, incorporates reviews and blurbs) to prepare the copy that will appear on the book cover.

3. *Manuscript and cover copy to the copy editor.* (See discussion below.) The copy editor reads the manuscript, checking for errors, and returns it to the editor, for transmission to author, with comments, suggested revisions, and queries. Author revises and returns the ms. to editor, who returns to copy editor.

4. *Design memo to designer.* In some houses the editor will forward a memo to the designer indicating preference for specific typefaces, etc. In others, a copy of the copy-edited ms. will be sent directly to the designer. The designer will make all pertinent choices of typeface and style, size, and art.

5. *Design complete. Designed ms. and art out to comp.* The "comp" is the compositor, the person who is going to set the type. He or she will depend on instructions provided by the designer and various editing marks on the manuscript (see below.)

TIMETABLE: Expect at least two or three months to pass between Step 1 and Step 5.

6. *Sample page and galley to publisher.* The publisher approves a sample page and sample galley proof. The galley proof is a long sheet of paper on which the text is printed as it will appear in the book, typeset and sized to fit the page.

7. *Cover concept meeting.* Some publishers schedule a meeting between the editor, designer, and perhaps the publicity director to discuss ideas for the (front) cover. In some houses, however, this decision is left to the art director.

8. *Galleys arrive at publisher, are forwarded to author.* The first galley proofs arrive, and a copy of them is forwarded to the author for proofreading and corrections. Unless the book is exceptionally long, you should be able to read the galley proofs and have them back to the publisher within a week or two. If the publisher has decided to send out bound galleys for advance publicity, the uncorrected proofs are bound at this time.

TIMETABLE: Add another two or three months for Steps 6 through 8. From final manuscript to galley proofs in six months is about right.

9. *Author returns corrected galley proofs to publisher.*

10. *Dummy begins.* The designer pastes up the type so as to create a "dummy," a model of the finished book.

11. *Galleys and dummy to comp.* The corrected proofs and the dummy return to the compositor, who will make the required corrections and set up the pages according to the dummy model.

12. *Final art to comp.*

13. *Cover mock-up to author.* A rough copy of the book's cover is sent to the author. (Not all houses include this step!)

14. *Page proofs arrive at publisher.* These proofs show the book in its paginated form. Authors do not usually receive a copy of page proofs to review.

15. *Cover mechanical to printer.* The mechanical is the final, camera-ready copy from which the cover is printed.

16. *Index from author or indexer to comp.* If the book has an index, now is the time to insert it, since we already have page proofs to tell us which pages contain which material.

TIMETABLE: These late steps will require at least two months, longer if the index is particularly complicated.

17. *Printer's blues to publisher.* The "blues" are the finished pages, so named because they are produced in blue ink. They offer the absolutely last opportunity for the publisher to spot an error.

18. *Cover proof to publisher.* The final proof of the cover.

19. *Bound books.* The first books arrive from the press—usually a few samples come first, followed by the major shipment. The first copy is sent to the author.

20. *In stock.* The books arrive in the publisher's warehouse and publisher begins shipping them to the bookstores.

TIMETABLE: Another month or so is required for these last steps. The total production schedule is about ten months in duration, but up to a year is normal (given occasional problems and delays).

Granted, the production schedule described above is greatly simplified. It is a composite based on schedules we've seen from both small and large publishers, and is meant to give you a basic idea of what happens to your book after it leaves your hands and before it comes back nicely bound and ready for sale.

The Copy Editor's Role

After you and your editor have decided the manuscript is in its final form, the next person to keep you honest will be the copy editor. Copy editors are born Virgos, perfectionists, nitpickers. They must have the greatest patience for fine detail. It's their job to question every little quirk in your manuscript, usually referring to some insuperable authority like the Modern Language Association or *The Chicago Manual of Style*. Some publishers declare allegiance to a particular dictionary and make all their authors conform to its spellings. Remember that the copy editor is your friend, not just an annoyance, and appreciate the many instances in which he/she helps you say something in a more exact fashion. Forgive the fact that copy editors will call you on deliberate turns of speech that are "brilliant" prose to you but incorrect verbiage to them. If you make up words or freely use contemporary slang, your copy editor may become the bane of your existence; yet, even the most professional author and editor *together* can miss errors that the copy editor snags, fortunately, before the book goes to the typesetter.

More: Copy editors often act as fact checkers for a nonfiction manuscript and can save embarrassment for both authors and editors; with a fiction manuscript, they make sure characters, physical characteristics, and the time frame remain internally consistent. As the last professional editor to handle your manuscript, the copy editor can be your salvation. Just remember that the additional time and careful attention to detail the copy editor gives you can save you from committing grievous errors in the manuscript that somehow make it as far as the typesetter. You want your manuscript error-free and unblemished before it gets set in type.

The author's interaction with the copy editor is usually directed through the editor. Personal contact is rare. The copy editor will expect your replies to any queries in roughly a few weeks' time, unless greater urgency has been expressed. The author and copy editor will occasionally disagree on some point, and the book's original editor may step in as an arbitrator. Technically, you, as author, have the right to insist on having it your way, but remember, it's the copy editor's job to know what's correct.

Typesetting

The author is not likely to have any direct contact with the typesetter. The copy editor gives typesetting directions by marking up the manuscript. (See some printer's markings below.) Typesetting can generate a whole new set of errors. Innocent typos occur that happen to spell out real words—the word "park," for example, substituting for the word "part," although these types of errors get much more subtle than that. In reading along, your eye doesn't see a typo, but the meaning of the sentence is totally changed. Gross typos are usually quite visible, but double articles often escape notice: "The park is near *the the* pond." And then there's the old nemesis, the dropped line: You're reading along and all of a sudden something is drastically missing.

Of course your publisher will have a professional proofreader go over the galleys, but our best advice is to have your galleys (those long, unbound sheets of set type) *read and reread by at least three competent persons*, including yourself. Most literary contracts (see chapter 4) contain a clause giving the author the responsibility of reading proofs. You will be amazed at the typos and errors a second and third reader, in addition to the author, can uncover. The author can almost be accused of being too close to the material; a fresh person, unfamiliar with the book but a good, knowledgeable reader, will see differently. It wouldn't hurt to have five or six good readers go over your proofs, but you probably won't have the time. Two extra readers are the minimum necessary, in our experience, if you want to make sure no typos slip through the net.

When correcting your galley proofs always use a pencil rather than a pen and use standard proofreading marks, which you'll find in *Webster's New Collegiate Dictionary* (and a number of other dictionaries). They're easy to learn. A few examples follow:

delete	℘	close up	◡
space	＃	paragraph (indent)	¶
upper case	charles	lower case	¢harming
italicize	charles	to add	∧

Timetable Deadlines

Deadlines become even more important in production than they were during the creation of the manuscript. In particular, the publisher will need you to read and correct galleys on time, because every delay generates a domino effect of delays in subsequent stages of the project. Time on the press is scheduled well in advance and is expensive. Probably the very worst thing you could do to your publisher is to start revising material that is already set in type and on galleys; these revisions are costly, can be charged back against your royalties (see the fine print in the contract, Chapter 4), and push the production schedule back.

The Index

If your nonfiction book requires an index, it will be your responsibility (not your publisher's) to provide one, but the index will be the last chore you perform before publication. Before you can index the manuscript, you must have achieved a final edited book in page-proof form, so you know which page of the finished book each topic will appear on. Although computers can now speed up the indexing process considerably, you and the publisher will need to build extra time into the production schedule.

9 The Publishing Process

While your book is going through the arduous production schedule, a simultaneous and equally complex process is under way at the publisher's editorial offices. These in-house functions include creating the publicity items and promotion campaign, designing and placing advertisements, coming up with a concept for a cover, writing dust-jacket and catalog copy, preparing fact sheets for the sales personnel, etc. If you're fortunate, a great deal of advance thought and work goes into preparing for your Day of Publication.

The Launch

While your book is in production the publisher should already be well into its *launch schedule*, which means the planning and preparation for its appearance in the bookstores. Launching a book, like launching a ship, is a complicated process of bringing all engines to gear on one focus: in this case, the successful debut of your book on the market. Some of the steps in the launch are:

The catalog announcement. Most publishers issue a catalog of new titles twice a year (spring and fall), in addition to maintaining a general catalog of all their back stock (previously published and still in print) titles. The announcement of your forthcoming

book in the catalog is the first public volley in what you hope
will be a lot of publicity. It's also the sales rep's primary tool in
selling your book to the bookstore owner. If the publisher thinks
your book is likely to sell well, the catalog announcement may
be a full page with a reproduction of the cover, or you could be
relegated to a paragraph or two, sandwiched in between other
books. Much depends on:

Positioning. Publishers, in the wisdom of their experience,
decide early on which of their new books is likely to attract the
most sales and "position" the book in order of priority of importance. Some books will get a large advertising budget and ener-
getic promotion; others will get much less, but some help; still
others, deemed to be of interest only to a limited market, will be
published quietly, without ads or fanfare.

Who makes the decision on what "position" your book will
get? The ultimate responsibility lies with the marketing director, but in the larger publishing houses it may be arrived at after
a meeting involving your editor, the promotion manager, and
the sales representatives.

What factors are considerations in positioning a book as a
"lead" as opposed to a "midlist"?

1. Popular taste. Is your book the kind that the public may
turn into a best-seller?

2. The publisher's strongest sellers. Does your book fit into a
category that the publisher has already had success with?

3. In-house enthusiasm. Has your book impressed the editors
and sales reps? Are they excited about selling it?

Brochure or advertisement copy. If the book is to be advertised
either in publications or by a brochure or flyer, the text should
be prepared and the ads ready for press well before the book
comes out. That's just one reason why publishers can use "blurbs,"
or comments on the book by other authors or noted critics,
several months before day of publication—those authors and
critics are mailed bound galley proofs about three months before
finished books are available. A press release is also written and
prepared for mailing out with the early review copies.

Publicity planning. The publicity director issues the press
release and, if you've been asked to go on tour to publicize the

book, will book you well in advance (sometimes months ahead of time) to appear on television or radio talk shows, at booksellers' conventions, in bookstores, on college campuses, at writers' workshops, or wherever your book can be effectively sold. She or he will also prepare the mailing list of review copies to be sent to newspapers, magazines, and independent reviewers.

You, the author, can help the publicity director by providing cleanly typed names and addresses of reviewers, authors, and others who should get review copies as early as possible once the book is in production. Copies mailed to solicit "blurbs" have to go out first, as you want the "blurb" comments to be useful in promotion and maybe even appear on the front or back cover.

Promotion planning. A marketing team including the advertising manager, publicity director, marketing director, and promotion manager is responsible for planning whatever special marketing efforts will be made for your book. These could include posters, cardboard display stands for the bookstores, special discounts to booksellers, lapel buttons, bumper stickers, or any creative idea tied in to your book.

Note that one major difference between promotion and publicity is that the publisher pays for one and not the other. Promotion is paid advertising of one kind or other. Publicity is exposure the book gets in the public media, whether newspaper reviews, TV talk shows, news coverage, or feature interviews. As we mentioned before, the publisher pays for the travel costs when an author goes on tour but not for the publicity itself.

If you have a good idea for promoting your book, share it with the promotion manager. Quite often the author is aware of promotional opportunities in his or her local area that the major publisher may know nothing about. We caution you, however, against continually harassing the promotion manager with letters and calls and fresh ideas beyond the point at which the company has decided your book is completely launched. Authors have a way of thinking that the book should be continually advertised and promoted, while publishers, because of other obligations, have a way of giving up that effort within a month of the day of publication.

Publicity and promotion are discussed at greater length in Chapter 15, "Self-Promotion, the Writer's Best Friend."

Day of Publication

About a month before what has been announced as the Day of
Publication, you should receive the first, finished copy, complete with dust jacket adorned with a picture of yourself that
flatters your left profile. (This applies mainly to hard covers, as
most paperbacks don't use an author's photo.) Congratulations!
The first few nights you may want to take it to bed with you so
you can stroke it, open it at random, and read from it, or sigh
contentedly as you look at your name on the cover.

10 | Major Publishers: Going for the Gold

Are you going for a major house, a small press, or considering publishing your book yourself? All are viable options that can lead to celebrity and profit. Close your eyes and imagine your book in print. Visualize the cover, your name on it, the dedication page (in which you dedicate the work to a loved one). A toast to you! You're in print! Who's your publisher?

Advantages of a Major Publisher

Whether you admit it or not, you'd rather your book be published by a major, world-renowned publisher than a small press for obvious reasons:

- Likelihood of a better advance on royalties
- Wider distribution
- More reviews
- Greater advertising and promotion budget
- Higher prestige

When asked who is publishing your book you coolly reply "Random House" and even your Aunt Minnie from Smallsburg will have heard of that firm, and probably say so. "Oh, I've heard of Random House. They're *big* publishers!" Being published by a major house is a feather in your cap. However, it may also be a pain in your posterior.

The single greatest advantage is in distribution. Books of major publishers can reach into every bookstore, drugstore paperback rack, airport newsstand, and library in the country, and you have a much greater opportunity for an audience. A big paperback publisher, for example, will give a mass-market book a first-press run of at least 40,000–50,000 copies.

The greatest frustration in dealing with a major house, however, is that unless you are a best-selling "celebrity" author, you can easily get lost in the huge bureaucracy and vast field of competing authors, and your book may seem to become just one of many in the catalog, with nobody to push it, nurture it through, *care about it.*

It seems incredible to the uninitiated, but major publishers do publish many books they can't afford to advertise or aggressively promote on an individual basis. Despite having invested thousands of dollars, they'll let a book fend for itself (or surrender the promotional chores entirely to the author) when they should (from the author's point of view) be advertising and promoting it relentlessly.

What most authors don't understand is that a single promotion manager at a major house may have a dozen or more new titles to push every month. Major promotions are planned well in advance, and by the time your book's been off the press for a month, it's as good as finished in terms of publicity, advertising, and promotion. While you think it's just a baby, the promotion manager is swamped with a crowd of younger babies to nurture. Sorry to say, but if the major publisher hasn't planned the ads and promotion for your book months before publication, it won't do so months afterward. (Well, there are rare exceptions to this rule, when an unheralded and unpromoted book suddenly takes off, surprising everyone but the author, and merits a late advertising campaign.) So plan your own campaign to try to make it happen. Talk it up with your editor; ask for a conference with your regional sales rep and the firm's sales manager and publicity director well ahead of pub date.

A great deal depends on the sales force, which will adopt certain titles for a greater push based on its assessment of a good market. Your editor prepares the materials with which your book is presented to the salespeople at a sales meeting, and can help generate enthusiasm for it among the traveling reps who call on bookstores through his/her personal efforts.

Some publishers send the editor to the sales meeting, offering you, as author, the best shot. If your editor can make an effective pitch to the sales staff, your book may get special attention. What you want to do is build a *climate of anticipation* for the book in advance of its publication!

Salespeople and editors both get enthusiastic when they've read your book and liked it. That's fundamental. Good word of mouth publicity *within* the major house may portend a good seller.

Your Friendly Editor

Your only hope of surviving contact with a major house, in fact, is your friendly editor. She or he is the link between you, a living talent eager to be exploited, and the major publisher, a glittering monolith. From that first day when you ride the elevator to the twenty-second floor and find your editor's tiny cubicle through a maze of warrens, dozens of offices, and hundreds of books and manuscripts stacked on the floor, you know that without this one person's help, you'd be overwhelmed.

A good editor tends a flock of writers with the firm hand of authority and expertise and the tender caress of sympathy and admiration for an author's angst and talent. She or he should feed your body and mind, through the publisher's lunch and the vital exchange of ideas. The editor will lead you by the hand through the morass of personnel who will have some role in your book: the copy editor who niggles over semicolons, the designer who creates your cover, the publicity director who books you onto the *Phil Donahue* show, the promotion manager who designs the flyers, advertisements, etc. You may even be taken around to meet the editor in chief if your publisher is not *too* mammoth. Everybody you meet and every department you interact with, including the all-important bookkeeping department, which issues your checks, will work through your editor.

Chances are the editor is also the person who originally liked your work and persuaded the house to publish it, so you've got a good friend there. A major-house editor is swamped with work and has numerous other authors to consider, so don't make unreasonable demands on his/her time, but go to your editor first for whatever needs you have.

When You Lose Your Editor

So important (almost romantic, but not in the sexual sense) is the relationship between writer and editor that it can be a devastating trauma if your editor quits the job before your book is published, which often happens in this age of rapid turnover and movement of editors from house to house. A really powerful editor can even take authors along to the new publishing house, but that's rare. What usually happens is that your book is left with the original publisher, an orphan assigned to some new editor who may or may not like your style.

When you lose your editor try to remain calm—and don't try to make the editor feel guilty (it won't help!)—but do plan on expending even greater personal energy to promote the book. Try very hard to find a new friend within your major publishing house, but if it doesn't work out after this book, you may consider going back to your friendly editor, switching to the new house for your next book. After all, a good working relationship with your editor is the entire salvation in having to deal with the faceless policies of major publishers.

Editors and authors don't stay together, married in literary productivity, as in former years. Not only do editors change jobs, but writers change publishers with regularity, and not necessarily because they were unhappy with the previous one. A book that is just right for Bantam may not be of interest to Harper & Row, and vice versa. As author, you go pretty much where you find the most interest in your project.

My only novel, Tropical Detective Story, *was signed to E. P. Dutton Co. when my editor, Susan S., was there. But she left the job between the time I finished the book and its publication. The book was reassigned to*

Continued

Continued

Hal S., the editor in chief, but he died of a heart attack at a tragically young age. By the time the novel appeared in print in 1972, it had no editor, I had no personal friends left at Dutton, and I was living in India, wearing a loincloth and searching for a guru.

Well, actually, I had one friend left at Dutton then: Maureen C., the bookkeeper. It doesn't hurt a writer to develop a friendship with the person who issues your checks. I enjoyed dropping in on Maureen to pick up my money, and could call her directly to find out when it would be ready. We'd chat about each other's families, my books, children, whatever, and she even patiently and faithfully mailed my checks to foreign addresses, American Express, and other mail drops while I was on the road.

Big-House Production Blues

Major houses give the writer the least control over the physical qualities of the book. They all have in-house art departments, which they prefer using, for economic reasons, to free-lance artists, designers, or illustrators. If your book is conceived with special design features or much art and illustration, you need to have the artist's work protected by and included in the contract. Beware that the art director and/or production director will be greatly annoyed if you bother the department all the time, attempt to reject the cover design, or otherwise try to manipulate the physical production qualities, as authors have been known to do. That kind of act puts you in the dreaded category of a "difficult author," and that reputation gets around major publishing circles. Writers tend to want the most expensive production, while publishers lean toward economy, but more than that, it's simply not efficient for a major house to have every author overlooking the production work. There are too many different expectations, personalities, styles, and levels of expertise to accommodate.

For more about production, see the preceding chapters "Manuscript into Type" and "The Publishing Process."

"Sell" a Book by its Cover

About covers: The subject is rarely mentioned in a literary contract, and in practice the author's control over the cover varies greatly from house to house. Many authors never even see their cover until the book is published (especially true with mass-market reprint publishers) but with a hardcover book and a major house, you're likely to get an advance copy of the design and/or an early glossy print of the full-color cover. Unless you have a guarantee of veto power over it in the contract, you can assume you have no power to change it, even if you hate it. (And, yes, authors have been observed to faint upon seeing a naked couple locked in passionate embrace sprawled over the cover of what had been a rather sedate novel.)

But I *have* known a few occasions when an author strongly objected to a cover, causing the cover to be withdrawn and replaced with another just to keep the peace. Since the cover is one of the last stages of production work, it can be a major nuisance and/or delay for the publisher to have to change it— which probably explains why no publisher is eager to give the author control. Authors are often eccentric, and egocentric enough to be terribly sensitive about their covers.

The dust-jacket copy (the description and account of your book that appears inside the cover) is almost invariably written by someone other than the author—usually the copywriter, editor, promotion department, or publicity director. As with the cover itself, dust-jacket copy is seldom submitted to the author for approval.

If you "can't tell a book by its cover," you certainly can *sell* a book that way. Most of us tend to trust the house's art department professionals in this regard.

Control Over Your Manuscript

The one thing you may have absolute control over is the content of the manuscript itself. Editors' suggestions are not mandatory commands, but advice calculated to strengthen the book. If you work well with the editor, the combination of your efforts will produce a finer book than you could have produced alone. But ultimately it is still the author's province to compose, and rewrite the words, and authorize each one for publication.

(In genre publishing, the house often rewrites the manuscript after it's been submitted. The same is true with "adult fiction" or porno publishers.)

The publisher, in turn, has one ultimate control, which is the privilege of declining to publish the book because the manuscript is unsatisfactory. So, a delicate balance ensues. While you as author may have complete authority over the content of the manuscript, if you refuse to make revisions the editor thinks are essential, you could wind up looking for a new publisher.

The most important aspect of choosing a major house editor is to find one you *can* work with, someone who's on your wavelength. Then you shouldn't have any problem accepting some editorial direction.

Hard Cover or Paperback?

When we mentioned earlier that hardcover books get more reviews, we didn't mean to diminish the power and growth of the original paperback. (An "original paperback" is a new work that's never been published in hard covers.) For many books, the paperback route is the most direct and profitable.

Years ago, the hardcover edition *always* preceded the paperback by at least six months to a year. Nobody would pay more for the hard cover, it was reasoned, once the paperback was available. Today, some publishers take the simultaneous approach, bringing out a small number of hard covers and a much larger press run of paperbacks at the same time. The hard copies are strictly for reviewers, libraries, and those rare collectors who still prefer a cloth binding—"a real book." The general public goes for the soft covers and much lower price. Books have become more expensive as the cost of paper has multiplied many times over the past decade. Some say that books will eventually be published on floppy diskettes that we "read" on a computer screen, because the world's supply of paper will run out. Others

point to the eventual development of synthetic paper. We doubt
that either eventuality will come about anytime soon.

Trade vs. Mass-Market Paperbacks

There are original trade paperbacks and original mass-market
paperbacks. The former, as we've noted elsewhere, are mainly
available in bookstores while the latter are sold in many other
outlets such as supermarkets, newsstands, drugstores, and train
stations. The original trade paperback is usually the same size as
a hardcover book and can be very handsomely produced; it's
cheaper than a hard cover but not by that much. Lately we've
seen the price of trade paperbacks ranging from $4.95 to $14.95.
A major publisher will go for the original trade paperback route
in cases where the book is expected to command a market
smaller than mass market—a first printing may be as modest as
5,000 copies—or where the book requires a large format, such as
cookbooks and how-to books meant to lie flat. Art and fine
photography seem to do well in original trade P.B.

The original *mass-market* paperback may be the least prestigious kind of book but it stands an excellent chance of outsell-
ing all others. Seldom reviewed, these rack-sized editions hit the
supermarket shelves for a relatively brief period, and, if not sold,
are "pulled" (removed) and the return copies destroyed after
their covers have been ripped off. This kind of paperback has the
shortest life in print but can reach the greatest number of readers. A great deal of genre fiction is published as original mass-
market paperbacks. While a mass-market reprint of your book is
highly desirable, a mass-market *original* is less so, unless you
are working in a genre (such as romance or Gothic).

The store manager, by the way, doesn't select individual mass-
market titles to stock the way a bookstore chooses hardcover or
trade paperbacks. A distributor simply delivers the paperbacks in
bundles, calling on the store every month or two in order to
deliver new titles and remove the unsold earlier releases.

The advantage to you of being published in original mass
market is the rapid sale of potentially huge numbers of copies.
It's not uncommon for a mass-market publisher to do a first
printing of 100,000 copies, and if your royalty was 49½ cents a

copy (or 10 percent of a $4.95 cover price), that's a chance to earn $50,000 in a few months. "Production" writers, who turn out mass-market originals in profusion, can make a fine living at it.

Backlist, Midlist, or Listless

When publishers talk about "backlist" they mean those previously published books that are still in demand and kept in print year after year. *Winnie the Pooh* and the King James version of the Bible are backlist items stocked by every bookstore. "Midlist," which is where most books wind up, are stock-in-trade books published to some success but which are not top sellers. We now have a crisis among so-called midlist authors, writers who have never commanded a huge readership, in finding a publishing contract. Their middle-of-the-road sellers aren't as profitable anymore, and the major publishers would rather go with a stable of sure-fire hits. Printing and paper have shot up in price. TV and video cassette recorders have taken people away from us. People are reading more books, but they're all reading the same ones. The little guy is getting squeezed out. One doesn't want to be midlist but we have to accept the fact that the odds are heavily stacked against most of us becoming best-selling authors! Midlist is perfectly respectable, indeed a triumph in itself. It just gets tougher every year to make a living there.

Funny there isn't any category for "bottom-of-the-list" books. The bottom, I suppose, is the day your book goes out of print. It's happened to the best writers.

Where you want to be, of course, is at the top of the list, on the first or second page of the publisher's catalog, one of the new titles being pushed, advertised, promoted, destined for fame and riches. Destined, indeed, to become backlist. How publishers decide which books to feature depends on management and editorial policy, but here the sales personnel exert their greatest influence. More on that in Chapter 14, "On the Shelf Between Austen and Zolotow."

Use this chart as a general guideline but don't lose sight of the basic rule that everything depends on which publisher you have. Some small presses have excellent distribution in partnership with a major house, and some major houses give close personal attention to their authors.

MAJOR VS. SMALL-PRESS PUBLISHERS—AN AUTHOR'S GUIDE
Rating: * Poor **Fair ***Good ****Excellent

Category	Major publisher	Small-press publisher
Attention to personal needs	**	****
Control over production	*	***
Distribution	****	*
Advertising	***	*
Advance on royalties	****	*
Reviews	***	** (and growing)
Royalty rate	(no substantial difference)	

If your book is being published by a major house, congratulations. The next chapter explains the many real advantages of small press publication, but most books will surely sell more copies in the big leagues.

11 | Small Presses and Self-Publishing

Advantages of Small-Press Publishing

Being published by a major house is gratifying to your ego and adds something to your purse (though it may not quite pay the rent for a year), but there are substantial advantages to being published by a smaller press. The greatest of these is simply the personal attention your book will receive from its editor and publisher, and remember that your small-press book is still available to major publishers for reprint purposes. It's in print in some form that can be noticed and/or republished. It's on the market and can build a sales history. A large number of books that originated with a small press have eventually reached the highest limbs of the best-seller lists.

We mentioned earlier the case of Seattle's Madrona Publishers and the book *Volcano*. Also consider the huge success that Berkeley, California's, North Point Press had with *Son of the Morning Star* by Evan S. Connell. The publishing house, under the direction of Jack Shoemaker, has consistently produced books of the highest quality and proven that it can sell its books in major-house numbers.

Typically, the small press compares to the major house like this:

• *advance on royalties*, if any, is likely to be smaller, but royalties will be paid out sooner for that reason

• *distribution* is totally different and varies widely from house to house, but generally can't compete with major publishers

• *reviews* are more accessible than they used to be; small-press books are getting more attention

• *advertising and promotion* budget is much smaller, and the author carries more responsibility for publicizing the book

• *prestige* level depends on the house; the better ones are as reputable and prestigious as the majors.

Approaching the Independent Publisher

Officially the smaller presses call themselves "independent publishers." Check the Yellow Pages of your local phone directory for the names and addresses of small-book publishers in your vicinity, then find out what kinds of books they publish. You can research the shelves of your bookstore, looking for independently published titles, or call or write the publisher, asking for a catalog. You could be surprised by the variety of local publishing in your area. Also check the *International Directory of Little Magazines and Small Presses* (Dustbooks, Box 1056, Paradise, CA 95969), the annual editions of *The Pushcart Prize, Best of the Small Presses,* which contains a listing called "Outstanding Small Presses," and the *Cosmep Catalogue,* published by the International Association of Independent Publishers (P.O. Box 703, San Francisco, CA 94101).

How Big Is "Small"?

You may find yourself confused about the exact definition of what is "small." ther aren't any established standards at which a publisher goes from small to medium to large. The best rule of thumb is simply the number of titles a firm produces in a year:

• 1 to 5: a "mom and pop" operation
• 6 to 20: likely three or more people working full-time
• 21 to 50: too big to be considered small, easily a dozen or more employees

The other consideration, of course, is how many copies of each title the publisher brings out. Some do a first press run of

500 or a thousand, others much more. Be sure to know what level of business a publisher does before tailoring your approach to it.

Where to Find Small Publishers

While small publishers exist everywhere, they tend to be most numerous and successful on the West Coast, where sheer distance from the New York hub makes local publishing more attractive. Berkeley, California, is itself a microcosmic publishing capital and home of Bookpeople, the largest and farthest-reaching distributors of small-press books, and a company called Small Press Distribution (1814 San Pablo Avenue, Berkeley, CA 94702), which operates a retail bookstore, mail-order catalog business, and wholesale distributorship of 4,000 titles from 300 independent publishers located all over the world.

Don Ellis and his Creative Arts Book Co. in Berkeley is the essence of what a small press should always be: friendly, low-key, original, and thriving. Ellis started out in 1968 as a printer and in 1976 started publishing books printed on his own machinery. He hooked up with novelist Barry Gifford to produce a series of books by distinguished American writers, including the last two books authored by William Saroyan. Creative Arts also reprints classic out-of-print American novels such as the Jim Thompson thrillers. "The thing about having your book published by Don Ellis is that the guy himself is always going to be there for you," Gifford says. "Oh, he can't match a New York advance, but he's helped writers out of his own pocket, and every book he publishes is a substantial investment to him. He'll keep the book in print and available and really care about it."

The Friendly Editor and Publisher

Friendliness and caring may well suit your needs as a beginning writer more than the high-stress world of major publishing. Your small-press publisher is a close friend, somebody you can drop in and visit, go out drinking with, and confide in when it comes to literary matters. You may be able to play an important role in decisions regarding the production of the book, and you could very well be your own marketing manager too. The book, so important to you, as author, is also enormously important to the publisher, who has only a limited number of titles, so he can't afford to ignore any of them.

Jumping from Small to Major

Your chances of jumping from a small press to a major house by selling reprint rights to your book depend on convincing the larger publisher of its marketability. If you can sell the first few thousand copies of the Little Publisher edition, a major house may be able to sell many thousands more with the advantage of wider distribution. Alicia Bay Laurel brought out the first edition of her book *Living on the Earth* with a tiny Berkeley company in 1971, but Random House picked up the rights and went on with it to great success (over a quarter of a million sold in trade paperback). Alicia's San Francisco-based agent, Jerome Dollarhide, sold the rights to Random House and in the process signed Alicia up for several new books.

The author, agent, or the original publisher can submit a book published by a small press to a major house for paperback reprint consideration just as one would a manuscript. It helps greatly to have generated some reviews and to have a sales history to which to refer. It's a phenomenon of the 1980s in New York publishing that small-press books have been going for large reprint money more often than ever before.

There's yet another way to make the transition from small to major publisher, which is to use your small-press-published book as testimony to your writing ability when you query the major-house editor on a new project. If the editor reads and likes your small-press book, you could be rewarded with a contract for a new book from the major house.

Secondary Distribution

Just because small presses don't have the enormous distribution powers of the majors doesn't mean they can't get your book around. There are a number of alternative distributors (sometimes called "secondary distributors") who handle small-press books, and if a particular title exhibits early success, there's precedent for major distributors taking it on. Some small publishers actually maintain a national direct outreach into thousands of bookstores (the small press I owned in Seattle sold books at one time or other to over 5,000 different stores) and groups of small publishers have banded together to hire traveling sales reps. For a more detailed look at distribution see Chapter 14, "On the Shelf Between Austen and Zolotow."

The heaviest part of your small publisher's responsibility, of course, is somehow getting the book into the stores . . . and that can involve the author as well. At the most basic level you can and should carry the book around to bookstores yourself, ask to see the manager or buyer, and talk that person into ordering a few copies. (This is just one of many methods of self-promotion that we discuss further in Chapter 15, Self-Promotion, the Writer's Best Friend.") In some cases the publisher may be willing to leave books on consignment just to get them onto the shelves with some visibility. Since small-press distribution cannot be as thorough as with a major house, it never hurts to push your title anywhere you can place it.

Mail order still works surprisingly well for some kinds of small-press books. If your book speaks to a constituency represented by the readership of a given magazine or newspaper, you can advertise with a clip-out coupon and sell the book one at a time directly to the reader. Classified ads are inexpensive and sometimes effective. We recommend that you experiment selectively with your advertising dollar, keeping close track of how many orders you generate with each publication. Use a code in your address to identify the source of the order; if you advertise your book in *Organic Gardening*, for example, have people write to your address plus "Dept. OG."

Bookpeople

How big is the small-press movement? Well, the R. R. Bowker Co., publishers of *Publishers Weekly*, thought enough of it to initiate *Small Press* magazine in 1983, a periodical that deals only with the business of small publishing. And Bookpeople, the small-press distributor, has grown over twenty years into a sub-stantial force.

This is the way Bookpeople in Berkeley works: The retail bookseller doesn't have the time or energy to keep separate accounts with every small publisher; it's just not worth all that paperwork, billing, returns, etc., to deal with a publisher who may do only one book you want in your store. But a single account with Bookpeople can give the bookseller hundreds of titles from a wide variety of small publishers. The publisher sells the book to Bookpeople for 60 percent off the retail price, and Bookpeople sells it to the store for 40 percent off. The books are usually left on consignment, so the publisher doesn't get paid until the books are sold.

(Bookpeople is not the only distributor of small-press books, of course, just the most established. With the great proliferation in small-press publishing in recent years, even Bookpeople can't stock anywhere near all the titles, so they have become quite selective. It's an accomplishment to place your book in the catalog, one which is guaranteed to generate some sales.)

Self-Publishing vs. Vanity Presses

There is a noble tradition of self-publishing in this coun-try that dates back to Thoreau and Benjamin Franklin. Publishing your own book is certainly an acceptable and respectable enter-prise if you find that regular publishers aren't interested or if you just want to maintain absolute control. You automatically become a small publisher when you bring out your own book. But sending your manuscript to a vanity press and paying someone else to print and bind it is something that we don't recommend. Generally the distribution of vanity-press books is poor to non-existent, and for the thousands of dollars these outfits charge to publish your book, you probably could publish it yourself at regular commercial printing rates.

But we'd be remiss if we didn't point out right here that producing a book is not an easy task.

Making It Yourself

Setting type and doing your own design and pasteup is a lot of fun if you have the creative talent to handle it. With the advent of word processors and sophisticated desktop printers, good-looking type can now be set much faster and cheaper than before (see our discussion of word processors in Chapter 8). Basically, anyone with type set to a specific page size and a pot of glue can paste up "boards" of pages of a book. Those boards are then photographed ("shot") by a printer's camera and the negatives used to create plates. You can do it very simply, or you can raise it to a high art form.

Most self-publishers don't actually own a printing press, so the author's creative level of involvement ends with the finished boards—kind of a master, or original, copy of the book, which is then turned over to a printer and binder. There are endless varieties of type to choose from, and the overall design of the book can range from the conventional to the unique.

Prestype or Letraset (trademark) is in widespread use, especially with smaller publishers and self-published books. These are transfer letters that you rub off a plastic sheet onto paper to make camera-ready type. In recent years the variety of prestype available has become staggering; for a few dollars a sheet you can get any imaginable typeface as well as thousands of graphic designs. You wouldn't want to set the actual text of the book with transfer letters—too tedious—but it's perfect for heads and larger type as well as borders and bylines.

The binding may be spiral, comb, glue (or "perfect binding" for trade paperbacks), a hardcover binding with signatures and stitching, or just two staples holding the book together in the middle. If you're planning to make your book yourself, check our Lit Biz Reference Sources for the titles of books to lead you through the mechanical process. Two of our favorites are Clifford Burke's *Printing It, a Guide to Graphic Techniques for the Impecunious*, and Dan Poynter's *Self Publishing Manual: How to Write, Print, and Sell Your Own Book*.

We are rapidly becoming a nation of instant-printing addicts, and there is likely to be a copy shop in your town that can rush you into print. You can start with as few as a hundred copies or go to a big-web press, fork out serious money, and do thousands of hard covers. Whatever course you take, when you make it yourself you've got absolute artistic control over the finished product, and absolute responsbility for getting it circulated to the reading public. You distribute the book any way you can—through small-press distributors, directly to bookstores, by mail-order-coupon advertising, or selling single copies at your public appearances. It's an adventure worth the taking, and most people who've published their own books will tell you they're proud and happy with the results.

Others will tell you it's a great big headache keeping track of all the shipping and accounting, and they're actively seeking a publisher to take over the rights so they can get out from under the hard work for small pay.

Notes on Self-Publishing

If you self-publish a book, you'll be on really intimate terms with all these production details unless you hire a graphic artist to produce the master for you. If you've got the time, creative ability, and access to materials to set your own type and paste up your own board, go for it!

Otherwise, try to find an artist who can design the book, get the type set, and broker the printing and binding arrangements for you, all at a combined price within your means. Such artists are listed in the Yellow Pages of the phone book under "Commercial Art" or you can ask local printers or publishers for a reference to one. That way, you simply pay the producing graphic artist and don't have to run around shepherding the book through stages of production. Alternately, of course, you can pay the artist only to produce the master boards, then haggle with the printers and binders on your own. You might save money that way, but we've found that a hardworking graphics professional should know the printing ropes, get a commercial discount, and actually save the self-publishing author some production costs.

Finding a printer and binder on your own is a matter of careful searching. Starting from the Yellow Pages of the phone book, you can call printers, describe your project (how big a book, how many pages, whether or not color illustrations are involved, how many copies you want to print, and so on) and get a "quote" or price estimate. A good printer will ask intelligent questions about aspects you may not have considered and will get back to you with a price quote, guaranteed, in writing. By all means, though, shop around and get competing estimates. By sheer exposure to the printing industry you'll pick up technical jargon and come, eventually, to a better understanding of the trade.

A large printing press may do its own binding, but most printers send their finished pages to a bindery to be bound in hard cover or paperback. Typically, a printer's quote will include the cost of binding, but check the fine print (or simply ask) to be sure. You can find a bindery on your own, just as you did a printer, but it's extra work, and you may not be thrilled to receive thousands of loose pages of your book off the press.

Whichever route your book takes through production, whether with a mammoth publisher and a promotion schedule, or a tiny local printshop, it's always a small miracle to see it born, healthy, and ready for the shelf.

A Word About University Presses

While not precisely the same thing as a small press, the American university press is a special category of independent publisher and a very healthy one. Although originally chartered as educational institutions, university presses have enjoyed a lot of success even in trade publishing in recent years. Ohio State University Press did well with the best-selling ". . . And Ladies of the Club" by Helen Hoover Santmyer, and the University of Washington Press has achieved prominence in the art-book field. Norman Maclean's wonderful reminiscence of growing up in early twentieth-century Montana, A River Runs Through It, has been a strong seller for the University of Chicago Press for a decade.

Traditionally, however, the university presses have published the scholarly work of professors. When writing a query letter to such a publisher, you should include a full description of your academic background, degrees, and/or special honors, and scholarly publication credits if you have them. In many cases a university will recognize life achievements as a valid substitute for academic credits. Some university presses also publish poetry and fiction, so don't overlook this potentially excellent kind of publisher if your book is suited to one.

Promoting and Publicizing Your Small-Press and Self-Published Book

In Chapter 15 we talk about promoting your book, whether it's from a large or small publisher. With the small publisher the promotion effort (which depends to a great extent on the author, even with a major house) can become *entirely* the author's province. You might have to do it all yourself.

A good small publisher will take care of mailing out review copies and press releases to newspapers and magazines, and may even be able to afford a few advertisements. But it's a rare small press that employs a full-time publicity director who can book you onto radio and TV talk shows, for example. To do that you've got to call the station, ask to speak to the person in charge of booking guests on the show, and deliver your pitch. You'll probably want to follow that up by mailing a review copy of the book, a press release, and personal letter saying (in a nutshell) "Nice to talk with you on the phone, when can you book me on the show?" You might be surprised at how easy it can be.

Start with the local talk shows in your area that are within a day's trip from your home. Watch and listen to find out what kinds of authors they book as guests. You can't just book yourself on one of the network heavyweight shows, but every city of any size has local shows with names like "Good Morning (City)" or "(City) After Dark" that are always eager for fresh talent and interesting new ideas and are quite approachable. Since you don't have a publicity director vouching for you and aren't representing a major publisher, be prepared for the station (more so if it's TV than radio) to want to interview you in person before putting you on the air.

Press releases and review copies should get you covered in print, radio and TV talk shows are accessible avenues of broadcast coverage of your book, and the telephone is your best ally in making arrangements and (gently) pressuring the media to notice your small press or self-published work. But nothing seems to help a book that is published outside of mainstream houses quite as much as personal appearances by the author.

The Personal Appearance

By "personal appearance" we don't mean how your hair is styled or what you're wearing. As an author you can make a personal appearance almost anywhere. Just a few suggestions:

—in a bookstore, where (by arrangement) you autograph books. See also Chapter 16, "Owning a Bookstore";

—in a shopping center, where you give a demonstration of what your how-to book teaches. For example, if it's a cookbook, you could set up a portable kitchen and demonstrate how to make a certain dish; if it's a crafts book, you demonstrate the skills involved;

—at a school or university or in a writers' workshop setting, where you may read from your book or deliver a lecture;

—at a civic luncheon, PTA meeting, or evening library function, where you've wheedled an invitation to address the audience;

—at a regional or national booksellers' convention (which may require either your publisher's sponsorship or renting a booth to get in the door), where you shake hands and hype your book directly to bookstore owners;

—at any convocation of "spin-off" industries or groups related to your topic. If you'd written about having an abortion, you might make a personal appearance at a Planned Parenthood meeting; if your novel is set in Korea in 1952, perhaps you'd address the Korean War Veterans convention; if yours is a book of poems, seek out the Poetry Society's monthly meeting; if it's a children's book, how about a personal appearance and story-telling time at the library's children's room? You get the idea. Appear!

And, of course, always carry a boxful of copies of your book to sell directly to the audience!

12 | Newspapers and Magazines, for Ink-Stained Wretches

Paying the Rent

Writing for newspapers and magazines serves the author in at least two important ways. First, it provides an available outlet for short pieces of writing or chapters and excerpts from a book; second, it provides income to sustain the writer while he or she works on the book. Perhaps more to the point, it is easier for a beginning writer to sell an article or story to a periodical than a whole book to a publisher.

Books are our principal stock in trade at Lit Biz 101, but every working writer knows the value of newspapers and magazines for regular exposure of your work, at professional rates, that can make the difference between starving and making a good living. In fact, since book royalties come due in such a protracted way, and magazine payments are relatively easier and quicker to extract, free-lance work for periodicals may be the most effective way to pay the rent.

Refer back to Chapter 6, "Money and Perks," for the discussion of collecting your pay from magazines and newspapers. You'll recall the publications pay either "on acceptance" or "on publication," and that sometimes a "kill fee" is paid if your article or story doesn't make it into the publication.

Researching the Market

When deciding which magazine to query for your article or story, you should know the market well. While *LMP* is invaluable, it's hard to get around *Writer's Market* (an annually published book) as the definitive source of information on periodicals and what they buy, how much they pay, and who to write to. The magazines are divided into categories so you can quickly locate the region of interest for your work. The general formula is that *Writer's Market* tells you these things about the magazine:

1. The frequency (monthly, weekly. etc.)

2. The audience ("for blue-collar, family-oriented women" or "primarily male, thirty-six years old, interested in engineering," etc.)

3. The number of free-lance manuscripts bought per year or percentage of content that is free-lance-written

4. How payment is made (on acceptance, on publication, etc.)

5. Which rights are bought (first serial, exclusive, etc.; beware that when selling "all rights," you are surrendering just that)

6. How to submit (is a stamped self-addressed envelope necessary, do they prefer a query letter or complete manuscript, how much in advance should you submit seasonal material? etc.)

7. How long before you get a report or reply?

8. What they buy (particular field of interest)

9. Length requirements

10. What they pay

11. Special tips ("prefers to see more articles about such-and-such, prefers articles with photos," etc.)

Writer's Market is available at most libraries, and when you skim over the thousands of listings your mind may reel at the limitless markets and possibilities for free-lance submissions. You have nothing to lose by sending your queries and manuscripts out, although an enormous amount of patience and unswayable self-confidence may be required before you see the first acceptance letter and/or check.

DIFFERENT KINDS OF MAGAZINE AND NEWSPAPER RIGHTS

Rights	Definition
First serial	First-time publication in a periodical
Second Serial	Material has already appeared in another periodical
One time	Material may be used only once; copyright remains with the author
All	Rights to every possible development from the story, including film or book adaptation

Fiction in Magazines

Alas, we don't have general-interest magazines that publish fiction in the same numbers we once did. But a few major magazines still buy it, and many small literary (or "little") magazines thrive on it. Among those that pay for short stories are *The Atlantic, The New Yorker, Saturday Review, Cosmopolitan, Family Circle, Good Housekeeping, Mademoiselle, Playgirl, Redbook,* and *Woman's Day.* The literary magazines that do pay some money for fiction include *Antioch Review, The Paris Review, The Denver Quarterly,* and *Pulpsmith.*

There are plenty of publishing opportunities and the short story is a traditional form that is never going to disappear. Moreover, short stories can lead to a collection published in book form. They are still and will always be popular, although the number of big-money magazines publishing fiction has dwindled. If you're willing to accept modest payment, there are hundreds of smaller periodicals eager for good fiction.

Nonficton Articles as Book Proposals

Timely nonfiction magazine or newspaper articles have quite often resulted in full-length books. Sometimes the author can use a published magazine piece as part of a book proposal to a publisher in which she/he proposes to expand the subject matter into volume form. The fact that the work is already being publicized in the magazine has established a reading audience, and in many cases the article can only touch on the highlights of a topic that could fill a book.

You can also reproduce a magazine piece as one of the chapters in your book, assuming you have sold the magazine only one-time publication rights and not "all rights." Authors make entire books out of previously published stories, and you'll often see a note on the copyright page to the effect that parts of this book "appeared in somewhat different form" or "originally appeared" in certain periodicals.

The Magazine Query Letter

If you have a good idea for a magazine piece, query the editor just as you would a book editor, with a one-page letter describing what you want to write or have written, stating its length, and detailing your past publishing credits. Begin by reading the periodical in question so you have a clear notion of the kinds of work it publishes. You'll find magazine and newspaper editors are always on the hunt for new material and fresh ideas. We've noted that one of the easiest acceptances a beginning writer can locate is the Sunday magazine section of a smaller-city newspaper (as long as the section is locally produced and not a nationally syndicated insert like *Parade*). You may find it tough to crack *The New York Times Magazine*, but considerably easier to approach the Sunday *Weekend Living* editor at the Monterey, California, *Herald*.

A magazine editor takes a good look at your letter of inquiry. If the letter itself is poorly typed, with misspellings or awkward writing, he or she is likely to toss it aside with the weary sigh of a much-beleaguered reader. If you propose to write something, it should be directly related to the kind of material that magazine normally carries, well represented by an intelligent letter that also establishes your past credits, and offered at a specific length, price, and deadline. Don't press the patience of an overworked editor, but try to establish why your article will be of peak interest in the near future.

Sample Magazine Query Letter

Jane L. Joyce
1313 Ulysses Way
Dublin, CT 00000

November 5, 1987

Ms. Heloise Medium
Young Gal Magazine
000 Madison Avenue
New York, NY 10000

Dear Ms. Medium:

Thanks for a lively November issue of Young Gal. I think you're doing a great job reporting on the trends, fashion, and music that young gals today really go for.

I'm doing research now for a piece that will have a lot of appeal to your readership. It's called "How to Tell If Your Boyfriend is Cheating," and it's a serious approach to the question. I'm interviewing fifteen girls whose boyfriends were caught cheating on them. They tell how they felt and what the telltale signs were of a deteriorating relationship.

The piece will run about 2,000 words, and I can deliver it in time for your annual March issue on "Spring Vacation Dates." Do you think you could use it? I enclose my latest clips from Teen Meet magazine. The price of 50 cents a word quoted by Writer's Market is acceptable to me. Hope to hear from you soon.

Sincerely yours,

Jane Joyce

Daily Newspapers

Now consider the differences between newspapers and magazines as markets for your work. Daily newspapers generally have their own editorial staff and use wire services like AP and UPI; free-lance opportunities may be limited to the guest essay or editorial on the op-ed page, the Sunday magazine feature piece, or the Sunday book review section. Be advised that the average Sunday book review pays the writer somewhere between nothing at all (but you get to keep the book) and $75.

Getting a job as a daily newspaper writer can often be the first step toward eventually having your books published, and many good novelists started out writing obituaries on the midnight shift. Most newspaper work, however, lacks both glamour and much room to get creative in your writing. The *Lawrence* (Massachusetts) *Eagle-Tribune*, which gave me my first writing job when I was seventeen, was not interested in any flighty prose so much as it was concerned with my getting the names, ages, and survivors of the deceased in proper order (I was the writer of the obits). I also spent many midnight hours hanging around the station house with the local cops, trying to generate crime copy from the log.

Weeklies

Weekly newspapers are now thriving around the United States, and are much more likely to buy free-lance articles and photography. The pay may not be much, but a weekly-paper editor is generally more approachable and the material is less strictly news, with more room for feature stuff, even fiction.

Types of Magazines

Magazines can be weekly, monthly, quarterly, whatever, and can range from pulpy newsprint and a staple binding to high-gloss, elegantly bound prestige publications like *Vanity Fair*. Research the magazine market thoroughly, using tools like *Writer's Digest* and *LMP*, because there is an endless variety of them out there, appealing to every conceivable special interest. There are magazines of regional interest, magazines for plumbers, for skiiers, "city" magazines, Sunday-insert national magazines that arrive with the weekend newspaper, even magazines about magazines (*Magazine and Bookseller* will give you a free subscription if you're professionally involved).

Doing Business With a Magazine

Most magazines pay their writers by the word. The editor will tell you how many words he/she wants, the magazine issues a simple contract for the article, with a "kill fee" included in case the magazine doesn't accept the finished piece. Typically, the kill fee should be about a third of what you would have been paid if the magazine had used your piece. Always, of course, determine whether the magazine pays "on acceptance" or "on publication." Even that may be negotiable if they want your piece badly enough.

Magazines have a longer "lead time," or time required to prepare an article for publication, then newspapers do. Most of the larger monthly magazines are put to bed two months before the issue date. Editors are thus eternally searching for material that will seem new and fresh in several months time. The competition for original ideas is fierce; nothing could be worse than coming out with coverage of something that's been previously "done" or done better. If yours is the first nonfiction article on a new trend, you may be able to command a good price from a national magazine.

Mistakes Not to Make with Editors

Jeffrey Whitmore, who for years edited the slick monthly Monterey Life, *brought his Lit Biz 101 students examples of some of the lamebrained, unbearably egotistical, and/or obnoxiously pushy letters he'd received from would-be authors. Worst of all, he said, are the poets. Every magazine that publishes any poetry at all is swamped with submissions. Accept it gracefully if the editor tells you he won't be accepting new poetry for a year. Most of all, don't try to press an idea that's been rejected, and don't promise an article of such sweeping import that you can't deliver it.*

Magazine Excerpts

Excerpts from new or about-to-be-published books make excellent fodder (some would say filler) for magazines. When your book is sold to a major publisher, your editor or agent should be pushing individual chapters of it to the magazines, taking advantage of the first-serial subsidiary rights (see above, Different Kinds of Magazine and Newspapers Rights). Payment depends on the size of the circulation, which means it could be nominal or extravagant. As author, you'll find those occasional scattered payments for excerpts a delightful peppering of your income, a series of bonbons, "gravy" income beyond the primary royalty and good publicity for the book as well.

Magazine Payment

Small literary quarterlies listed in *Writer's Market* sometimes offer payment in terms of free copies of the magazine and a subscription, while *Playboy* offers a minimum of $3,000 for an article or story and $4,000 for the "Playboy Interview." There is a full range in between, so it's difficult to pinpoint any kind of standard. Just be sure that payment terms are defined in advance and that you're willing to sell your work at the going rate. A thousand bucks for a first-time publication of an article in an average-circulation national magazine is probably a decent middle-of-the-road payment, and remember that a reprint of a work that has already appeared in another periodical will bring a significantly lower price than first-time rights.

13 | Publishing Your Own Magazine

If you enjoy writing and want to expand your involvement with other writers and Lit Biz professionals, you might consider publishing your own magazine. It gives you an outlet for your own work, allows you to stay in contact with other writers and editors, and can lead to finding a publisher for your book or publishing it yourself.

If you have the ink in your veins, as the old cliché says, you won't be able to stop yourself from this undertaking, which is also fraught with economic dangers. Publishing your own magazine is a dream that many, including myself, have succumbed to. I've done it more than once in my life but at the moment I edit a small, nonprofit, literary quarterly called *Creative States*, which is great for the cause of literacy, but of course doesn't earn money. It operates in the red, which is possible for non-profit arts organizations because sponsors and contributors can deduct their donations for tax purposes. But even big, glossy magazines have a difficult time turning a profit, and the whole business is precarious enough to put off all but the most dedicated of investors.

Editorial Content

The first thing any magazine needs is a concept of its editorial content. What kind of writing and photography do you want to publish? Is there a clearly identifiable market you are aiming this magazine toward? (Advertisers definitely want to know *who* is reading it.) Do you know enough writers, illustrators, photographers, etc., who will provide original work at whatever price you can afford to pay (even for free)? Have you got the stuff, got something to say?

Assuming you do, the fiendish attraction of bringing out a magazine is that it's so much cheaper than publishing a book. With a little donated time and energy from layout and typesetting people and a quick-and-dirty press job, you can have a reasonable-looking magazine on the streets for a manufacturing cost of under a dollar each.

If you just said "That sounds too easy," go to the head of the class. The donated time and energy is likely to be your own and that of your friends. A good layout person is a creature of talent and endless capacity for tiny details, an artist. If your design and layout person is inexperienced, it's going to show in the published magazine. And typesetters get around $50 an hour (although you can set your own type if you have access to one of the new computer desktop printers.)

Advertisers

Advertisers, if you can get them, are the entire foundation of a magazine's financial stability, but the small literary magazine may actually depend more on subscribers than ads. If you've wondered how the big magazines can offer subscription rates at a third of the newsstand price *and* a "free" digital watch ("with your paid subscription"), it's because the paid subscription circulation of the magazine directly determines the advertising rates. Certain larger mags are willing to "lose" money on each subscriber because they gain it back in higher ad revenues. They can charge more for an ad if they can prove their number of readers has increased.

How to convince advertisers to spend money to reach the readership of your magazine? Major periodicals have audited circulations, so the advertiser knows exactly how many people will receive his message and quite a bit about those people's spending habits: 47 percent own a VCR, 61 percent have two or more cars in the family, 88 percent earn more than $25,000 a year, etc., etc. (They get these funny figures through all kinds of surveys of apparent reliability, but I remain skeptical.) *Unaudited* magazines, like my little literary quarterly, rely on goodwill from advertisers who take our assertions on faith. (Of course we don't even claim that our readers own BMWs or Rolls-Royces, just that they are literate readers, mostly college educated and middle class.)

You can solicit advertising from any business, whether it's local or national. Approach local merchants on a personal basis, showing them your magazine and explaining to them the advantages of reaching your readers. Bigger businesses and nationally oriented companies usually work through an advertising agency, and it's the agency executive you must convince. Telephone the company's corporate headquarters and ask for the name of the agency and person to contact; there may also be an office for advertising and public relations you can speak to.

Be assured that although it's not easy to sell advertising space in a new or unknown publication it is possible. Don't give up too easily. Offer a free trial ad if it comes to that. Also, we've found that other magazines have been willing to exchange subscription ads with us; no money changes hands, but *Creative States* solicits and finds new subscribers among the readership of *Publishers Weekly, Mother Jones,* and *Writer's Digest.* The usual procedure is that the larger publications such as *PW* will run one ad for every four ads in the smaller publications, such as *Creative States.*

Keeping to a Schedule

Although producing a magazine may be more economically feasible than publishing a book, the publication then commits you to reproducing it on whatever schedule you've announced, supposedly for the indefinite future. As long as you're soliciting subscriptions for the next six, twelve, or however many issues, you've got a moral obligation to keep publishing the rag, even though creditors may be howling. Distributors get angry and tend not to want to carry your magazine if you're chronically late on arrival. Subscribers, especially, expect and anticipate every issue and notice when it doesn't get there on time.

Subscriptions

Subscriptions are something you have to drum up in any way possible, starting with personal friends and family, mailing lists and ads. If your magazine has a specific market appeal, you can advertise it in other publications already reaching that market. It's worthwhile paying the post office 37 cents each for those Business Reply postcards whereby people can subscribe, pay no postage, and be billed later. Make it easy on them or they won't subscribe at all.

Give deadbeats a couple of extra issues while continually dunning them with form letters: "We know you won't want to miss our upcoming special issue on Tahiti . . ."; "We know you wouldn't deliberately cheat a nonprofit literary quarterly, Mr. JONES . . ." (inserting the personal references via computer mail-merge); "Your personal DIGITAL PENDANT is waiting for your paid subscription. . . ."

And here's a tip from a very small magazine publisher: When you bill a person for a subscription, always enclose a stamped envelope addressed to the magazine, so the subscriber has merely to write out a check and send it back. Some people, if forced to address an envelope and affix a stamp to it, won't get around to doing it for months.

Finally, use the oldest pitch in the world because it still works: Offer a free, no-obligation copy of your magazine with a subscription. Tell the potential subscriber "If you don't like the publication, write 'cancel' on the invoice, return it to us, and owe nothing. The first issue is yours to keep with our compliments!" A few people will take advantage of this scam, just to get a free magazine, but the vast majority who subscribe will pay.

Magazine Distribution, Major and Secondary

Magazine distributors conventionally take a 50 percent discount on the retail price of copies sold and destroy the returned copies after tearing off the covers. Distributors are remarkably cooperative for the most part. If you publish your magazine with any regularity at all, and have at least some sales attraction, you may get distributed in most major U.S. cities by "secondary distributors" (those who distribute smaller magazines).

Major distribution is available only to periodicals that print a large number of copies on a reliable schedule. That level of publishing is beyond the boundaries of this elementary approach.

Those cooperative secondary distributors have elaborate rules about paying that assure them at least sixty to ninety days leeway *after* receiving the *next* issue of the magazine to pay for the *previous* one, less returns of course. Did you get that? You bring out Issue Number One, sell a distributor a thousand copies, and the distributor pays you for the 410 copies actually sold, having destroyed 590 returns, three months after you've shipped him Issue Number Two, which itself may have been published months after Number One. The net effect is that the publisher gets paid late and short, and the distributor has nothing to lose. If your magazine happens to go under, you can't even collect for the last issue you sold to a distributor; usually by contract, he's obliged to pay only on receipt of a new issue. It's just the nature of the biz. But wait, there's a good side.

On the "pro" side of the coin, the distributor will get your magazine out to readers who would never otherwise see it. The advertisers can be told that your publication, however small, is being read in New York, Miami, Los Angeles, and Seattle too. Your publication needs the legitimacy of being available and visible on newsstands. New subscribers will come from copies sold that way: Always include the postage-paid return-reply postcard for subscriptions; the U.S. Postal Service charges only $50 a year for the permit, and it's well worth it.

Staples or Glue, Glossy or Newsprint?

Production values vary wildly. We did a magazine with a press run of 2,500 copies, black and white with one overlaid color on the covers, on pulp newsprint, for under a thousand dollars in 1985. Or you can do a full-color job, print on glossy stock, and order 50,000 copies for a budget of $100,000 per issue. The best way, obviously, is to have enough capital to ride out whatever number of issues is likely to be necessary to raise the advertising revenue that would support the production costs.

Depending on where you live, you should be able to get some competing bids from printers and figure your production costs in advance. If there's only one printer in your area, consider that you can deal with printers at a distance through the mail—although most people who publish a magazine like to be physically at the press to catch last-minute errors and problems.

You get the capital from your Uncle Harry, the local bank, or the none-too-shrewd investors with whom you have culled favor. Just don't bet the house mortgage on your ability to make a profit with a magazine.

Publishing Book Excerpts

As publisher of a small magazine, you may be able to purchase an excerpt from a new book for a token fee, as long as bigger publications aren't vying for it. Second-serial reprint rights (after the initial publication), even to work by famous authors, are often available for a hundred dollars.

Small-Magazine Network

The Coordinating Council of Literary Magazines (CCLM) is a nonprofit clearinghouse that assists literary publications. Write to them at 2 Park Avenue, New York, NY 10016. For trade news of the regular commercial magazines we recommend *Magazine and Bookseller* (401 North Broad Street, Philadelphia, PA 19108). And see the Lit Biz Reference Sources for more addresses related to the magazine business.

14 | On the Shelf Between Austen and Zolotow

This chapter gets into the business of bookstore economics from the writer's point of view. Even if you, as author, can't change or otherwise influence this end of the business, it's important that you know the financial realities of publishing your book. Authors have a tendency to be ignorant of the difficulties of doing business as a bookseller or publisher. But the better you understand these related branches of the industry, the better you'll be able to help your publisher and local bookseller sell your book!

Your book makes the long trip to the bookstore from the publisher's warehouse one of three ways: by mail or phone order, via a wholesale distributor, or directly from publisher to store through orders taken by a publisher's representative—a fancy term for a traveling salesperson. But this publisher's rep is as important to the success of your book as the editor was, or more so. The publisher's rep is the industry ambassador, the insider, the reluctant literary agent and direct link between publisher and bookstore. He or she may even advise the bookstore buyer how many copies of your book to order, and enthusiasm for your title among the reps can be an important step toward big orders and sales.

As an author, you can and should:

—get to know your local bookseller(s) on a personal basis; you'll want to autograph books in the store, perhaps, or seek an invitation to meet the publisher's rep;

—get to know the publisher's reps for your area; you may want to ask a rep to "agent" your book to an editor, or if your book's being published, you'll want to plan sales and promotion strategies with your publisher's rep;

—contact the bookstore buyer to restock your book when it's not on the shelf.

Direct Sales by Reps

In practice, reps are often given a quota for their territory on the number of copies they need to sell for each new list and bookstore account. The publishing house conducts sales conferences at which the reps are informed of the company's position and sales "handle," or selling approach, on each new title. Input from the reps at that conference can directly influence how many copies of your book the publisher will print! If the publisher has already decided your novel might be a big seller, it will tell its reps how and *how much* to push it, but often the reps' enthusiasm for a book can enhance the publisher's willingness to invest in it.

The rep then hits the road in his/her territory with a fairly clear notion of which new titles are positioned for enthusiastic promotion. If the publisher is planning a half million copies of a book coming off the press, naturally he'll back it up with appropriate advertising, promotion, publicity, and a whale of a pep talk to the reps. But *each* title should get special attention in the city or region where the author lives, so even a book with a small first printing can catch the attention of your local rep.

A good rep is a personable, articulate, and outgoing type, one who can develop a friendly and trusted relationship with the booksellers on whom he or she calls. With appointments made in advance, the rep goes from store to store, sitting down with each buyer for as long as an hour or two to go over the publisher's latest catalog, make recommendations, and write the order. Over a period of time, by visiting a store twice each year, the rep comes to know the bookseller and what kinds of book that store sells best. If a rep's recommendations have proved reliable and profitable in the past, the bookseller may be willing to go along with them and order accordingly.

Publishers need distributors to be sure, but they retain much more of the price of a book when they deal directly to the stores through their own reps. A distributor needs to get 55 to 60 percent discount in order to make a profit selling to booksellers at 40 percent off. If the publisher sells direct to the store at 40 percent, both bookseller and publisher prosper, and the rap earns a commission above salary.

It often happens that the publisher's rep and the bookseller develop an honest friendship aside from business. As owner of a bookstore, I was regularly feted by certain preferred salespeople. But our expense-account revels always had a serious business side to them. While dining or drinking with the rep I could make arrangements for an author to visit the store and sign books, or get talked into ordering a special counter display of some new paperback, or in turn urge the rep to read a manuscript one of my customers wrote—and possibly take it back to an editor in New York.

MEETING YOUR PUBLISHER'S REPRESENTATIVE

Headquarters approach	Call the publisher at its main office and ask for the name, address, and phone number of the rep in your area, then make direct contact.
Bookseller approach	Ask your local bookseller for a personal introduction to the publisher's rep. (Bookseller reference may get you a more personal reception.)
What to Ask	Start by asking the rep only to *read* a short excerpt from your work, or perhaps read your book proposal/query letter.
Follow-up	If the rep likes your work, he or she may be willing to read the whole manuscript, and/or recommend it to an editor.

Wholesale Distributors

In addition to buying direct from the publisher through the rep (or through mail and telephone order), the bookstores also buy from wholesale distributors. The trend, in fact, is that bookstores are doing an increasing amount of business with wholesalers. Distributors can really help the sales of your book by featuring it and/or promoting it to booksellers. Some of them operate warehouses open to the retailers, who shop for books with a rolling cart just as in a supermarket. As co-owner of a bookstore in Seattle, I made a monthly trip to Raymar Northwest, a giant distributor in Bellevue (a nearby suburb). Its long aisles were stacked with books of all major publishers, and the center aisle featured piles of special-promotion titles—books that Raymar Northwest had decided were of particular appeal. The special visibility these books got virtually assured that they would sell better than most and wind up in all but a few Northwest area bookstores.

Raymar was a trade-book distributor, specializing in hard covers and trade paperbacks, although it also sold mass-market paperbacks. We also used Riches and Adams, a mass-market distributor and magazine wholesaler that dealt *mainly* in rack-sized mass-market paperbacks. The hardcover publisher calls its distributor a "wholesaler," while the mass-market publisher calls that same distributor a "jobber." Mass-market paperbacks are also distributed by magazine wholesalers. Most bookstores have access to these three distinct types of distributors, even if only by mail or telephone contact. These distributors:

—offer the bookseller the convenience of buying titles from many different publishers from a single source;

—sell at more or less the same wholesale discount the publishers themselves offer (40–45 percent is the usual range), so the price to the bookseller is competitive;

—usually require a minimum order, making it inconvenient to order a single copy of a book;

—may be able to provide the books faster than the publisher can, particularly if the bookstore is a great distance from the publisher's warehouse;

usually will accept returns, within the time limits set by
the publishers;
—in the case of jobbers and independent magazine wholesalers, will sometimes provide assorted titles delivered monthly
and remove unsold copies of older titles.

Chain Bookstores

Chain stores can be vitally important to the success of a book.
Independent booksellers have long been complaining that the
big chains are driving them out of business. Giants like B.
Dalton's, Waldenbooks, and Crown Books get a much better
discount on every book because they can order for all their
stores out of one central office and buy in huge quantities. They
can advertise heavily, offer best-sellers at a discount price, and
they're usually well located in shopping malls or downtown
areas.

And if there is a certain sameness to the chain stores (they do
tend to look alike, with the modern fixtures and shopping-mall
ambience), the books are not the same at all. Many franchises
are managed by a local owner, who selects his store's inventory.
If you hand-sell your own book to the local chain-store owner
(who likely will be happy to stock a few copies if you're a local
resident and promise to tell people to buy it there), it might even
help get you into more stores in the chain. If a book does well
with one store in a chain, and the manager reports its success to
the home office, other stores in the chain may order it.

Even if the chain store is not locally owned, it will have hired
a manager who probably has the authority to special-order or
take on consignment a book from a local author, so the tactic
generally works. However, what you really benefit from is selling the national office a large number of copies that it distributes around to its many outlets. Your publisher is probably
wooing Dalton and Walden to order in quantity!

The chains *are* very good when it comes to sensing the public
pulse and following trends in best-sellers. They are sensitive to
what's selling, they communicate within the organization to
their member stores, and they can really help your sales.

Are Small Bookstores Extinct?

There is simply no shaking the industry's gravitation toward the big chains, but we're great lovers of the independent bookshop, one with personality and a distinguished inventory, a friendly owner, a free cup of coffee, and Bach on the stereo. As long as real *readers* exist, the small bookstore will not completely disappear.

Sales Tactics to Booksellers

We've discussed how the wholesalers and reps sell books to the stores. The author can also play a big role.

A: If your book is published by a publisher
1. Visit the bookstore and urge the buyer to contact your publisher's rep and order some copies. Always point out if you are a local resident and/or expect local publicity, reviews, etc.
2. Offer to appear at a book-signing event to which you can invite your friends, family, co-workers, and any special interest groups that might like your book. The bookstore will sometimes pay for a local newspaper advertisement and provide refreshments.

B: If your book is self-published
1. Try to sell it directly to the store. Ask to see the buyer, then deliver your pitch. If you're willing to leave them on consignment, it should be easy to place a few copies on the shelf. If the bookseller has to pay on invoice, she or he is likely to order conservatively.
2. The mail-order approach is popular with both authors and publishers as a way to reach bookstores. Booksellers regularly get swamped with mail advertising for new books, but most of them do read this material, so you've got a chance for a reasonable return.

"I Can't Find It in Any Bookstore!"

What if your book's out, the rep and distributor and chain store have all been properly notified, and yet you just don't see your book in most bookstores you walk into? Thousands of authors will tell you that this is precisely their problem. Nobody can buy the book if it's not on the shelf.

In general, your editor is the first person to go to with questions about how well or poorly you're selling. But there does reach a point after the book's out where the editor can't do much more for it and you, as author, have to carry the ball.

It's permissible to telephone the publisher's rep (whom you should know) or your local book distributor to inquire how your book is doing, as long as you don't harass him or her with repeated calls. Maybe the distributor hasn't stocked your book but would be willing to order a few copies from the publisher; maybe your book's in stock but just isn't moving very fast; maybe you need to do more self-generated promotion (we'll get into the details of self-promotion in the next chapter). It's important to stay calm. As mentioned above, it might be out of your editor's hands at this point (remember, they don't do the actual selling to bookstores or distributors) but you should still try to work with your publisher to correct the problem and, at the very least, inform your editor of your actions so that you maintain a rapport through this crucial period in a book's life. Remember, your editor has every reason to want your book to succeed and sell too.

On the Shelf Between A and Z

You're in the stores. You and every other competing writer from Jane Austen to Charlotte Zolotow, among books of every publisher from Harry N. Abrams' art books to Zebra's romance paperbacks. The casual browser just looking for something to read can pick you up, look you over, take you home. But any bookseller will tell you that more books are sold to people who come in the store looking for a particular title, looking for a book *they have heard of,* than to those who wander in to peruse the new arrivals on the shelf. What you want now is publicity, indeed celebrity!

15 | Self-Promotion, the Writer's Best Friend

Publisher's vs. Author's Promotion

We've established in earlier chapters that if your book is published by a major house, it will have the services of a publicity director and promotion manager. If you publish it yourself, or if it's published by a very small press, you could be the whole of the promotion staff. But even books published by major houses do benefit from the author's self-promotion.

Back in Chapter 9, "The Publishing Process," we were talking about the *launch*—the things your publisher does to publicize, promote, and generally sell your book. If the publisher's done a great job and the book's a hit, you could be one of those lucky authors who just stays home and collects royalties. But chances are if you have the right kind of nonfiction project, or if you're a natural-born media personality, the publisher's launch is going to *include* your getting out in the world to make public appearances, give interviews, do talk shows, charm booksellers . . . in short, help your own cause through self-promotion. Just be sure to inform your editor of your efforts! The editor and local sales rep can get the word out to the house. And you could even find yourself like Callan Pinckney, who made a failure into a success by promoting her book alone after the publisher had more or less given up on it.

A Self-Promotion Success Story

Pinckney is the author of *Callanetics* (written with Sallie Batson), a weight-loss book that hit near the top of the best-seller lists in 1986, although it was published in 1984 (by William Morrow & Co.) and initially didn't sell all that well. It's an exercise and fitness plan that promises you'll get "ten years younger in ten hours," a near-miraculous claim. But the real miracle is how Callan Pinckney turned a mediocre seller into a national sensation.

After Morrow sent the author on a modest publicity tour in 1984 and the first printing of 10,000 copies of *Callanetics* sold out, a second printing of 5,000 copies seemed to be mired in the warehouse. The publisher had done all that seemed possible for the book, but sales had trickled down and the promotion campaign was over. But not for Pinckney herself. She decided to put her own money behind it. She reportedly ran up $1,000-a-month phone bills in her apartment, calling TV talk shows and booking herself into appearances. First, she did a series of TV appearances in her native South; then she got on some shows in New York; then Oprah Winfrey's morning show in Chicago gave her a boost, and eventually she made a big splash on *Donahue*—all through tireless self-promotion. At this writing *Callanetics* has over 300,000 copies in print and is number three on the best-seller list published in my local newspaper.

Following a lively paperback-rights auction, Avon Books bought the mass-market rights to *Callanetics* from Morrow for a reported $187,000 advance, and a videotape version is being made. Of course weight loss and fitness are popular topics, and almost every year brings its new best-sellers in those categories, but *Callanetics* is a best-seller that appears to have succeeded mainly through the author's own never-give-up attitude toward promotion, even when the publisher was satisfied with modest sales. In publishing circles, it's an inspiring story.

A Self-Promotion Sob Story

Not every self-promoting author does as well as Callan Pinckney did. Author Victor Kiam, the owner of Remington Products, spent $1 million of his own money promoting his book *Going for It!*, which, like *Callenetics*, was published by William Morrow. *The New York Times* reported that three months after its publication—and after Kiam spent the money, much of it on radio and TV advertising—the book had not reached the best-seller lists. Morrow had 136,000 copies in print, but the book needed to sell 350,000 copies just to break even.

Agent Julian Bach told the *Times* that *Going for It!* was a big success in England, Australia, and New Zealand, but *Times* reporter Edwin McDowell reported. "[The book's] mixed performance so far has done little to change the traditional book industry view that a best-seller is much more dependent on favorable word-of-mouth publicity than on saturation advertising."

The Rigors of the Road

Self-promotion, as crass as it sounds, is your best friend when it comes to moving your book. You have to be ready to do it with verve and boundless enthusiasm, even if it means loading up your own automobile with books and knocking on radio producers' doors; sleeping on your college roommate's living-room floor; putting up with ignorant questions from radio and TV interviewers who haven't read a word of your book; traveling uncomfortably and staying in sterile hotel rooms; humiliating yourself before every newspaper reporter and college dean you find, and autographing copies of the book with fond regards to any stranger who'll buy one.

Sounds like fun, doesn't it? Well, it is! And as vain and immodest as it is, it probably makes more difference in the selling of books than any other factor. An aggressive author who's out there pounding the media trail, appearing in bookstore autograph parties, giving lectures or demonstrations, generating newspaper stories is definitely the best salesperson for the book. When booksellers hear their customers say "I saw the author on TV," they rush to their purchase-order pad. If two people in a single day come in asking for a book that's been featured on TV, the store will probably order at least a dozen in anticipation of demand.

The ABA Booksellers' Convention

Self-promotion for your book should begin well *before* it is published, and one of the best ways to reach booksellers is at their periodic conventions. The regional Booksellers Associations have annual conventions, but the granddaddy of the form is the national convention of the American Booksellers Association (ABA), held every Memorial Day weekend in a major American city. The ABA is the national trade association of retail booksellers, and its convention is designed to draw headlines and TV news coverage to the book business. Movie stars and Olympic athletes, celebrity authors of books they may or may not have actually written, autograph books for long lines of patient admirers. Ex-Presidents and other politicians give windbag speeches that are covered by all the papers. Everybody deplores the decline of literacy and vows to do something about it.

But the ABA is also like a giant annual clambake for the entire publishing industry. Every major publisher in the country and a large number of smaller ones send representatives; editors, executives, reps, agents, and authors are all there, pressed together with tens of thousands of booksellers, the ABA's membership, in one huge conference center. But the gathering is not open to the public, you can't just walk in and register. You have to be sponsored by your publisher or, if you've self-published a book, pay a substantial amount for exhibitor registration. (Some small presses band together and share a booth.) Contact the American Booksellers Association at the address listed in Lit Biz Reference Sources at the back of this book well in advance of the event.

If your book is soon to come out, the ABA may give you a chance to talk it up with bookstore buyers from coast to coast. If you haven't found a publisher for your book yet, here's an assembly of them, each with a public booth where you can meet editors and discuss your project. If your book is already out in hard cover, you may be searching for a paperback publisher, or you may be autographing books or speaking on one of the many panels. The ABA is simply a circus, but great territory for promoting your work, provided you have a legitimate reason for attending and are disciplined in setting goals for yourself.

You may even get into the pattern of attending the ABA every year. Then you find that you meet the same friends there, good folks that you don't get a chance to see any other time of year, so a great, steaming billowing family reunion takes place. Rumors and gossip are everywhere as people swap tales of the publishing biz. Parties are all the rage, and you are considered lucky if invited to the "in" affairs. Conversations run like this:

"Say, Mary, what parties are you going to tonight?"

"Well, I'm starting at the (mammoth publisher) champagne reception for (movie star author) at the Sheraton Palace, then at eight o'clock (prestigious paperback house) is opening up in the Green Ballroom at the Hilton, but the best party will be after ten at the (noted distributor) Small Presses Ball."

Every publisher worth its salt has to outdo the other in lavishness of partying. With luck you can find oysters on the half shell, caviar, steak tartare, fabulous hors d'oeuvres and pastries, a full cocktail bar and dance band.

Small-Press Fairs

While the ABA annual is the biggest booksellers convention, it is far from the only one. The small-press publishers have their own kind of ABA in the annual New York Book Fair in October. This convention focuses on smaller publishers and always occurs in New York, although its location there varies. In recent years it's met in Madison Square Garden and on Fifth Avenue, covering several blocks, which tells you it's not a small group! The New York Book Fair is the largest single gathering of minor presses and their people, but other major cities also have a small-press book fair, and in some places a library or daily newspaper will sponsor a book fair.

Regional Bookseller Conventions

Many booksellers belong to a regional booksellers association, and the regional group may hold an annual convention, like a mini-ABA. Most of the large publishers sponsor a booth, and small publishers from within the region are there also. Some of the regions cover vast amounts of territory. The Pacific Northwest Booksellers Association, of which I was a member, brought together bookstore owners from all of Oregon, Washington, British Columbia, Alaska, Idaho, and Montana. Their annual convention hosted several thousand people and was a good environment for doing business as it was less hectic than the national convention.

The intrepid author of a soon-to-be or recently published book would do well to get the publisher to sponsor him or her at *every* booksellers' gathering within reach. But the regional book fair could be more useful and accessible to you than the national ABA.

Working the Convention Floor

The publisher and author have different methods of working the book convention crowd. At a trade fair the publisher really wants to make its pitch to booksellers, in hopes of getting their orders for its new books; at a book fair open to the public, the emphasis shifts to selling books at retail. The publisher sets up a booth to display its titles and is anchored to that location, doing business with those who come by. The author, on the other hand, is free to roam the convention hall, striking up conversations with assorted booksellers and publishers (identified by their color-coded name tags) he or she may encounter. Wear a name tag that boldly announces the title of your book, and it doesn't hurt to pass out leaflets, flyers, or other advertisements for it.

Blurbs

Earlier we defined blurbs as comments on the book, usually from other authors or noted critics. These endorsements are best received well before publication in order to be helpful. They are useful in attracting the attention of both reviewers and potential readers when featured in the publisher's press release and advertisements and on the jacket or cover of the book.

Ideally, your blurb comments will come from established, famous authors to whom you or your editor has mailed a copy (in galleys) in fervent hopes of a comment. You can help your editor by thinking up writers to approach for a blurb or offering to write the pleading letters yourself. Certain authors will be more inclined to help if another author, rather than an editor, appeals for help. Some writers are generous about giving out blurbs, while others fiercely refuse to participate in the custom.

Quite a few authors turn out to have "blurbed" *each other's* book so you have to ask yourself if it's an "I'll scratch your back and you scratch mine" situation. The really world-famous authors are swamped with requests for blurbs and don't have time to read all the books people send them, but some of them may be worth the try if your material is related to their interests. A beginning baseball writer, for example, might try to fetch a blurb from Roger Angell of *The New Yorker*, America's premier baseball writer; for a children's book you might approach Beverly Cleary or Maurice Sendak. Midlist authors and locally famous ones may be more generous with comments, since they are not as often approached and may be seeking the publicity value in having their names printed on the jacket or in the ads for another writer's book.

Criticism and Reviews

There's nothing better than good reviews and nothing worse than none. In other words, even a bad review is preferable to being ignored by the press. Most people don't read or retain the negatives. Your publisher should take care of mailing review copies to book reviewers for newspapers and magazines and forwarding clippings of your reviews to you, but here also the author can be instrumental in generating reviews and other kinds of press. Do you know of local, community, or special-interest national magazines or newspapers that would be interested in your book but may not be known to your publisher? Call them up and get the name of the editor or reviewer to whom the book should be sent! Then get your publisher to mail it out. You may send a follow-up letter a month later if no review has been forthcoming—something polite along the lines of "We sent you a copy of the book last April and are wondering if we may look forward to the pleasure of your notice or review?" Be prepared to work closely with the publicist assigned by the publisher to your book.

You'll be surprised at the variety of publications that might review your book. If you, or even your spouse, works for a company that publishes an employee magazine, you're a cinch for a mention at least. If your college and/or high school puts out an alumni newsletter, your former classmates would love to read about your book and may even run out and buy one. Special-interest publications with smaller circulations may have more room to pay attention to your book than *Time* or *Newsweek* would, although of course you'd rather be in *Time* than in the *Podunk Prairie Press*. And *The New York Times Book Review* published on Sundays continues to wield enormous power and influence. A good review there can be one of the key elements that "make" a new book.

Wherever your good reviews appear they can always be re-printed and quoted selectively in advertising and further promoting of the book. Some publishers go to disgraceful lengths in taking a reviewer's comments out of context so that a mediocre review sounds like a rave. Watch out when you see a publisher using a single word from a review. "Original!"—*Washington Post*. The full quote might be: "This novel is certainly original, but disappointing."

Use good reviews and blurbs to full advantage in advertising or writing to every possible outlet for the book you can afford to contact.

The "Big Book" Campaign: Different Kinds of Media

A big-book campaign calculated to push a title on to the best-seller list will frequently include an exhausting schedule of personal appearances by the author on TV and radio talk shows as well as the campus and lecture circuit. But even a lesser-budgeted campaign can easily result in your being booked on the talk shows if your work is of some topical interest and you are at ease in front of the microphone or on camera. And then there is the considerable world of print journalism to pitch, exploit, or otherwise use to your advantage. Newspapers and magazines don't print book reviews only; most also run feature stories, interviews, or news coverage when a book or an author's story warrants it. Let's consider these different kinds of media and how to use each in self-promoting your book.

The Publisher-sponsored Publicity Tour

If your book has a publicity-tour budget, the scenario unfolds like this: The publicity director at your publisher's office sets up a schedule of author appearances, hands you a sheaf of tickets and itinerary of hotel reservations with stern instructions to save your cab receipts and restaurant tabs if you want to be reimbursed, and pushes you out into the cold. (If you're lucky, however, your publicist might accompany you or the publisher may appoint its local reps to escort you around.)

Assuming you're on your own, you are suddenly in Buffalo, Syracuse, or Rochester rumbling around in taxis, trying to live up to a schedule that has you in a different place every ninety minutes. The publicist will appreciate your absolute punctuality, as will the TV and radio hosts, many of whom work with only minutes to spare, and if you fall behind schedule by as much as only fifteen minutes, you *must* call ahead to your next appointment to advise. Some days, through no personal fault but a succession of things like bad traffic, weather, and other acts of God, the beleaguered author is late for every appointment in succession and spends the whole day frantically calling ahead to later commitments.

Exhausting it is. Far from being given star treatment, the author in many cases will be handed a plastic cup of coffee. You're lucky if it's real coffee, not instant. You sit outside the TV studio, nervously chewing on a Danish or smoking cigarettes while waiting to get on the air. Then it's two or three minutes of mindless banter under the blistering lights and you're off again, replaced by a Colgate-Palmolive commercial. Then you jump into a cab headed for the next ordeal.

Over the course of doing this kind of promotion for a couple of weeks, the author may feel lost at times, despairing of the efficiency of this system (Are these talk shows really selling my books? Why aren't the books readily available in every store? How come *The Frugal Gourmet* gets the window display and I get buried in the cooking section? etc. etc.) and just plain frazzled by the constant exposure and interrogation. It's worth hanging in there. We know for certain that broadcast exposure ties in well to the sale of books, and don't you feel a moral obligation to jolt those TV viewers out of their seats and into the nearest bookstore?

TV and Radio Talk Shows

TV and radio shows are frequently hungry for talent. They pay nothing to the author or publisher, you appear on their shows for the publicity value, so the shows are getting free entertainment and the book free exposure. The interviewer who questions you about the book will almost certainly give you a chance to review the questions before going on the air, and will almost never have *actually read* the book. That used to annoy me until I realized that an interviewer who hasn't read the book can only spout complimentary phrases off the publisher's own promo sheet, which provides me with an opportunity to steer the conversation.

I wrote a book for Atlantic Little Brown called *Cosmic Profit*, a study of entrepreneurs who'd started their own businesses, and the publisher arranged a tour that included numerous radio and TV appearances. On one radio station in Philadelphia I was interviewed by a woman who started off by saying, "You call your book the *Cosmic Prophet*. Is this a book about astrology, or are you promoting the thoughts of some guru?" She continued in that vein, confusing "profit" for "prophet," until I set her straight. Her embarrassment was so profound that I had to talk nonstop for a minute until she recovered.

The worst thing on a talk show is dead air. It helps if you can talk a blue streak even when the questions you're being asked are less than intelligent. Whatever else happens, make sure that you and the host or hostess repeat the title of the book as often as possible and, if on TV, show the cover to the audience at home. The odds of your publisher being able to book you on the network shows with big ratings, shows like *Good Morning America* and *Donahue*, are fairly slim, but if you can get on a show like that you're virtually guaranteed to acquire a raft of new readers. TV talk shows produced by a local station for its own viewing market are a comparatively easy mark. Many of them are hungry for material and are overlooked by publishers trying to mine the national shows. You could be of service pointing out the smaller ones to your publicity director. And local radio is even easier to penetrate.

Radio-Phone Publicity

Using the telephone to call in to radio shows is extremely effective publicity, as well as inexpensive. It's relatively easy to convince your publisher to undertake this type of publicity if they haven't thought of it themselves. The publicist makes arrangements with radio talk shows all over the country, and you are interviewed on the shows just as if you were in the studios in person. If it's a call-in type of show, listeners can call and ask you questions by dialing their local radio station, even though you may be thousands of miles away. The station invariably pays for the call, sometimes using an 800 or WATS number. The best part of radio-phone publicity is that you often don't have to leave your own home to do it!

But radio-phone interviews, like in-person interviews, are scheduled tightly, so you *must* be at your phone at the time prearranged by the publicist. If you're "good on the phone," you can do a half dozen to a dozen such interviews in a sitting. If you're working out of your home, by the way, be sure to advise your friends and family *not* to call you during times when you expect to be conducting radio-phone interviews. Generally the radio station has to call you, get you on the line, and hold you there for a few minutes before the hosting interviewer comes on. Then you're live in Cleveland, or wherever the show is broadcasting from.

Print-Publicity Ideas

Here are a few ideas for print publicity beyond what your publisher is probably doing to generate reviews and "off the book page" coverage:

—Both publisher and author should have a good supply of press releases (printed on the publisher's letterhead) and send them out liberally to any newspapers or magazines that might be interested.

—Consult *Bacon's Publicity Checker* (Bacon Publishing, 14 East Jackson Street, Chicago, IL 60604) for names of editors and reviewers.

—Is your book a news item, aside from the book review section? Do you make a "startling revelation" or "throw fresh light" onto a question or issue? If so, your book may be a news item suitable for the paper's main section, with a juicy headline. A wide cross-section of books do qualify for this distinction. Newspapers love to run items like "Fat Women More Passionate Lovers, New Book Asserts" and "Stress May Lead to Insomnia, Researcher Says." If in any remote way your nonfiction book can be said to contain information that has not previously been brought to the public, it's *news*. Leak it to the wire services and newspapers via a press release and/or telephone calls to the editorial department.

—What about you, personally, is interesting or unusual? You, as author, could be a good *feature item* for the newspaper's "Life-style" or "Arts" section. If you were a ship captain or war hero, there's an adventure feature. If you're a mother and wife who has just sold her first novel to the movies, that's a feature story of another kind, the Cinderella variety. If you've traveled widely, or have come out of extreme poverty, or learned to write in English as a second language after fleeing persecution in a foreign land . . . if you're different or interesting, as many authors are, you may be feature material. Issue a press release with glossy black-and-white photo attached.

—Does your novel take place in a historical setting or a geographical location that makes it of news interest to a particular interest group or region? Get in touch with that local historical society and regional newspapers. There's no guessing what might follow.

Lecture and College Circuits

Libraries, religious groups, civic clubs, and schools all sponsor lectures by authors. The speakers' circuits are also terrific vehicles for getting the word out. Lectures and college readings usually pay the author an honorarium, but addressing a luncheon meeting of a civic club may not. These promotional opportunities are likely to be viewed as small potatoes by your publisher and hence fall most naturally into the area of self-promotion. Whether paid or not, you want the exposure of speaking in public, which can also generate newspaper copy. (*Do* make sure the press is invited by means of a press release and cover letter, which you can help the sponsoring organization prepare.)

Professional speakers' bureaus exist in every major city. They book authors onto the lecture trail in exchange for a percentage of the payment. It's worth looking into if your subject is educational or of particular appeal to a campus audience or a broad general public. Only the foolishly modest or wildly rich author would neglect to bring a pile of fresh books to sell after the lecture or reading.

Promotional Giveaway Ideas

Fresh promotional giveaway ideas crop up at every ABA and other booksellers' conventions. Everything from T-shirts to aprons and tote bags can be imprinted with your promotional message. Publishers sponsor contests, give away matchbooks and pencils, and advertise books with 800-number TV/telephone pitches. But you, the author, should be able to come up with fresh ideas that relate to your book specifically. If you've written a cookbook, you might want to offer sample bites of your favorite dishes from a portable kitchen set up in the bookstore next to a pile of hardcover copies. You might peddle your travel book through travel agency offices and in airport newsstands. The Dodgers' one-time flaky outfielder, Jay Johnstone, sold his autobiography in the stands at Dodger Stadium in L.A. until the team made him stop; his risqué adventures with wine and women were considered unfit for family consumption.

Ask yourself (or ask your publisher): What can we offer for free as a giveaway to stimulate sales of the book? Are you prepared to pay for it yourself if the publisher doesn't think it's an appropriate use of promotional dollars?

Bookstore Promotion

We've made frequent reference to the bookstore autograph party in previous chapters, but it seems worthwhile to add a few thoughts here because the bookstore appearance is still the average author's favored way of promoting a book. The autograph party falls under the realm of self-promotion because in most cases the author (not the publicist) makes the arrangement with the local bookstore.

To make your autograph party as successful as possible, pay attention to these details:

—Plan the party far enough in advance to allow time for your publisher to ship an adequate supply of books, and for newspapers and magazines to run your press release and/or advertisement.

—Have plenty of copies of the book on hand—leftover unsold copies can be returned to the publisher.

—Try to use a bookstore that has or can create an open space for partygoers to stand around and chat.

—Always serve some kind of beverage, preferably inexpensive boxed white wine (less staining than red wine if spilled) and a nonalcoholic alternative like cider. Food is optional, but keep it simple—cheese and crackers are popular.

—In addition to press publicity, promote the event to your personal network; invite everybody in your circle of friends, colleagues, family, etc., with a printed invitation in the mail.

Great Self-Promotion, a Parting Tale

While the Callan Pinckney story is a great example of self-promotion for a nonfiction how-to book, one of the best publicity stories for a novel was that of Famous All Over Town, *published by Simon and Schuster and written by "Danny Santiago." Santiago was presumed to be a young Hispanic writer. He won the* Redbook *magazine fiction award and was nominated for the Pulitzer Prize for* Famous All Over Town, *the story of a Mexican-American juvenile delinquent growing up in the tough barrio of East L.A. But just after the book came out it was revealed that Santiago was really Daniel James, an aristocratic seventy-seven-year-old living in a posh castle in the Carmel Highlands on the coast of California. James had been a radical in his youth and was blackballed during the 1950s Hollywood Red scare. His career as Daniel James the writer was destroyed so he took up the "Danny Santiago" name as a disguise but didn't publish* Famous All Over Town *under that name until 1984.*

Continued

Continued

The news of Danny Santiago's true identity had been kept secret from the author's own agent and his publisher! He'd dealt with them entirely through the mail. The story broke in the New York Review of Books *in an article by James's friend, John Gregory Dunne (who had the author's full cooperation), and promptly landed on page one of* The New York Times, *was featured in the weekly news magazines, on network television, and in wire-service news items around the world. Dan James's thirty years of hiding paid off.* Famous All Over Town *has been sold to the movies.*

16 Owning a Bookstore

The Author as Bookseller

As an author, you may be enough of a book lover that you find yourself interested in owning or managing a bookstore. Very often the clerk who sells you a book is writing one on the side. Whether or not you get into the retail end of the business, however, it's helpful to understand the terms, mechanics, difficulties, and profit factors. They affect the performance of your book and the amount of your royalty check.

Some booksellers tell me that any chapter on "owning a bookstore" ought to be Chapter 11, the Federal Bankruptcy Act. No, it's not that bad of course. I owned a series (not exactly a "chain") of three bookstores for seven years in the 1970s and, at their best, they provided a living in the dignified company of upright volumes. At their worst they provided a pile of debts beyond payment, nightly stress and anxiety, divorce, bank repossessions, and corporate despair.

But a bookseller is a special breed of person. She or he simply loves books and can't imagine selling automobiles or insurance or something more sensible. With very careful management, and quite a few nonbook sidelines at higher profit, even a small independent bookseller can succeed in business.

Markets and Locations

Location is as important to a bookstore as it is to any other kind of retail operation. The bookstore will never make it if it's put on Skid Row or way out on some lonesome valley road. (I did the former and have a close friend who did the latter. We opened our second Seattle bookstore in a downtown waterfront zone that was under restoration and lived to regret it.) A successful bookstore should be located in a spot where the reading public is already bound to be—in a shopping center, near a university, next door to a post office. Of course the location will also have a strong impact on the kind of books it can sell. A bus-station paperback rack deals largely in best-seller fiction, while a college bookstore stocks fine-art books, quality fiction, and textbooks.

Knowing the Market

After running a bookstore for a while one gets a very clear idea of what sells and who buys what. And from that the bookseller can make reasonable guesses about what will sell in the future. This skill of prognostication is perhaps the key to successful bookselling. One doesn't want to either (a) get stuck with a lot of books that don't sell in the particular store or (b) run out of a popular title that customers really want. If the store orders a lot of books that don't sell, it's tied up capital in deadwood. Most of these copies, of course, can be returned to their respective publishers, but the store loses money (many publishers give back slightly less than what was paid) and has to do a ton of paperwork, pay for shipping, and wait for credit. Run out of a popular book and you've lost a sale; chances are the eager reader can find the book in another store sooner than the small bookseller can get it back in stock.

If you're wondering how well your book will sell in the local market, you need go no farther than your local bookseller for a professional opinion.

Discounts

The primary concern of a bookseller is of course how much he or she has to pay for the book. That is determined by the publisher's discount. A common standard for a hard cover is 40 percent, so that a $10.00 book costs the bookseller $6.00. That's an apparent profit of $4.00, and at first glance it would seem that with a 40 percent markup *and* the option of returning books that don't sell, one should be able to make a decent living. Yet most booksellers report their actual margin of profit at 1 to 2 percent, if they turn a profit at all.

Paperback discounts and returns procedures differ from hard covers. It depends on the publisher and the type of paperback. The more expensive trade paperbacks offer a higher discount and are returned entire; mass-market paperbacks give a smaller discount and may require the bookseller to tear off the cover, discarding the book, for returns.

In any case, every point on the publisher's discount is crucial to the bookseller. The difference between buying at 40 percent off or 42 percent off is 2 percent, or *double* the profit if the store operates on 2 percent profitability. If one can get the discount up to 45 percent, one is making a substantially better margin. One way to get a higher discount is, of course, purchasing in greater volume, and here the independent bookseller is at a hopeless disadvantage compared to the chains. Shipping expense is also a major factor in the cost; usually the bookseller has to pay, but some publishers will offer free shipping with a prepaid order.

The reason cards, calendars, stationery supplies, and other nonbook items often "carry" a bookstore is that they come with much better discounts—typically 50 percent—and are returnable, with shipping paid by the supplier.

The (Dismal) Economics of Bookselling

The margin of (more or less) 40 percent is eaten away by costs of inventory, overhead, taxes, salaries, insurance, and common, unavoidable losses, such as books that get shopworn or shop*lifted*. First, the store has to pay for the books that are on the shelves, including thousands that won't sell in a year's time and will eventually be returned. Meanwhile, those nonsellers represent money tied up and earning no interest. Most states also have an inventory tax, so the nonsellers are hurting double when taxed on their face value. Overhead, such as rent and utilities, can be a killer; if a bookseller is paying high rent to be located in a busy shopping center, the bookstore must more or less sell books hand over fist all day to break even. Salaries cut further into the margin, although bookstore clerk salaries are among the lowest in the country.

This insight into the economic weakness of publishers' principal outlets should offer you, as an author, some idea of the economics of Lit Biz as a whole. You can work more effectively as an author if you don't have the attitude that your publisher is rolling in money and trying to cheat you. How healthy can publishers be if they're waiting to collect from a community of outlets as fiscally anemic as booksellers?

How Booksellers Find Their Merchandise

Publishers' catalogs are must reading for the bookseller. Whether the books are to come from a distributor, directly by mail order from the publisher, or through a rep, the bookseller's first news of it is the announcement in the catalog. I never had time for Faulkner once I started reading Farrar, Straus & Giroux catalogs. As we've already discussed, authors want their books featured toward the front of the catalog, with a full page to catch the bookseller's eye. But a careful manager will read every new book announcement, small or large, searching for those titles that are likely to sell to his or her specific customers.

Returns and Credits

As we've noted, returns constitute a fair amount of hassle to booksellers as well as publishers and absorb costly employee time and energy. Every publisher has a different return policy, so the bookseller has to keep impeccable records. Some publishers will accept returned books within six months of the invoice date (the date it was bought, not the date received); others give a year, or even eighteen months. One has to establish a filing system that calls to attention the titles of books that are up against their returns deadline every month. (More and more of this record-keeping is computerized, but plenty of bookstores still keep manual files on every publisher and supplier. Within two or three years the accumulated paper constitutes a fire hazard.)

The books to be returned must be in "salable condition," a highly idiosyncratic designation. (The exception, as noted, is mass-market paperbacks, which are returned with stripped covers.) Books that have been on the shelf for months may well be battered, dog-eared, or torn. One takes these losses stoically, it really can't be helped, but makes a record of them for income-tax deduction purposes. After assembling all the books going back to a particular publisher, the bookseller may even be obliged to fill out a form and use a special mailing sticker so that the publisher can identify the account and issue proper credit. It can take a month just to get that sticker sent, but sometimes the publisher's rep can provide it during the sales call.

Once the returns are shipped it will take a month or two for the publisher to credit the store. Some also nick the discount a little—books bought at 40 percent off, let's say, are bought back by the publisher at 38 percent. In any case, the bookseller is glad to be rid of the unsold copies and you, as the author, must sadly count black sheep who've returned to the fold.

Sidelines, or How the Croissant Saved Faulkner

After all that gloom there has to be a good side or two. We've mentioned that nonbook items often make the difference between surviving or perishing in the book business because they come at a better margin and don't sit on the shelf as long. These "sidelines" have lately come to include espresso coffee, pastries, audio and video cassettes, computer disks, little high-intensity lamps, stuffed Garfield the Cat dolls, posters, greeting and blank note cards, trendy Japanese pens, T-shirts, aprons, Hello Kitty stickers, and just about anything else one could think of. As a bookseller, one has to make serious decisions about how much of this stuff the store can handle. Our original bookstore took a haughty attitude and refused to stock sidelines or even popular paperbacks we had deemed unworthy or trash literature. After a few years of suffering with low incomes, however, we ended up operating a store inside the Seattle Aquarium that sold key chains, film, touristy T-shirts, and so forth with abandon.

But sidelines aren't the only silver lining. There's Christmas, the bookseller's salvation. While all retail stores do more business at Christmas, the impact on bookstores is spectacular. It's been estimated by the American Booksellers Association and regional booksellers associations that the average bookstore can do 40 or 45 percent of its annual business in the month of December alone. If you think about it, that means that in December the store does about *ten times* its normal daily business. It's a wonderful feeling to carry those sacks of dollars to the bank—three times a day. Books and calendars make excellent, affordable gifts and people who wouldn't buy a book if their lives depended on it any other time of year will do so at Christmas. And they'll buy a heavy, full-color, expensive coffee-table book!

Remainders

Special outlets can bring new sales to the store. Remaindered hardcover books, which are available from specialized distributors, can be offered on a bargain table near the front of the store and serve to lure readers in. One has to be careful with remainders, however, since they are not always returnable and occasionally may arrive in less than mint condition.

Building a Loyal Clientele

One of the great joys of bookselling is the feeling that one really is serving the reading needs of the community and making a contribution toward literacy. The bookseller gets to know his or her regular customers by first name, and knows what kinds of books they like to read. A loyal customer will even wait several days or weeks to get a book by special order that might be available instantly in some other shop. To build that kind of loyalty you have to treat the reader well, cheerfully assist in locating a book, consistently find and stock outstanding titles, and patiently listen to everyone who walks in the door. For some reason bookstores attract their share of nut cases, but we must be polite. What I liked best about owning a bookstore was the contact with young people who love to read. Such a child still exists in America, thank God. I loved the teenagers who hung out in the balcony, fervently discovering Kerouac for two hours before sheepishly buying a greeting card. To hear them talk about favorite books and writers, to see the excitement in their eyes as they describe the thrill of reading Thomas Wolfe's *You Can't Go Home Again* . . . almost took me back there.

17 | Lit Biz 201, 301, and 401

We had a joke at the original Lit Biz 101 class. If Lit Biz 101 consisted, as it did, of twenty students working with a faculty member, then:

Lit Biz 201 is five students working with a professional faculty member on some specific project, such as an issue of a literary magazine or an anthology;

Lit Biz 301 is a one-on-one experience between student and faculty member, a pure collaboration on a piece of writing or publishing project;

Lit Biz 401, you have sexual relations with your faculty member and publish a book of your own;

Lit Biz 501, the graduate level, you're too neurotic to have sexual relations with your faculty member and too blocked to finish your new book.

Seriously, now that you're nearing completion of Lit Biz 101, you should consider some of the many ongoing courses and programs for writers. The book review section of your Sunday newspaper has listings of writers' seminars, gatherings, and/or readings and autograph sessions taking place in your area, and *The Writer* magazine (in its May issue each year) features listings of writers' conferences to be held at various places around the country.

Writers' Associations

Definitely consider joining one of the many writers' associations that are listed in our Lit Biz Reference Sources. Remember that there are special associations for particular types of writing, like the Mystery Writers of America, the Academy of American Poets, the Society of Children's Book Writers, etc., ad infinitum.

Lit Biz 101 heartily thanks both The Authors Guild and the American PEN Center for their good work for authors. Be warned, however, that you cannot become a member of PEN unless you are nominated—write to them for details. And don't confuse The Authors Guild, which represents book authors, with the Writers Guild of America (WGA), which represents screenwriters.

Writers' associations not only help organize and protect authors' interests, they also provide pertinent trade information through newsletters and mailings.

Writers' Workshops

A writers' workshop can be extremely valuable to you if you make the most of it. You don't need to be a published author to attend the typical workshop, but some of the better ones will ask you to submit a sample of your writing on which your admission will be based. The very famous ones, such as the University of Iowa summer gathering, are difficult to get into, but most are fairly open if you've got the price of tuition.

Try to find a workshop that is sponsored by a university or other reputable nonprofit organization, or one whose faculty includes published authors you respect. The greatest value in a writers' conference may be the interaction between the beginning writer and the seasoned pro. Some authors are good teachers and can effectively communicate to an audience how they write and how to improve your writing; others simply offer a sympathetic ear and a critical reading. When you're trying to break into a writing career, nothing is as helpful as a real editor or author's comments on your work. And attendance at a variety of these gatherings, or at the same one year after year, can result in the kind of networking—helpful in getting published, "blurbed," and promoted—we mentioned earlier.

There's also something marvelous about what happens when you throw a crowd of writers together in one place. The exchange of ideas, conversation, and arguments stimulates the mind, exhilarates the soul, and activates the thirst. Clink! You might learn a lot from a famous author who's had a few drinks. Or you might just have a good time.

Writers' Colonies

Colonies are places where writers can retreat and work without interruption or distraction. Most are located out in the country, typically on the estate of some deceased benefactrix. Some colonies are listed in the PEN book *Grants and Awards Available to American Writers* and *LMP* and quite a few of them are receptive to unpublished or beginning writers. If you've been thinking that you'll never get that book finished until you can have your own little cabin in the woods, breakfast delivered on a tray, a typewriter and stack of paper and *no* phones, *no* job, *no* kids bugging you, then a writer's colony may be the answer.

> *A classic example of a good one is the MacDowell Colony in New Hampshire. It's in a beautiful setting, far from the city. Each writer gets a little house and has absolute privacy in which to work. Every night a communal dinner is served in the big dining room. The cost of staying there is modest and scholarships are provided to the needy writers. Nobody is allowed to bother you, and you can't even bring your own spouse or be visited by friends (unless the spouse also qualifies as an artist or writer). An admissions committee makes the decision on who gets to enroll there based only on the writing samples you send in and not on your publishing history (or lack of it). I've known a number of writers who benefited from staying at MacDowell, but I backed out of a reservation to go there myself because I fell in love just beforehand and they wouldn't let me bring along the object of my affections.*

Correspondence Schools

Writing classes offered by mail are numerous, too, and some of them are legitimately educational and helpful. You will find these courses advertised in the back pages of all the writers' magazines. Many colleges and universities offer some type of creative writing course by mail and give college credits for successful completion. For a list of those schools and what kind of courses they offer, write to the National University Continuing Education Association, at 1 Dupont Circle, Washington, DC 20036.

Grants

Grants and awards are of enormous importance to the working writer. Many a fine novel or book of poetry would have been impossible without the assistance of a foundation or government National Endowment for the Arts (NEA) grant to the author. Unfortunately, there is never enough to go around in the way of grant money, so the competition is fairly stiff, but perseverance and a methodical commitment to applying for grants can pay off. Even more unfortunately, the Reagan Administration in 1987 was seeking to cut back the NEA's allotment.

The most comprehensive source of information on grants that we know of is the aforementioned *Grants and Awards Available to American Writers*, published by PEN. The most prestigious writing award in the world is the Nobel, in the United States the Pulitzer. The leading writer's grant is the NEA's Literature Program fellowship, worth $20,000. In 1986, according to author and Literature Director Frank Conroy, 94 fellowships were awarded out of 1,866 applications, which works out to 1 in 20 odds, better than the state lottery for sure. (But you have to already be published in order to qualify. Write to the NEA Literature Program, Washington, DC 20506.)

Teaching Writing Instead of Writing

Teaching provides a living to many aspiring writers. Not to put the knock on English teachers and professors, without whose influence we might not have become writers, but did you ever wonder how many of them have an unpublished manuscript, usually a novel, in the desk drawer? Come out!

Ultimately, nobody can teach you how to write well. One can teach the rules of our language: spelling, punctuation, grammar, syntax, and so forth. You can learn the ropes of Lit Biz, the commercial end of things. But to write well you have to first have the talent and then the self-discipline, willpower and/or tenacity to practice and perfect the skill—maybe for years, maybe for a lifetime. And you have to have something to say—a story to tell, a tale so beautiful, strong, and real that it won't stay inside but demands to be written and subsequently read.

Pomp and Circumstance

Congratulations on completing this mini-course of study! What follows is a good sampling of Lit Biz Reference Sources you can use to further crack into the writing game. If you've read every chapter of the book, you should have a fairly basic but comprehensive understanding of all aspects of our business, from the actual creation of your work to its publication and marketing to the reader.

As an author myself, I sincerely appreciate all the writers who care enough to keep the craft alive. We live in perilous times, with illiteracy on the rise. If you have further questions, don't hesitate to write to me at PO Box 22438, Carmel, CA 93922. Like most writers, I like to get mail and try to answer all of it.

Our Lit Biz 101 students were "graduated" with a genuine parchment diploma. You, dear reader, deserve at least as much. Write and get published; live long and prosper.

Special Section: How to Submit

For All Categories of Writing

SUBMIT IN STYLE: Use 8½-by-11 inch, standard typing paper; manuscript should be clean, freshly typed, and free of errors and misspellings; always include a stamped, self-addressed envelope for return of material; always include a copyright notice on the title page of your material, whether or not you have already obtained the copyright.

Nonfiction

(See Chapter 1, "Nonfiction, or Facing the Facts," and the sample query letters therein.)

Includes:

Anthologies	Ghostwriting
Autobiography	How to
Biography	Humor
Collaborations	Journalism
Cookbooks	Travel
First-person narrative	

Step 1: Researching the Market

- Examine publisher's catalog, advertisements, existing titles, research publishers through *Literary Market Place, Writer's Market,* etc.; search for a publisher who is already involved in producing the kind of book you are writing.

- Importance of contacts: Pursue any connection to an editor working in your field of nonfiction.

Step 2: Initial Query

- One-page query letter describing your nonfiction book project and including length, delivery date, and production details (photos, illustrations, etc.), as well as your previous publishing credits.
- Query follow-up: If you have not heard from an editor after one or two months, follow up with a letter asking for a reading and response to your query.

Outline and Sample Chapters

Step 3: Book Proposal with Sample Chapters.

- If editor responds favorably to your query letter and asks to see more material, send a careful outline with specific chapter-by-chapter description of your nonfiction book, plus several sample chapters, not more than fifty pages total. Expect a reading time of one to three months before reply.

Step 4: Negotiation

- If the house has decided it wants to publish your book, either the author or agent negotiates with the publisher on the terms of the contract. Or the publisher may hold out the possibility of publication if specific revisions are made, or ask to see a larger section of the manuscript, or the whole book, before it decides whether to offer a contract.

Fiction

(See Chapter 2, "Fiction, or Making It All Up," for in-depth discussion and sample query letter.)

Includes:
The novel
The short story
Genre fiction

Step 1: Researching the Market

- Use *LMP* and *Writer's Market*, etc., to know which publishers and magazines are buying fiction; stay abreast of the fiction market and best-sellers; read what's out there!
- For genre fiction (science fiction and fantasy, mystery, Gothic, romance, Western, etc.) locate the publishers who specialize in the genre.
- Importance of contacts: Pursue a connection to any editor working with fiction, contact the editors of novelists whose work you admire.

Step 2: Initial Query

- One-page query letter describing your novel (with plot summary) and including length, delivery date, and your previous publishing credits. Compare your work to that of an established novelist writing in your field.
- Query follow-up: If you have not heard from an editor after one to two months, follow up with a letter asking for a reading and response to your query.

Step 3: Sample Chapters or Finished Manuscript

- Usually sample chapters or a finished ms. is requested by an editor who has responded positively to your query. Most publishers will need to see a novel finished and entire before they can decide whether to publish it, but follow the editor's instructions on how much to submit at this stage.
- The short story is always submitted to a periodical in finished form. A proposed book of short stories may be represented by several sample pieces.
- Expect a reading time of one to three months for reply.

Step 4: Negotiation

- The author or agent negotiates with the publisher over the terms of the offered contract, exactly as in nonfiction. Motion-picture rights may be more important to the novel than to the nonfiction book.

Poetry, Children's Lit, and Screenwriting

(See Chapter 3, "Poetry, Children's Lit, and Screenwriting," and sample query letters therein.)

Poetry

Step 1: Researching the Market

- Read the poetry magazines, quarterlies and anthologies to study their tastes in poetry; submit your poetry to magazines and publishers whose existing poetic output inspires you.

Step 2: The Query Letter

- This letter or letters, in the case of poetry, is likely to be more personal than that for nonficton or fiction. Always include one or more completed poems and ask for the editor's critical assessment.

Step 3: Negotiation

- Payment for poetry is likely to be small or nonexistent except in terms of free copies of the book or magazine. However, published poets do qualify for grants and honorariums.

Children's Literature

Steps 1 through 4 (under Fiction): As above (depending on whether project is fiction or nonfiction) with these special considerations:

Age Level
- Always establish the age level of the work; age level is determined by the publisher's standards of vocabulary and reading skills in the average youngster.

Illustrations
- Do not submit illustrations with the query letter. Submit illustrations with the manuscript only if the editor has agreed to consider them. Send copies, never the original art, in the mail, until and unless you are delivering art under contract.

Screenplays

Major differences in submitting are:

Script Agent
- The query letter is likely to be written to a script agent rather than directly to a producer.

Treatment
- A brief treatment, or summation of the motion-picture screenplay, is sent to generate interest before submitting the full script. However, the producers or studio must see the entire script before deciding whether to buy the rights to it.

Magazines and Newspapers

(See Chapter 12, "Newspapers and Magazines, for Ink-Stained Wretches," and sample query letter therein.)
Major differences in submitting are:

Query letter
- The query letter is brief and may lead to an article assignment via telephone discussion with the editor.

Topicality
- Timing is of the essence: The magazine or newspaper article should be planned to be of topical, timely interest when it is scheduled to appear. The writer must submit on deadline!

Negotiations
- Negotiations for payment are simpler, with many publications offering a single-page "agreement," like a brief contract, and "kill fee" if your piece is not used.

Additional Comments About Submitting

Multiple Submissions
- Multiple submissions are usually acceptable, but always advise the editor in your cover letter if you are submitting your work to more than one publisher.

Photocopies
- Never submit your original manuscript until you are delivering under contract and have safely made a copy for yourself; otherwise submit copies and retain the original.

Perseverance
- Submit often and don't give up easily. When your work is rejected try to resubmit it (with a fresh cover letter) to another publisher as soon as possible.

Special Section:
Simple Things Nobody
Ever Told You

A Miscellany of Odd Facts About Lit Biz

• DON'T REJECT REJECTION. If you get a rejection letter from an editor or publisher, don't push it. Don't write back demanding a fuller explanation of why you were rejected or asking to get a second reading. Go on to resubmit your work to another house.

• DEVELOP A RELATIONSHIP WITH YOUR PUBLISHER'S BOOKKEEPER or royalty manager. This person pays your royalties and may well be the only stable contact you keep at a major publishing house, since editors change jobs with frequency.

• USE YOUR PERMANENT ADDRESS and type it on the material you submit. If you are likely to change your residence, use a post-office-box address or the safest address for your immediate family.

• THE AVERAGE TYPED PAGE, on 8½-by-11 inch paper, double spaced, with reasonable margins, contains about 250 words and is roughly equal to one page of a finished book.

$$100 \text{ pages} = 25,000 \text{ words}$$
$$200 \text{ pages} = 50,000 \text{ words}$$
$$300 \text{ pages} = 75,000 \text{ words}$$

• MAKE COPIES OF EVERYTHING YOU WRITE and retain your original manuscript.

• KEEP A CALENDAR OF LITERARY EVENTS to help you improve your contacts in the industry. Using your local newspapers and our Lit Biz Reference Sources, make a note of and plan to attend: booksellers' conventions and gatherings, writers' workshops, bookstore autograph parties, seminars and classes, readings, anywhere editors and other writers are likely to be.

• USE THE MANUSCRIPT RATE. Manuscripts and books qualify for a special postal rate, special fourth class, which is much cheaper than first-class mail and still relatively swift and safe. At this writing, the rate is 69 cents per pound.

• COPYRIGHT ANYTHING but a title or idea. Under the new copyright law, you can take out a copyright even on unpublished material. Always include a copyright line on your material before mailing a copy out: © Copyright 19__, by _____ author's name.

• DON'T SEND ORIGINAL ART through the mail. Send copies unless you are delivering art under contract, in which case be sure to insure the shipment appropriately.

• MULTIPLE SUBMISSIONS are acceptable as long as you advise the editor and publisher that you are submitting the same work simultaneously to more than one house.

• A STAMPED SELF-ADDRESSED ENVELOPE is your best guarantee of return of your materials.

• SUBMIT PHOTOS WITH MAGAZINE ARTICLES but not with book proposals; the average magazine will be more interested in an article that comes with photos or at least indicates that photos will be forthcoming.

• KEEP RECEIPTS. Much of your travel and office expenses may be tax deductible if you are a self-employed writer.

• MAKE A TAPE RECORDING whenever possible when conducting an interview. It will be your most reliable record of what was stated. If your interview subject refuses to be taped, keep lengthy and complete notes until at least three years after publication of the interview.

• NONPROFIT, TAX-EXEMPT STATUS is available to literary publications that publish poetry, fiction, and creative nonfiction, according to IRS standards under Section 501(c)(3) of the tax code.

• SUBMIT ON DISKETTE. Certain publications and book publishers today appreciate your submitting the work on computer diskette. Always make a hard copy (a printout on paper) as well.

• SPECIALIZE. Develop your reputation in one or more specific fields of writing—travel, high tech, cooking, etc. Approach the specialty publishers organized by categories in *LMP* and *Writer's Market*.

• AUTHOR'S PHOTO is the author's responsibility to provide to the publisher. Not all books use an author's photo, and not all publishers pay for one. Check with your publisher. Choose your best shot and send it well in advance of day of publication, while your book is in production.

• COPYRIGHT CERTIFICATE is generally obtained by the publisher; check your contract to be sure. INTERNATIONAL STANDARD BOOK NUMBER (ISBN) is the publisher's responsibility to provide.

• KEEP YOUR PRESS KIT available on file, including copies of your reviews, a press release describing your book, and a photo of yourself. Send it out whenever a publicity opportunity arises. (But don't duplicate the efforts of your publisher in this regard.)

• DON'T GIVE UP. If you believe in yourself as a writer, don't be discouraged by any number of rejections. Many well-known writers suffered extensive rejection before breaking into print.

Addenda:
Lit Biz Reference Sources

A. Other Books and Periodicals

Adventures in the Screen Trade
by William Goldman
Warner Books, 1983

American Library Directory
R. R. Bowker Co., 1986
Revised and updated biennially

American Odyssey: A Bookselling Travelogue
by Len Fulton and Ellen Ferber
Dustbooks, Paradise, California, 1975

The Art of Literary Publishing
by Bill Henderson
Pushcart Press, 1980

Aspects of the Novel
by E. M. Forster
Harcourt, Brace, and Co., 1956

The Author's Handbook
by David Bolt
Interbook, 1986

Ayer's Directory of Publications
Ayer Press, Bala Cynwyd, Pennsylvania
Published annually

Bacon's Publicity Checker
Bacon Publishing Co., Chicago Illinois
Revised annually

Beginning Writer's Answer Book
Edited by Kirk Polking and Rose Adkins
Writer's Digest Books, 1984

Book Reviewing
Edited by Sylvia Kamerman
The Writer, Inc., 1978

Books in Print
and
Subject Guide to Books in Print
R. R. Bowker Co.
Published annually

Books: The Culture and Commerce of Publishing
by Lewis A. Coser, Charles Kadushin, and Walter W. Powell
Basic Books, 1982

The Business of Book Publishing: 35 Experts on Every Phase and Function of the Publishing Process
edited by Elizabeth Geiser with Arnold Dolin
Westview Press, Boulder, Colorado, 1985

Chicago Manual of Style
13th edition, 1982
University of Chicago Press

The Complete Book of Scriptwriting
by J. Michael Straczynski
Writer's Digest Books, 1982

The Complete Guide to Self Publishing
by Tom and Marilyn Ross
Writer's Digest Books, 1985

The Complete Guide to Writing Non-Fiction
American Society of Journalists and Authors
edited by Glen Evans
Writer's Digest Books, 1983

Contemporary Authors
Gale Research Co., revised and updated, 1986

Copy-Editing: The Cambridge Handbook Desk Edition
edited by Judith Butcher
Cambridge University Press, 1983

COSMEP Catalogue
edited by Christine Paffrath
International Association of Independent Publishers
San Francisco, California
Annual

The Craft of Interviewing
by John Brady
Random House, 1977

Editor and Publisher International Yearbook
Editor and Publisher
Annual

The Elements of Style
by William Strunk, Jr., and E. B. White
3rd edition, 1986
Harper & Row

Gadney's Guide to 1800 International Contests, Festivals and Grants in Film & Video, Photography, TV-Radio Broadcasting, Writing, Poetry, Playwriting & Journalism
by Alan Gadney
Festival Publications, Glendale, California, 1980

Getting Published: The Writer in the Combat Zone
by Leonard S. Bernstein
William Morrow, 1986

Grants and Awards Available to American Writers
14th edition, 1986–87
American PEN Center

Handbook of Nonsexist Writing for Writers, Editors and Speakers
by Casey Miller and Kate Swift
Harper & Row, 1981

How to Be Your Own Literary Agent
by Richard Curtis
Houghton Mifflin Co., 1984

How to Get Happily Published
by Judith Appelbaum and
  Nancy Evans
NAL Plume, 1982

*How to Publish, Promote and
  Sell Your Own Book*
by Robert L. Holt
St. Martin's Press, 1986

*How to Self Publish Your Own
  Book and Have the Fun and
  Excitement of Being a Best Sell-
  ing Author*
by Melvin Powers
Wilshire Publishers, 1984

How to Sell What You Write
by Jane Adams
Perigee Books, 1985

How to Write a Book Proposal
by Michael Larsen
Writer's Digest Books, 1985

*In Cold Type: Overcoming the
  Book Crisis*
by Leonard Shatzkin
Houghton Mifflin Co., 1983

*International Directory of Little
  Magazines and Small Presses*
edited by Len Fulton and Ellen
  Ferber
22nd edition, 1986
Dustbooks, Paradise, California

Law and the Writer
edited by Kirk Polking and
  Leonard S. Meranus
Writer's Digest Books, 1985

*Literary Agents of North
  America, 1984–85*
Author Aid Associates, New York,
  New York

Literary Agents: A Writer's Guide
by Debby Mayer
Poets and Writers, Inc., 1983

*Literary Agents: How to Get
  and Work With the Right One
  for You*
by Michael Larsen
Writer's Digest Books, 1986

Literary Market Place
 R. R. Bowker Co.
Revised and updated annually

Make More Money Writing Fiction
by James Frenkel
Arco, 1984

*Mass Market Publishing in
  America*
by Allen Billy Crider
G. K. Hall Co., 1982

Maybe You Should Write a Book
by Ralph Daigh
Prentice-Hall, 1977

*MLA Handbook, for Writers of
  Research Papers, Theses, and
  Dissertations*
by Joseph Gibaldi and Walter S.
  Achtert
2nd edition, 1984
Modern Language Association

*New York Times Manual of Style
  and Usage*
edited by Lewis Jordan
Revised edition, 1982
Times Books

*On Writing Well: An Informal
  Guide to Nonfiction*
by William Zinsser
3rd edition, 1985
Harper and Row

The Poet's Handbook
by Judson Jerome
Writer's Digest Books, 1986

Printing It: A Guide to Graphic Techniques for the Impecunious
by Clifford Burke
Wingbow Press, Berkeley, California, 1974

Publicity for Books and Authors: A Do It Yourself Handbook for Small Publishing Firms and Enterprising Authors
by Peggy Glenn
Aames-Allen Publishing Co., Huntington Beach, California, 1985

Publishers Weekly

Pushcart Prize: Best of the Small Presses
edited by Bill Henderson
Pushcart Press
Annual

Readers' Guide to Periodical Literature
H. H. Wilson Co.
Revised and updated annually with supplements published semimonthly

Simple and Direct: A Rhetoric for Writers
by Jacques Barzun
Harper & Row, 1985

Small Time Operator: How to Start Your Own Small Business, Keep Your Books, Pay Your Taxes and Stay Out of Trouble
by Bernard Kamoroff
revised edition, 1986
Bell Springs Publishing, Laytonville, California

The Travel Writer's Handbook
by Louise P. Zobel
Writer's Digest Books, 1984

Word Processing Book: A Short Course in Computer Literacy
by Peter A. McWilliams
Ballantine, 1984

The Writer's Directory, 1986–88
St. Martin's Press
Published biennially

The Writer's Handbook
edited by Sylvia K. Burack
50th edition, 1986
The Writer, Inc., Boston

Writer's Market (Current Year)
edited by Bernadine Clark
Writer's Digest Books
Published annually

Writers at Work: The Paris Review Interviews
edited by George Plimpton
Viking
Published annually

Writers Guild of America Theatrical and TV Basic Agreement
Writers Guild of America, New York and Los Angeles, 1981

The Writing Business: A Poets and Writers Handbook
by the Editors of *Coda*
Poets and Writers, Inc.
Pushcart Press, 1985

Writing for the Soaps
by Jean Rouverol
Writer's Digest Books, 1984

B. Associations, Organizations, and Services for the Writer

Academy of American Poets
177 East 87 Street
New York, NY 10028

Poets who have *not* had a book of poems published are invited to apply for the annual Walt Whitman Award ($1,000 and publication of your book).

American PEN Center
47 Fifth Avenue
New York, NY 10003

Publishers of *Grants and Awards Available to American Writers*, U.S. headquarters of an international writers' society offers emergency loans to published authors in need. Membership is by nomination only.

American Society of Journalists and Authors
1501 Broadway, Suite 1907
New York, NY 10036

Members are professional free-lance writers. The society has regional chapters in southern and northern California, New England, Washington, D.C., and Madison, Wisconsin, and publishes a Code of Ethics and model Letter of Agreement for free-lance magazine articles. Membership is by application to the Membership Committee and open to professional free-lance writers of nonficton.

Associated Writing Programs
Washington College
Chestertown, MD 21620

An educational service agency, it publishes a list of creative writing programs in American colleges and universities.

Author Aid Associates
340 East 52 Street
New York, NY 10022

Provides listings of agents (its own membership of about 400) to whom you may submit your query or manuscript. (*Literary Agents of North America*, see Lit Biz Reference Sources above).

Author's Guild, Inc.
234 West 44 Street
New York, NY 10036

The closest thing we have to a union. The Guild seeks to protect the rights of authors worldwide, provides emergency loans, hosts international conferences, publishes an "ideal" literary contract from author's point of view. More than 5,000 professional writers are members; membership open to writers who have published a book within seven years (self-published books excluded) or were published in a periodical of general circulation within a year and a half. Apply to the Membership Committee.

Coordinating Council of Literary Magazines
2 Park Avenue
New York, NY 10016

The CCLM has a number of programs to assist writers and literary magazines, including a newsletter and several grants. Magazines that publish mainly fiction, poetry, and creative nonfiction and are organized as nonprofit and tax exempt, qualify for membership and/or assistance.

Copyright Office
Information and Publications Section
Library of Congress
Washington, D.C. 20559

Write here for the forms with which to copyright your work, published or otherwise.

COSMEP
International Association of Independent Publishers
P.O. Box 703
San Francisco, CA 94101

Small-press publishers' trade association, publishers of the COSMEP catalog and other books; displays its members' publications at book fairs and booksellers' conventions.

Independent Literary Agents Association
c/o Elaine Markson Literary Agency
44 Greenwich Street
New York, NY 10011

Another source for names of literary agents to whom you may submit your work. This association of agents is smaller than the Author Aid Associates and special for agents who work independently of the large agencies.

International Writing Program
University of Iowa
School of Letters
Iowa City, IA 52242

The prestigious Iowa Writers Workshop is administered by the university and open to students whose writing sample meets the standards of the admission committee. Write for details.

ISBN (International Standard Book Number)
1180 Avenue of the Americas
New York, NY 10036

Every published book has, or should have, an ISBN. It's easy to register via a simple form and identifies the book for ease of reference worldwide. Your publisher takes care of getting it; if you self publish a book, apply by mail for an ISBN.

Modern Language Association
575 Lexington Avenue
New York, NY 10011

Publishers of the definitive *MLA Handbook* and an academic association of English professors dedicated to preservation of and correctness in the language.

Mystery Writers of America, Inc.
150 Fifth Avenue
New York, NY 10011

Sponsors the Edgar Allen Poe Award and is very active in helping its members. Chapters in New York, New England, the Midwest, northern California, southern California, and Colorado, with an at-large chapter for others. Affiliate membership available for unpublished writers.

National Association of Science Writers, Inc.
P.O. Box 294
Greenlawn, NY 11740

Membership open to those who write science-oriented material for publication; association offers classes, a job placement service, and publishes a directory of member free-lance science writers. Associate membership available.

National Endowment for the Arts
Literature Program
1100 Pennsylvania Avenue NW
Washington, DC 20506

Grantors of the most significant writers' fellowship for published authors in the nation, as well as fellowships for literary publications and translations. NEA is a federal agency; the literature program director is novelist Frank Conroy.

Poetry Society of America
15 Gramercy Park
New York, NY 10003

Membership is by election by the Executive Board. Members submit five poems for consideration; associate members include critics and teachers and honorary members are invited by the board to join. The society exists to promote poetry and aid poets in America.

Romance Writers of America
5206 F.M. 1960 West
Suite 208
Houston, TX 77069

Science Fiction Writers of America
68 Countryside Apartments
Hacketstown, NJ 07840

Sponsors the Nebula Awards for excellence in science fiction and fantasy writing. Holds conventions, publishes a newsletter (*Forum*); membership open to anyone who has had a science-fiction piece published.

Society of Authors' Representatives
P.O. Box 650
Old Chelsea Station
New York, NY 10013

A major source of listings of agents. Founded in 1928, this association of agents offers a brochure. Send a stamped, self-addressed envelope.

Society of Children's Book Writers
P.O. Box 296
Mar Vista Station
Los Angeles, CA 90066

Supports excellence in the children's book field though awards, conferences, and publications. Full membership is open to anyone who has had a children's book published within six years; associate membership open to children's book writers, unpublished or published.

Western Writers of America, Inc.
Meridian Road
Victor, MI 59875

Sponsors the WWA Spur Awards for the best Western writing. Active members must have three Western books or twenty-five Western stories published; associate members have one or five articles published on Western themes. Services include a members' magazine.

Writers Guild of America East
555 West 57 Street
New York, NY 10019

Writers Guild of America West
8955 Beverly Boulevard
Los Angeles, CA 90048

The national union of scriptwriters; you must have sold a script to be eligible for membership. Covers the fields of radio, TV, and motion pictures. The WGA is the only writers' union with actual legal clout; it maintains basic agreements with all major production studios, and represents virtually all the screenwriters working in Hollywood.

Glossary of Lit Biz Terms

ABA American Booksellers Association, the trade association of book retailers; sponsors the annual ABA convention.

ABRIDGMENT Short, or edited, version of a book published in volume form.

ADULT BOOKS Sexually explicit, or so-called pornographic, literature.

ADVANCE Amount of money paid to an author out front as a kind of guarantee or loan against future royalty payments on a book.

AGENT Person who represents the author in negotiations with the publisher and other businesses and takes a commission on the author's earnings.

BACKLIST Publisher's term for books available and in print year after year beyond initial publication.

BOOK CLUB Membership buying club that acquires the rights to selected recently published books and offers them in special editions at reduced prices, by arrangement with publisher and author. Those with the largest memberships are the Literary Guild and Book-of-the-Month Club.

BOUND GALLEYS Printer's proofs of the book bound together. Bound galleys are sent to reviewers and authors from whom an endorsement "blurb" is requested.

COLD CONTACT Contacting an editor (usually by mail or phone) without prior introduction; unsolicited query letter or submission of manuscript.

CONDENSATION Shortened or edited version of a book in volume form, sometimes bound with other books in one volume.

CONTRACT Legal agreement between publisher and author setting forth the terms of publishing a book or other version of author's work.

COPYRIGHT Legal ownership of original written material.

CREATIVE PROSE Usually fiction or "creative nonfiction," including essays and autobiography, but not including journalism.

DEFAMATION Damage to the reputation of a person or persons by publication of untrue or libelous material.

DELIVERY Presentation of a manuscript from author to publisher. Publisher determines acceptability of manuscript thereafter.

DOT MATRIX Basic kind of computer printer and type formed by the placement of multiple dots on the page.

DUMMY A pasted-up set of large white cardboard "boards." The pasteup artist glues the type down in place on the boards, exactly as it should appear in print. The dummy is the model that is used to create the final boards from which the book is printed.

DUST JACKET Detachable paper wraparound jacket to a hardcover book.

FEATURE Newspaper story separate from main news section; includes interview, "style," or "perspective" coverage.

FICTION Not fact. Invention, made-up story or novel.

FIRST SERIAL Rights to publish written work for the first time in a periodical or newspaper, one time only.

FLUSH LEFT Copy that lines up on the left margin.

FOREIGN RIGHTS Rights to publish written work originally published in English into foreign languages for sale in other countries.

GALLEYS Printer's proofs of the book on long sheets. The author reads the galleys, checking for typos.

GHOSTWRITING Writing on behalf of another person, as in writing the autobiography of a celebrity.

HACKERS Computer users; those who write computer programs and compose on word processors.

INDEPENDENT (or ID) Magazine distributor who also distributes mass-market paperback books.

JOBBER Paperback distributor; sometimes called "wholesaler."

KILL FEE Sum paid to an author whose assigned magazine article has been ultimately rejected for publication; usually about a third of the full price offered for the article or story.

LAUNCH Process of marketing a new book before and during its time of publication, including publicity, promotion, advertising.

LEAD TIME Time required by a newspaper or magazine to prepare an article for inclusion.

LETRASET (See also Prestype.) Type that is pressed onto paper from a film original.

LIBEL Damaging a person's reputation by publishing untrue and defamatory statements or allegations.

LINE In publishing terms, the kind of books or category of publications that a given publisher offers.

LMP *Literary Market Place;* perhaps the most comprehensive annual listing of publishers, editors, etc.

MASS-MARKET PAPERBACK Popular, rack-size (6 ¾-by-4 ¼ inch) paperback that receives widespread distribution—from airports to drugstores to bookstores.

MECHANICAL The final master copy on boards, which is photographed and then printed.

MIDLIST Position publisher assigns book deemed to have modest sales expectations—not a best-seller.

MODEM Device linking the computer with telephone for phone-generated transmission of messages and/or copy.

MOVIE RIGHTS Rights to adapt written material for film presentation.

MULTIPLE SUBMISSIONS The practice of submitting a manuscript or sample to more than one editor or publisher at a time.

NOVELIZATION Creating a novel from an existing script of a film or television production.

OBSCENITY Written or other matter which appeals to prurient interest and lacks any social value.

OPTION CLAUSE Clause in the literary contract by which the author grants the publisher the right to make the first offer to publish author's next book-length work.

ORIGINAL PAPERBACK A book published for the first time in paperback, with no preceding hardcover edition.

OVER THE TRANSOM See Slush.

PAGE PROOFS Printer's proofs of the book set up in pages, as the final book will appear.

PERFECT BINDING A kind of glue binding for trade paperbacks.

PERSONAL APPEARANCE Author's appearance in public or on TV or radio media for the purpose of promoting the book.

PICA Measurement of type size: regular body type in a book is usually from 6 to 10 picas. An inch-tall headline or chapter head might be 24 to 30 picas.

PLAGIARISM The act of reproducing another's thoughts or work in writing, claiming it to be one's own original work.

PLATES Metal sheets by which pages of the book are mechanically reproduced on the press.

PRESTYPE See Letraset. Type that is pressed onto paper from a film original.

PUBLICIST Arranges publicity for author and book; includes writing press releases and booking author tours.

PW *Publishers Weekly* magazine, the trade journal of the publishing industry.

QUERY Letter to an editor describing the writing work an author wishes to submit for consideration.

RADIO-PHONE Promoting a book by talking on radio shows via long-distance telephone connection.

REMAINDERS Copies of the book remaining unsold when it goes out of print.

RETURNS Books returned to the publisher by the bookstore or distributor as unsold leftovers.

REVERSION Process of returning rights to the author when a book has gone out of print.

REVIEW COPIES Books given away to reviewers and newspapers for critical comment. No royalties are paid on these copies.

RIGHT JUSTIFICATION Copy that lines up on the right margin.

RIGHTS Legal term meaning ownership of written work and its derivatives and the enjoyment of its proceeds.

ROYALTY Sums of money paid to a writer for published work, usually based on a percentage of retail cost of the book and usually paid out twice a year.

SCRIPTWRITING Writing for the movies or TV in script form.

SELF-PUBLISHING Publishing or arranging and paying for the printing of one's own work.

SIGNATURE A section of book printed but not yet bound or folded—the number of pages that can be printed on one large sheet before cutting and folding. The folded section of a book is then bound together with other signatures either by sewing or glue.

SIMULTANEOUS PUBLICATION Publishing of a book in both hard cover and paperback at the same time.

SLUSH Unsolicited manuscripts that arrive at a publisher's office for publication consideration.

SOFTWARE "Program" usable and readable on a computer. The software is the actual system that tells the computer (hardware) how to produce your manuscript. The computer is like a stereo system, the hardware being the record player, the software the disk.

SPECS Specifications. These are instructions from the designer to the typesetter. The designer marks up your manuscript with specs indicating headline sizes, body text, choice of typeface, etc.

STATEMENT Formal accounting of royalties due and/or payable to author from publisher.

TERMS Agreed-upon payments and percentages of rights between author and publisher.

TERMINATION End or discontinuation of contractual agreement between author and publisher.

TRADE PAPERBACK Full-size paperback book, larger than rack size and frequently of same dimensions as hard cover but with quality soft-cover binding.

TYPO Error made in the typesetting by the printer.

VANITY PRESS Publisher that charges author a fee for the printing and binding of book.

VETTING Process of searching for legal problems or liabilities in a manuscript.

WARRANTIES Guarantees made by author to publisher of the legality and propriety of the manuscript.

WIDOW A single line of type at the end of a paragraph that gets carried over to a fresh page.

WGA Writer's Guild of America. See Appendix B in Lit Biz Reference Sources.

WORD PROCESSING Writing with computer equipment.

INDEX

Abridgments, 77
Accounting, 81–83, 105
Advance, 53, 72
Advertisements, 92–93, 128, 145
Advertisers, magazine, 161–62
Agents, 54, 92, 112–16
    activities of, 112–13
    finding, 113–14
    multiple submissions by,
        115–16
    nontraditional, 114
    publisher's rep as, 114–15
    for sale, 114
American Automobile Associa-
    tion (AAA), 8
American Booksellers Association
    (ABA) convention, 176–77
American Express, 8
American PEN, 5, 40, 196, 197
". . . And Ladies of the Club"
    (Santmyer), 149
Angell, Roger, 179
Another Roadside Attraction
    (Robbins), 32–33
Anthologies, 11–12
Antioch Review, 154
Arbuthnot, May Hill, 48
Art, 9–10
Atlantic, The, 18, 28, 41, 154

Atwood, Margaret, 31
Author-author disputes, 101
Author-publisher disputes, 100–101
Author's copies, 83–84, 106
Author's disclaimer, 24–25
Author's grants, 61–62
Authors Guild, 55, 196
Author's indemnifications, 64–65
Author's warranties, 54, 62–64,
    99–100
Autobiography, 7
Avon Books, 44, 174

Bach, Julian, 175
Backlist, 139
Bacon's Publicity Checker, 183
Bantam Books, 11, 44
Batson, Sallie, 174
Beacon Press, 13
Bernstein, Carl, 3, 96
Best Books for Children,
    48
"Big Book" campaign, 180–86
    bookstore promotion, 185–86
    lecture and college circuits,
        184–85
    print-publicity ideas, 183–84
    promotional giveaway ideas,
        185

"Big Book" campaign (*continued*)
  publisher-sponsored publicity
    tour, 181–82
  radio-phone publicity, 183
  TV and radio talk shows,
    182–83
Biography, 7–8
Black Lizard Books, 35
Blues, 123
Blume, Judy, 44
Blurbs, 178–79
Bly, Robert, 39
Body's Symmetry, The (Porche),
  39
Bombeck, Erma, xviii
Book clubs, 56, 78
Bookkeeping, 105
Bookpeople, 43, 145–46
Book proposal, 19–20, 21
Bookstore economics, 166–72
  authors and, 171, 185–86
  chain bookstores, 170
  direct sales by reps, 167–68
  out of stock books, 171–72
  small bookstores, 171
  wholesale distributors, 169–70
Bookstore ownership, 188–94
  author as bookseller, 188
  building a loyal clientele,
    193–94
  discounts, 190
  economics of, 190–91
  finding merchandise, 191
  knowing the market, 189
  markets and locations, 189
  remainders, 193
  returns and credits, 191–92
  sidelines, 192–93
Bradbury, Ray, 28
Braille editions, 76
Burke, Clifford, 147
Burroughs, William S., 96

Callanetics (Pinckney), 174
Capote, Truman, 2–3
Cassady, Neal, 96
Catalog announcement, 127–28

Chain bookstores, 170
Chicago Manual of Style, The,
  124
Children and Books, 48
Children's Book Council (CBC),
  46–47
Children's literature, 43–48
  age level, 44–45
  finished manuscript, 46–47
  how to submit, 203
  illustrations, 47–48
  query letter, 45–46
  trends in, 48
Cleary, Beverly, 44–45, 179
Coles, John, 111
Collaborations, 4, 5
College circuit, 184–85
Commodore computers, 119
COMPAQ computers, 119
Competing work, 91–92
*Complete Book of Scriptwriting
  The,* (Straczynski), 49
Computers, 119–21
Connell, Evan S., 141
Conroy, Frank, 198
Contacts, 17–18, 26–27, 115
Contracts, 52–93
  abridgments, 77
  accounting, 81–83
  advances, 72
  advertisements, 92–93
  author's agent, 92
  author's copies, 74, 83–84
  author's delivery of manuscript,
    65–67
  author's grants, 61–62
  author's indemnification, 64–65
  author's revisions, 67–68
  author's warranties, 62–64
  book clubs, 78
  braille editions, 76
  competing work, 91–92
  conclusion, 93
  copyright, 70–71
  defining terms of, 53–54
  direct mail order, 74
  editorial services, 67–68

Contracts (*continued*)
  foreign language editions, 80
  good, fair, 56–58
  interpretation, 91
  large discount sales, 76
  option to publish next work,
    90–91
  overstock and remainders,
    75–76
  performance and miscellaneous
    rights, 81
  promotional excerpts, 77–78
  publisher's acceptance of
    warranties, 64
  publisher's performance, 68–70
  purpose of agreement, 60
  reasonable, 60–61
  reprint editions, 78–79
  royalties, 73–76
  serial rights, 76–77
  small reprintings, 74–76
  subsidiary rights, 55–56, 76–81
  termination of, 84–90
  textbook sales, 79–80
Conventions, 176–78
Cookbooks, 11, 12
Coordinating Council of Literary
    Magazines (CCLM), 165
Copy editor, 118, 122, 124–25
Copyright, 54, 61, 70–71, 98–99
Correspondence schools, 198
Cosby, Bill, 1
Cosmep Catalog, 142
Cosmic Profit (Mungo), 182
Cosmopolitan, 154
Cover, 122, 123, 124, 136
Cover letter, 20
Creative Arts Book Co., 143
Creative nonfiction, 5–6
Creative States, 160, 162
Criticism and reviews, 179–80
Crockery Cookery, 12
Cult of personality, 25–26

Day of publication, 130
Defamation, 24–25, 94–96
Delivery, 54, 65–67

Delivery date, 21, 22
Dell Publishing, 14, 44
Denver Quarterly, The, 154
Designer, 122
Detro, John, 7
Dick, Philip K., 35
Dillard, Annie, 5–6
Direct mail order, 74
Discipline, 36
Discounts, 76, 190
Distribution, 168
  magazine, 163–64
  major publisher, 132
  poetry, 43
  secondary, 144–45
  self-, 148
  small presses, 142
  wholesale, 169–70
Doctorow, E. L., 12
Dollarhide, Jerome, 144
Donahue, 174
Dry It, You'll Like It
    (MacManiman), 11
Dummy, 123
Dunne, John Gregory, 187
Dutton Co., E. P., 134–35

EasyWriter, 120
Editions, 54
Editor, 133–34
  copy, 118, 122, 124–25
  friendly, 143–44
  losing your, 134–35
  magazine, 158
  as target, 14–15, 26
Editorial content of magazines,
    160–61
Editorial services, 67–68
Ehrlich, Gretel, 18
Electronic bulletin boards, 121
Ellis, Don, 143
Energy-sink, 36–37
Ephron, Nora, 96
Epson computers, 119
Esquire, 28
Even Cowgirls Get the Blues
    (Robbins), 33

Excerpts:
  in magazines, 158–59, 165
  promotional, 77–78
Expenses-paid travel, 108

Family Circle, 154
Famous All Over Town (Santiago), 186–87
Famous Long Ago (Mungo), xxi
Farber, Thomas, 4
Feast or famine, 111
Fiction, 24–37
  author's disclaimer, 24–25
  contacts, 26–27
  cult of personality, 25–26
  energy-sink, 36–37
  finished manuscript, 31
  first novel, 31–32
  genre fiction, 34–35
  how to submit, 201–202
  learning from mistakes, 33–34
  in magazines, 154
  muscling into print, 37
  paperback originals, 32–33
  pornography, 35
  query letter, 29–30
  reaching the editor, 26
  reading what's out there, 27
  second novel and beyond, 33
  short stories, 27–29
  trends in, 30–31
  writer's block, 36
Fictional nonfiction, 12
Fiction Collective, The, 32
Field, Syd, 49
Finished manuscript, 30, 46–47
First novel, 31–32
First-person narratives, 6
Floppy disks, 120–21, 137
Follow-up, 20
Forbes, Kathryn, xvii
Foreign rights, 55, 61, 62, 80
Free and damaged books, 74, 83–84
Fringe benefits, 106–107
Frohmer's, 8

Galleys, 123, 125, 126
Genre fiction, 34–35, 137
Getaway, The (Thompson), 35
Ghostwriting, 3–5, 112
Gifford, Barry, 143
Ginsberg, Allen, 39, 96
Giveaway promotions, 185
Going for It! (Kiam), 174–75
Good Housekeeping, 154
Grants, 198
Grants and Awards Available to American Writers, 197, 198
Graphic Arts, 148
Great Railway Bazaar, The (Theroux), 8

Hall, Donald, 39
Handmaid's Tale (Atwood), 31
Hard cover or paperback, 137–38
Harper's, 28
Heartburn (Ephron), 96
Heller, Joseph, 97
Hell of a Woman, A (Thompson), 35
Hennings, Carol Steinbeck, 7
Henry Holt & Co., 18
Heyerdahl, Thor, 8
Hinton, S. E., 44
His Way (Kelley), 7
Holst, Spencer, 28
Howl (Ginsberg), 39
How-to books, 10–11
HP Books, 12
Hughes, Howard, 100
Humor, 9
Huxley, Aldous, 103

Iacocca, Lee, 1
IBM, 100, 119, 120, 122
Illustrations, 22, 47, 135
In Cold Blood (Capote), 3
Indemnities, 64–65, 99–100
Independent Literary Agents Association, 113
Index, 123, 126
Insurance, 110
Intangible benefits, 110

Nonfiction (*continued*)

International Copyright Convention, 61, 62, 71

International Directory of Little Magazines and Small Presses, 142

Irving, Clifford, 100

Jacket, 122

James, Daniel, 186–87

Johnstone, Jay, 185

Journalism, 2–3

Kaypro computers, 119

Kelley, Kitty, 7

Kerouac, Jack, 28, 96

Kiam, Victor, 174–75

"Kill fee," 104, 152, 157–58

Lady Chatterley's Lover (Lawrence), 97

L'Amour, Louis, 35

Large discount sales, 75

Launching a book, 127–29
  brochure or advertising copy, 128
  catalog announcement, 127–28
  positioning, 128
  promotion planning, 129
  publicity planning, 128–29
  self-promotion and, 173

Laurel, Alicia Bay, 144

Law, the, 94–102
  author-author disputes, 101
  author-publisher disputes, 100–101
  copyright protection, 98–99
  if you get sued, 102
  libel and defamation, 24–25, 94–96
  obscenity, 96–97
  publisher-publisher disputes, 102
  warranties and indemnities, 99–100

Lawrence, D. H., 97

Lead time, 104

Lecture circuit, 184–85

Letraset, 147

Levant, Dan, 2

Libel, 24–25, 94–96, 99

Liberation News Service, xx, xxi, 12

Library of Congress, 54, 71, 98

Limitation on income, 105

Literary Agents of North America, 113

Literary contracts, *see* Contracts

Literary Market Place (LMP), 13, 26, 28, 107, 113, 153, 157, 197

Living on the Earth (Laurel), 144

Ludlum, Robert, 1

Lunches, 107–108

McDowell, Edwin, 175

MacDowell Colony, 197

McGraw-Hill, 16, 100

Maclean, Norman, 149

MacManiman, Gen, 11

Mademoiselle, 154

Madrona Publishers, 2, 141

Magazine and Bookseller, 157, 165

Magazines, 152–59
  articles as book proposals, 154–55
  collections from, 104–105
  doing business with, 157–58
  editors, 158
  excerpts from, 158–59
  fiction in, 154
  how to submit to, 204
  paying the rent and, 152
  payment, 159
  query letter, 155–56
  researching the market, 153
  rights, 154
  types of, 157
  see also Publishing your own magazine

Major publishers, 131–40
  advantages of, 131–33
  backlist and midlist, 139

Major publishers (*continued*)
 control over your manuscript, 136–37
 covers, 136
 editors, 133–35
 hardcover or paperback?, 137–38
 jumping from small to, 144
 production blues, 135–36
 small presses vs., 140, 141–42
 trade vs. mass-market paperbacks, 138–39
Manuscript into type, 117–26
 computers and softwear, 119–21
 control over, 136–37
 copy editing, 124–25
 electronic bulletin boards, 121
 ideal manuscript, 117–18
 index, 126
 printers, 121
 problems with, 135–36
 production schedule, 122–24
 timetable deadlines, 126
 typesetting, 125–26
 typewriters, 121–22
 word processors, 118–19
Massachusetts Review, The, 28
Mass-market paperbacks, 138–39
Matsen, Ric, 40–41
Maugham, W. Somerset, xix
Mechanical, 123
Meese, Ed, 97
Michaels, Leonard, 28
Michener, James, 1
Midlist, 139
Miller, Henry, 8, 97
Miller, Richard, 12
Minor, Bill, 28
Mistakes, learning from, 33–34
Modern Language Association, 124
Money and perks, 103–11
 accounting and bookkeeping, 105
 expenses-paid travel, 108
 feast or famine, 111
 fringe benefits, 106–107
 intangible benefits, 110
 limitation on income, 105
 magazine and newspaper collections, 104–105
 pensions and insurance, 110
 publisher's lunch, 107
 retirement, lack of, 111
 royalty collection, 103–104
 selling your own remainders, 108–10
 work-related deductions, 106
Monson, Dianne L., 48
Montana Books, xxii
Morris, Jan, 8
Morrow & Co., William, 174, 175
Mother Jones, 162
Movie rights, 55, 81
Multiple submissions, 115–16, 204
Muscling into print, 37
Mystery Writers of America, 35, 196

National Endowment for the Arts (NEA), 5, 198
National Review Press, 13
Newspapers:
 articles as book proposals, 154–55
 collections from, 104–105
 daily, 156–57
 how to submit to, 204
 paying the rent and, 152
 rights, 154
 weeklies, 157
New York Book Fair, 177
New Yorker, The, 28, 41, 154, 179
New York Review of Books, 187
New York Times, The, 10, 175, 187
New York Times Book Review, The, 180
Nin, Anais, 35
Nonfiction, 1–23
 advantages of writing, 1–2
 anthologies, 11–12
 autobiography and biography, 7–8

as book proposals, 154–56
collaborations, 4, 5
cookbooks, 11, 12
creative, 5–6
defined, 2
fictional, 12
first-person narratives, 6
ghostwriting, 3–5
how-to books, 10–11
how to submit, 200–201
humor, 9
journalism and reportage, 2–3
photography and art, 9–10
restaurant review guides, 9
review, 23
travel, 8–9
Nonfiction book project, 13–23
book proposal, 19–20, 21
contacts, 17–18
cover letter, 20
delivery date, 21, 22
editors, 14–15
follow-up, 20
illustrations and photos, 22
potential readers, 14
publishers, 13–14
query letter, 15–17
rejection letter, 18–19
review, 23
travel expenses, 22–23
North Point Press, 141

Oates, Joyce Carol, 28–29
Obscenity, 96–97
Oprah Winfrey, 174
Option clause, 54, 90–91
Out-of-stock books, 171–72
Outsiders, The (Hinton), 44
Overstock, 75–76

Page proofs, 123
Paperback originals, 32–33, 137
trade vs. mass-market, 138–39
Paris Review, The, 154
Patrons, 106
Pensions, 110
Performance rights, 55, 81

Perks, see Money and perks
Permissions, 63–64
Personal appearance, 151
Personal narrative, 6
PFSWrite, 120
Photography, 9–10, 22
Pilgrim at Tinker Creek (Dillard),
5–6
Pinckney, Callan, 173–74
Plagiarism, 65, 101
Playboy, 159
Playgirl, 154
Pocket Books, 25–26
Poetry, 38–43
distribution, 43
grants for, 40
how to submit, 203
income sidelines, 39–40
query letter, 42–43
where to submit, 40–42
Poets & Writers, Inc., 40, 41
Porche, Verandah, 39–40
Pornography, 35, 97, 137
Positioning, 128
Poynter, Dan, 147
Preppie Handbook, The, 9
Prestype, 147
Printers, computer, 121
Printing, 54
Printing It . . . (Burke), 147
Print-publicity ideas, 183–84
Procrastination, 36
Production process, see Manu-
script into type
Promotional excerpts, 77–78
Promotion planning, 129, 132,
150–51
see also "Big Book" campaign;
Self-promotion
Proofreaders, 125–26
Publicity planning, 128–29,
150–51
see also "Big Book" campaign
Publishers, 13–14
disputes between, 102
major, see Major publishers
performance of, 68–70

Publishers (*continued*)
  publicity tour sponsored by, 181–82
  small, *see* Small presses
Publisher's lunch, 107–108
Publisher's rep, 114–15, 166–67
  direct sales by, 167–68
  meeting your, 168
Publishers Weekly (*PW*), 13, 26, 31, 32, 145, 162
Publishing process, 127–30
  control over, 136–37
  day of publication, 130
  the launch, 127–29
  problems with, 135–36
Publishing your own magazine, 160–65
  advertisers, 161–62
  book excerpts, 165
  distribution, 163–64
  editorial content, 160–61
  production costs, 164–65
  scheduling, 162
  small-magazine network, 165
  subscriptions, 163
Pulpsmith, 154
Pushcart Prize, Best of the Small Presses, The, 142

Query letter:
  for childrens lit, 45–46
  for fiction, 29–30
  for magazines, 155–56
  for nonfiction, 15–17
  for poetry, 42–43

Radio-phone publicity, 183
Ragtime (Doctorow), 12
Random House, 144
Raymar Northwest, 169
Readers, potential, 14
Reagan, Ronald, 97
Redbook, 154, 186
Redford, Robert, xxi
Regional conventions, 177–78
·ection letter, 18–19

Remainders, 75–76, 193
  selling your own, 108–10
Reportage, 2–3
Reprint editions, 78–79
Restaurant review guides, 9
Retirement, lack of, 111
Returns, 82, 191–92
Reversion of rights, 54, 87–90
Reviews, 179–80
Revisions, 67–68
Riches and Adams, 169
Rights, 53
  subsidiary, 55–56, 61–62, 76–81
River Runs Through It, A (Maclean), 149
Robbins, Harold, 25–26, 31
Robbins, Tom, 32–33
Rogers, Rosemary, 31
Royalties, 53, 73–76
  accounting and, 81–83
  collecting, 103–104
  exceptions to, 74–76
  standard rates, 57, 73
Royalty statement, 54, 81–83
Rumble Fish (Hinton), 44

Sales, 53–54
Salespeople, 132–33
Salinger, J. D., 97
Santiago, Danny, 186–87
Santmyer, Helen Hoover, 149
Saroyan, William, xviii, 143
Saturday Evening Post, The, 28
Saturday Review, 154
Save This Car, 21
Scholastic Press, 44
Schwartz, Lynne Sharon, 6
Screenwriter's Workbook, The, (Field), 49
Screenwriting, 49–51
  how to submit, 203–204
Secondary distribution, 144–45
Second novel, 33
Self-promotion, 173–87
  blurbs, 178–79
  conventions, 176–78
  criticism and reviews, 179–80

Self-promotion (*continued*)
  publisher's promotion vs., 173
  rigors of the road, 175
  sales tactics to booksellers, 171
  sob story, 174–75
  success stories, 174, 186–87
  see also "Big Book" campaign
Self-publishing, 146–49
  promotion and publicity,
    150–51
  sales tactics, 171
Self Publishing Manual . . .
    (Poynter), 147
Sendak, Maurice, 179
Serial rights, 55–56, 61, 76–77
Sewanee Review, The, 28
Sheldon, Sidney, 26
Shoemaker, Jack, 141
Short stories, 27–29
Singer, Isaac Bashevis, 28
Sky, Penelope, 4
Small Press, 145
Small Press Distribution, 143
Small presses, 141–46
  advantages of, 141–42
  approaching, 142
  Bookpeople and, 145–46
  defined, 142–43
  fairs of, 177
  friendliness at, 143–44
  jumping to majors from, 144
  major publishers vs., 140,
    141–42
  promotion and publicity, 150–51
  secondary distribution by,
    144–45
  self-publishing, 146–49
  where to find, 143
Small reprintings, 74–75
Snail (Miller), 12
Society of Author's Representa-
    tives, 113
Software, 119–20
Solace of Open Spaces, The,
    (Ehrlich), 18
Son of the Morning Star
    (Connell), 141

Statement, 54, 81–83
Steel, Danielle, 26
Steinbeck, John, 7
Stock, 55
Straczynski, Michael, 49
Subject Guide to Books in Print,
    48
Subscriptions, magazine, 163
Subsidiary rights, 55–56, 61–62,
    76–81
  best share of, 57–58
Sunset Magazine Press, 13
Susann, Jacqueline, 31
Sutherland, Zena, 48

Talk shows, 174, 181–83
Taxes, 105
  deductions from, 106
Teaching, 198–99
Termination clause, 54, 84–90
Territorial rights, 55, 61
Textbook sales, 79–80
Theroux, Paul, 8
Thompson, Jim, 35
Total Loss Farm (Mungo), xxi
Tovell, Arnold, xxi
Travel expenses, 22–23
Travel writing, 8–9
Tropical Detective Story (Mungo),
    xxi, 134–35
Tropic of Cancer (Miller), 97
Typesetting, 125–26
Typewriters, 121–22
Typos, 117–18, 125

University presses, 149–50
Updike, John, 28

Vanity Fair, 18, 28, 157
Vanity presses, 146
Vermont Council on the Arts, 39
Vetting, 65, 95, 99
Volkswriter, 120
Vonnegut, Kurt, 25, 97

Warranties, 54, 62–64, 99–100
Warren, Robert Penn, 39

We Are Talking About Homes
(Schwartz), 6
*Webster's New Collegiate Dictio-
nary*, 126
Western Writers of America, 35
Whitmore, Jeffrey, 158
Woman's Day, 154
Woodward, Bob, 3
Word processors, 118–20, 147
WordStar, 120
Working title, 60

World rights, 62
Writers' associations, 196
Writer's block, 36
Writers' colonies, 197
Writer's Digest, 28, 35,
157, 162
Writers Guild of America (WGA),
49, 196
Writer's Market, 13, 26, 28, 35,
119, 153, 159
Writers' workshops, 196–97